D1396494

AGRIBUSINESS
IN THE
AMERICAS
BY ROGER BURBACH AND
PATRICIA FLYNN

MONTHLY REVIEW PRESS
NORTH AMERICAN CONGRESS ON LATIN AMERICA

Photo credits

Chapter 1: Texas Farmers Union, courtesy of *Food Monitor*; Chapter 2:
USDA: Murray Lemmon; Chapter 3: UN/FAO: Peyton Johnson; Chap-
ter 4: top, American Friends Service Committee, "Managing the Global
Plantation" slide show; bottom, World Bank Group: Larry Daughters;
Chapter 5: World Bank Photo: Tomas Sennett; Chapter 6: World Bank
Photo: Edwin G. Huffman; Chapter 7: World Bank Photo: Larry Daught-
ers; Chapter 8: *Del Monte Shield*; Chapter 9: Patricia Flynn; Chapter 10:
American Friends Service Committee, "Managing the Global Plantation"
slide show; Chapter 11: Patricia Flynn; Chapter 12: top, USDA: Paul
Conklin; bottom, USDA: Doug Wilson; Chapter 13: top, USDA: Jack
Schneider; bottom, USDA: Doug Wilson.

Library of Congress Cataloging in Publication Data
Burbach, Roger
    Agribusiness in the Americas.
    Includes bibliographical references.
    1. Agricultural industries—United States.
2. Agricultural industries—Latin America
I. Flynn, Patricia, joint author.   II. Title.
HD9005.B84   338.1'097   80-17114
ISBN 0-85345-535X
ISBN 0-85345-536-8 (pbk.)

Monthly Review Press
62 West 14th Street, New York, N.Y. 10011
47 Red Lion Street, London WC1R 4PF

North American Congress on Latin America
151 West 19th Street, New York, N.Y. 10011

Manufactured in the United States of America

10 9 8 7 6 5 4 3 2 1

Contents

Acknowledgments

This book would not have been possible without the many people who gave generously of their time, energy, and support throughout the years we worked on this project. Some shared information, insights, and their own research; some gave valuable critiques; some gave financial and others moral support; some helped in the innumerable tasks, from filing to clipping, that went into the book.

We would like to express special thanks and appreciation to those who collaborated most closely with us in producing the book: to Marc Herold, for sharing his data base on multinational investments (part of which he prepared for publication in the appendix here) as well as for his always provocative insights and critiques; to Hank Frundt, for helping in the final preparation of the appendix, as well as for his steady moral and intellectual support; to Sarah Stewart, not only for being invaluable as a research assistant and in helping with the final version of Chapter 3, but also for always being available for whatever task was at hand; to Mitchell Shoen, for his research assistance and perceptive critiques; to Dick Walker and Carol MacLennan, for helping us conceive of and then making a reality Chapter 1, and to Carol for her additional generous and invaluable help in everything from reading drafts to hunting for photographs; and to Karen Judd, our editor at Monthly Review, for her patient and skillful work on the final manuscript and in coordinating the myriad of tasks involved in production.

There are many others to whom we owe our gratitude for their support and assistance: Gonzalo Arroyo, Oscar Avila, Fred Beck, Walden Bello, Pepe Bengoa, Glenn and Marilyn Borchardt, Linda Briggs, Judy Butler, Carlos Fernando Chamorro, John Clements, Joe Collins, Alain deJanvry, Art Domike, Tim Draimin, Harris Gleckman, Fred Goff, David Hathaway, Cynthia Hewitt de Alcantara, Robert High, Robin Jurs, Salamon Kalmonovitz, Sherry

7

Keith, Leon Klayman, Al Krebs, Manuel Lajo, Frankie Lappé, Phil Levine, Susan Lowes, Salvador Mayorga, Dan Morgan, Bob Morris, Bob Norman, Orlando Nuñez, Jody Parsons, Elizabeth Patelke, Cheryl Payer, Charles Pillsbury, Mark Ritchie, Michael Roe, Mike Roland, Dahlia Rudavsky, Tom Seidl, Janet Shenk, Brian Sheppard, Paul Silverstein, Tim Smith, Steve Volk, Don Watson, and Eleanor Webster.

Finally, we are indebted to NACLA for the support of the organization and fellow staff members during the course of this project. We are also grateful to the many people whose support makes a unique research organization like NACLA possible.

Earlier versions of some of the chapters in this book originally appeared as articles in the NACLA's bimonthly publication, *Report on the Americas*.

Introduction

When we first began work in 1975 on the articles that formed the basis for many of the chapters in this book, the "world food crisis" of the early 1970s was still very much front page news. Serious crop failures in 1972–1973 (when world production actually fell for the first time in many years) sent shock waves through the world food economy. The general shift from over-abundant supplies to apparent scarcity, coupled with massive grain purchases by the Soviet Union for the first time, triggered a spectacular leap in world grain prices. People everywhere felt the pinch of soaring food prices, especially the poor. The spectre of massive famine threatened in the African Sahel, Ethiopia, and then Bangladesh. As a result of these disturbing events, many people in the United States and other countries began to ask questions about the real causes of the "food crisis." The research that went into this book grew out of that period of questioning.

Today, five years later, the food crisis has receded from the headlines and consequently from the forefront of public consciousness. But the concerns that motivated this book are as compelling as ever. They may not be the news of the day, but hunger and malnutrition are still a brutal reality for a shockingly large portion of humanity. In assessing the world food situation in 1978, the United Nations Food and Agriculture Organization (FAO) concluded that "little or no progress has been made toward the basic goal of the eradication of hunger and malnutrition." And, the FAO reported, "the number of malnourished people has in fact increased." Today, almost half a billion people, or one in eight of the world's inhabitants, are chronically undernourished.

One of the most widely accepted explanations of this situation is the notion that there are simply too many mouths to feed and not enough food to go around. In other words, as British economist Thomas Malthus first argued in 1798, overpopulation is the cause of hunger.

Over half a century later, Karl Marx offered a radically different explanation for the same massive poverty and starvation that Malthus observed. What appeared to be a problem of overpopulation in the mushrooming urban slums was, in Marx's view, a massive social problem created by the dynamics of expanding capitalism. In the countryside large-scale capitalist farms were closing in on the lands of small peasant farmers, forcing them into the overcrowded cities. These tens of thousands of unemployed appeared as a "surplus" population, but in fact they functioned as part of industrial capitalism's "reserve army of labor." Then, as now, this labor reserve—far from being superfluous to the system—was essential to ensuring capitalists a continuing supply of cheap labor. Their hunger, like their poverty, was an outgrowth of the social and economic organization of society.

Developments since Marx and Malthus wrote have only reinforced the view that social factors rather than scarcity are at the root of hunger. Over the past century the world's food supply has in fact tended to increase more rapidly than its population. Moreover, the potential for further dramatic increases in world production based on improved technology and opening up of new lands is substantial. For 1978, the same year that the FAO assessed an increase in the number of malnourished people, the U.S. Department of Agriculture reported dramatic rises in per capita world food output as compared to the previous decade. For the developed countries, per capita food production was more than 27 percent above the levels of the early 1960s, and for the forty-nine countries with the lowest per capita income it was 40 percent higher.

There is no denying, of course, that weather-induced crop failures occur and severely limit the supply of food. This was the case in 1972–1973 when world production actually dropped by 1.6 percent. Such shortfalls inevitably take their toll in human lives lost to starvation. But even in times of massive crop failure the notion of absolute "shortages" of food is highly questionable.

Contemporary food "shortages" exist only because of the way food is distributed in the capitalist world economy, which has very little to do with the absolute availability of food. While millions go malnourished, 35 percent of the world's cereal crop is fed to livestock because that is where profits are to be made. In an economic system where food is produced for and sold to the highest bidder rather than according to human need, hunger is more than anything a reflection of social inequality. In the third world, hunger is endemic principally because of the sharp inequalities that characterize the class structure of underdeveloped capitalist countries. The majority simply do not have sufficient income to afford an adequate diet, regardless of how much food is produced. Even in the most developed capitalist countries, the have-not classes are not immune to hunger and malnutrition. In the United States, a land of unsurpassed agricultural abundance, malnutrition affects over 25 million people, or over 10 percent of the population.

It is only in societies organized along socialist lines—where production and distribution is organized by the principle of social equality rather than private profit—that the possibility of ending hunger exists. China is a dramatic example. In spite of extreme population density, a low ratio of arable land to people, and a long history of mass famines, China has virtually eradicated hunger and malnutrition among its 900 million people.

Confronting the fallacy of neo-Malthusian arguments must be the starting point for any critical examination of the causes of the present food crisis. Neo-Malthusian notions have had a resurgence of popularity in the past decade as a plausible explanation of the crisis. Most alarming is the fact that the neo-Malthusian perspective dominates the thinking of those who have the power and the financial resources to mount an international campaign supposedly aimed at addressing the food crisis—namely, the United States and other governments of the capitalist world, such international financial institutions as the World Bank, private foundations such as the Rockefeller Foundation, and the multinational corporations.

Rationalizing their proposals with the misleading notion that the fundamental problem is an imbalance between population and food supply, these powerful forces have thrown their weight behind a two-pronged international strategy for dealing with the food crisis. The first aspect of this strategy involves a concerted international campaign to curb population growth. The particular focus of this campaign is third world countries, where methods of curbing population growth range from government-sponsored birth control programs to forced sterilization. The most pernicious of the neo-Malthusian population control solutions are "lifeboat ethics" and "triage." The first argues that since the world has only a limited number of "lifeboat seats" for feeding its population, many will simply have to be kept out of the boat and starve to death. Triage is a variant on the same theme: the world's poor countries should be divided into three groups, those who can be saved, those who cannot, and those in between. Resources should be concentrated on the first and third, and the hopeless cases should be abandoned.

Although neither of these solutions has been implemented, they are, in many ways, only more extreme forms of the population control solution. Instead of calling for the imposition of birth control, they and their advocates argue that the imbalance between population and food supply can be remedied through a "rational" policy of eliminating hungry people through starvation.

The second aspect of the strategy to solve the food crisis addresses the food production side of the equation. The race between population and food production can only be won, it is argued, if backward agricultural systems in the third world are thoroughly modernized in the mold of the capitalist world's most efficient and productive food system: namely, U.S. agribusiness. The development of agribusiness according to this model means more than the modernization of agricultural *production*. Just as in the United States, agribusiness in the third world means an integrated food system that extends from farm to factory to consumer—from food production to the manufacture of farm implements and pesticides to food processing and food marketing.* Besides *linking* agriculture to industry, agribusiness also means that agricultural production increasingly *resembles* industrial production, in the application of technology to control nature and increase productivity and in the use of wage labor. And

---

*The term "agribusiness" was first used in the late 1950s by a professor at the Harvard Business School, Ray Goldberg, to describe the integrated food system of the United States.

finally, as those who promote this model are well aware, the spread of agribusiness to the third world also entails a central role for the multinational agribusiness corporations that dominate the food system in the United States.

This "internationalization" of agribusiness is more than a *proposal* to end world hunger. It is, in fact, one of the main features of today's world food economy. Increasingly, agribusiness is the model for agricultural development in the third world. It not only determines how food is produced and distributed, but it also shapes the lives of millions of third world people who depend on agriculture for their livelihood.

One of the main purposes of this book is to analyze the workings and impact of agribusiness on an international scale. The reality is that agribusiness, far from being the solution, only aggravates the problem of hunger. For it entails not just the modernization of agriculture, but also the transfer of a particular model of economic development and social relations to the third world—the capitalist model. As such, agribusiness only exacerbates the social inequalities that, as we argued earlier, are the real causes of hunger. In both the United States and the third world, the growing dominance of agribusiness typically means that vast numbers of small farmers are continually being deprived of their means of production. Many are pushed from the land into the ranks of wage laborers in a gradual process of proletarianization. At the other end of the social scale, land, income, and resources are increasingly concentrated in the hands of the largest and wealthiest agribusiness growers who come to dominate production.

This transformation of social relations and class structures in the countryside as a result of agribusiness development is a central theme of this book. To examine this process in both the advanced capitalist countries and the third world we concentrate on two regions, the United States and Latin America. The United States provides us with a model of the most highly developed agribusiness system in the world. For its part, Latin America, has the most advanced capitalist agriculture in the third world, partly because of the relative strength of capitalist development in its other sectors.

As we show in several chapters, the distinct historical experiences of the United States as compared to Latin American countries, and the resulting differences in social and economic structures, have meant very different patterns of agricultural development. A highly developed industrial economy has nurtured U.S. agriculture and created the conditions for the early emergence of a highly developed agribusiness system. Yet the historical importance of the family farm has given U.S. agriculture its peculiar character. In spite of a high level of technical sophistication and productivity, family production units rather than large-scale corporate farms continue to characterize most sectors of U.S. agriculture. This is changing, however, as the continuing decline of the family farm and the growing concentration of land in the hands of large-scale agribusiness farms polarizes the class structure of rural America. These trends, along with their political reverberations through farm protest movements such as the American Agriculture Movement, are discussed in Chapter 1.

Latin American countries, however diverse in some respects, share a common history of colonial exploitation and more recent submission to U.S. economic and political hegemony. In contrast to the United States, this historical experience (common in many ways to other third world regions) has stunted and distorted their economic development in both agriculture and industry. Intense capitalist development in recent decades, however, has created conditions conducive to the rapid expansion of agribusiness. Unlike in the United States, this has occurred in a social structure already characterized by extremes of wealth and poverty in the countryside (where 7 percent of the population owns 93.8 percent of the land). The tens of millions of peasant farmers who have been pushed off the land into the ranks of the proletariat are usually unable to find jobs in industry (again unlike the United States' historical experience). As a result, the expansion of agribusiness in Latin America is an explosive social and political force in the countryside, as Part Two of this book describes in some depth.

In spite of these differences, what is remarkable is the extent to which modern agribusiness in Latin America has come to resemble that in the United States. In both regions, agribusiness production units run by an emerging agrarian bourgeoisie are increasingly similar. In the Bajío Valley of Mexico, the Cauca Valley of Colombia, and the Salinas Valley of California we saw fruit and vegetable growers who employed similar production techniques. They used the same hybrid seeds, bought the same farm implements, and applied the same fertilizers and pesticides. They were financed by the same banks, and sold to the same multinational corporations. The agrarian bourgeoisie of each valley were also involved in continual labor conflicts as they sought to hold down the wages of agricultural workers and to prevent them from forming effective unions. The same similarities are noticeable in other types of agricultural production as well. The new large-scale soybean farms of Brazil and Argentina also look like their counterparts in the Midwest and South of the United States.

The central role that U.S. multinational corporations play in the global expansion of agribusiness is another central theme of this book. The multinationals have extended their operations into every phase of agribusiness in nearly every corner of the globe.

In agricultural production, corporations like Del Monte and United Brands control vast stretches of farm land in Asia, Africa, and Latin America. Even more important is the role that U.S. agribusiness multinationals play in the more profitable facets of agribusiness: namely, input manufacture, food processing, and marketing. International Harvester and John Deere manufacture and supply mechanized farm implements to farmers from California to Brazil to Thailand. Giant food processors like Quaker Oats and General Foods bring the highly processed, nutritionally poor food products Americans know so well to millions of new overseas consumers every year. Dow Chemical and other pesticide manufacturers sell lethal chemicals like DDT throughout the third world, often unencumbered by environmental and safety restrictions. And MacDonald's and Kentucky Fried Chicken are springing up in most major cities around the world. Several chapters in the book analyze the global expansion of U.S. agribusiness, and an in-depth case study of the Del Monte Corporation presented in Part Three is a vivid illustration of both the dynamics and impact of multinational agribusiness in both the United States and the third world.

The U.S. multinationals are not just involved in expanding *within* other countries. They are also the crucial link in the global integration of agriculture through international trade. The flow of tropical commodities like bananas from third world producing countries to affluent markets in the industrialized capitalist countries is dominated by the multinationals. In the case of bananas it is three corporate food giants, each with sales in the billions— Castle & Cooke, United Brands, and Del Monte.

Multinationals also control the flow of many agricultural commodities from the advanced capitalist countries to the third world. Most significant in this regard is the stranglehold a handful of powerful corporations and the U.S. government have on international trade in grain, which is the world's main source of protein. Five corporations (the largest of which, Cargill, is highlighted in Chapter 13) dominate world grain trade, and the United States alone accounts for more than 60 percent of the grain entering the world market. This control over the world's grain supply gives these companies and the U.S. government tremendous power in the world food economy. The abuse of this power for national political and economic ends is a central concern of two chapters in this book, one on U.S. international food policy and the other on the U.S. food aid program.

Our hope is that the articles that follow will contribute to an understanding of the complex forces at work in today's world food economy. The topics covered in these articles are by no means exhaustive. But we believe that what emerges is a framework for analyzing and asking further questions about the world food system. We want to go beyond an exposé of the injustices and abuses in that system to an explanation of how these are embodied in the logic and dymanics of capitalism—the historically specific form of social and economic organization that has given rise to agribusiness.

The reason for stressing this perspective is essentially political in nature. The goal of our research is not just to denounce agribusiness for its inability to meet human needs, but also to provide people with the analytical tools of analysis needed to actively participate in social change. Without an understanding of how capitalism works it is impossible to develop effective tactics or strategies for transforming that system into one that can meet human needs.

PART ONE:

AGRIBUSINESS IN THE UNITED STATES

1. Crisis and Change in U.S. Agriculture: An Overview

by Carol MacLennan and Richard Walker

WITHOUT TODAYS FARMER
WHERE WILL TOMORROWS
FOOD COME FROM

HELP THE PEOPLE WHO ARE
TRYING TO HELP FARMERS
JOIN FARMERS UNION NOW

During the winter of 1978–1979, the nation's capital witnessed one of the largest and most militant demonstrations in recent years. The protest came from an unexpected direction. Family farmers, from the heartland of America, had organized a "tractorcade" to Washington and were blocking traffic in the capital to call attention to the crisis in the U.S. agriculture system which threatened the survival of the family farm. As their bright yellow, green, red, and blue tractors dotted the mall stretching west from Capitol Hill, the farmers lobbied intensely for a "fair price" on farm commodities in hopes of forestalling their economic ruin.

The farmers who participated were part of a loose-knit organization, the American Agricultural Movement (AAM), which came together in the fall of 1977 around a call for a nationwide farm strike. Originating in Colorado, the AAM gathered wide support in Kansas, Nebraska, Oklahoma, northern Texas, southern Georgia, Maryland, and Virginia. It caught on largely among grain, cotton, and small livestock farmers.[1] The movement grew rapidly in response to a sequence of lean years in which real farm incomes and profits plummeted. The last season that farmers did well was 1973–1974, and that was primarily due to crop failures in foreign countries and large wheat purchases by the Soviet Union which gave farmers new markets. From their peak in 1973, farm prices had fallen roughly 33 percent by 1977.[2]

The farmers' protest reflected a deepening crisis in American agriculture, one of the recurring bouts of "hard times" that periodically strike the farm sector. The farmers of the AAM are suffering from a "cost-price squeeze," caught between declining farm prices and rising high costs. This is not a chance occurrence: economic forces that have been at work in U.S. agriculture for over a century trap farmers in a vicious circle. They constantly try to increase productivity, but in so doing tend to overproduce for the market, driving down prices and incomes. When this happens it leads to bankruptcy for the weakest competitors, typically those who have gone deepest into debt in order to buy the very machinery, fertilizer, and other inputs which are essential to advancing productivity and staying competitive.

As a result, the numbers of family-owned and -operated farms has long been on the decline. Today the whole rural class structure is undergoing dramatic changes. Those who are likely to survive the crisis are not necessarily large agribusiness corporations, but a new breed of farmers, a prosperous agrarian bourgeoisie with roots in the traditional family farm. This new capitalist class will become more and more dependent upon wage labor and their farms will increasingly resemble factories in the fields. A different kind of survivor is the growing part-time farmer class which combines wage work in nearby towns and cities with farm work on its own land in an effort to hold off bankruptcy. Although the family farm still predominates in rural America,[3] it is conceivable that within a decade agricultural communities will be characterized by a polarized class structure, dominated by a small but powerful agrarian bourgeoisie on one side, with a large number of part-time farmers, or semiproletarians, on the other. What are the economic forces behind these developments?

Economic Pressures on the Family Farm

The farmers protesting the threat of bankruptcy and ruin are only the latest victims in a long tradition of cost-price squeeze casualties. Their plight recalls that of hardpressed farmers in the 1920s and 1930s whose mortgages were foreclosed by the millions after the Great Crash, or of the independent families of the 1880s and 1890s forced to convert in great numbers to tenants and sharecroppers. For decades, the family farm has been declining in numbers, yet the system of family farming still characterizes the overall structure of production in U.S. agriculture. The corporate farm has until recently made few inroads into farming.

A system of production characterized by family farm units may be called an "independent mode of production" (IMP)[4], a system of household producers who, owning their land and utilizing their own labor, produce commodities for commercial markets. With certain exceptions, most notably the southern plantation system, American agriculture has for over three centuries approximated the independent production system.

The critical feature which distinguishes a system of family farming from corporation-based factory farming is the use of family labor rather than wage labor. The family farm unit differs significantly from the capitalist farm unit in that no matter how mechanized, or how extensive the acreage, or how large the income, the primary input of labor on the family farm comes from family members. In contrast, large agribusiness firms owned by such companies as United Brands employ hundreds of wage laborers.

In spite of its persistence the family farm of today would be barely recognizable to a family farmer of 1830. The United States is unique in that it was settled by independent family farmers steeped in a commercial economy tied to the world market, who had access to vast reaches of land without feudal ties. The family farm system grew dramatically during the nineteenth century as millions of settlers spilled over the continent. Over the last century, however, with the development of capitalism in the industrial and manufacturing sector, farming practices have been tremendously affected. While the family farm has remained intact through all of this, the stress placed on its ability to survive has increased. Table 1 presents the long-run trends toward fewer and larger farms, increasing farm output and capital inputs (land, buildings, machinery) which provide a background for understanding the current squeeze on the family farmer.

The Productivity Treadmill

The most dramatic trend has been the rise in labor productivity. In an economy of small producers there is a built-in tendency for every family farmer to try to expand farm output, primarily by increasing the productivity of family labor. Besides the obvious goal of raising family income and purchasing power, other pressures work on the family to the same end: the need to pay off past debts, the need for a cushion against calamity, or the need just to maintain income in the face of periods of falling prices.

Most important, market competition forces all farm households onto a treadmill on which they must each run as fast as the rest in order not to fall behind—and faster than the others to get ahead. For example, if demand for farm commodities is constant and output rises, either because of new farms coming into production or old farmers producing more than before, prices will fall, reducing the income of any farm that does not increase its output proportionately. Even if demand is rising, the same dilemma occurs as long as production expands faster than demand. Paradoxically, fear of falling behind in the production race becomes an additional reason for every farmer to run a little faster.

Family farmers have two ways of increasing production: tilling more land (long the most common method) and improving yields per acre (see Table 1). Both require mechanization, given that continuation of the *family* farm means, by definition, that one must get the most out of the labor of the household. Higher yields per acre also depend on irrigation, fertilization, and improved varieties of seed. In other words, the production treadmill becomes a *productivity* treadmill, in which the way to prosperity and survival is to increase labor productivity and the size of landholdings (see Table 1).

As a consequence of the productivity race, the family farm system can, under the right conditions, be a dynamic one in terms of agricultural development. But this same drive to increase productivity also contributes to the financial undoing and gradual elimination of large numbers of family farms. The unplanned nature of the market, coupled with the desire of families to raise their income, ensures that there will be a tendency to overproduction relative to demand. Overproduction which in turn leads to falling prices and hence declining incomes. When income drops, many family farmers are unable to meet the costs they incurred in trying to compete. This is the essence of the cost-price squeeze that periodically plagues the small family farmer.

When prices are strong, each individual farmer hopes to take

Table 1
Basic Trends in U.S. Agriculture

A) *Non-Urban Popula-tion (percent)*

1840	90
1890	50
1970	25

B) *Farm Population (percent)*

1890	42
1910	35
1930	25
1950	15
1970	5

C) *Total Farm Acreage (millions)*

1850	293
1870	407
1890	623
1910	881
1930	990
1950	1161
1970	1102

D) *Numbers of Farms (millions)*

1850	1.4
1870	2.7
1890	4.6
1910	6.4
1930	6.3
1950	5.4
1970	2.9

E) *Average Size of Farm (acres)*

1850	203
1870	153
1890	137
1910	139
1930	157
1950	216
1970	373

F) *Size Distribution of Farms Over 1,000 Acres (thousands)*

1880	29
1969	151

G) *Total Farm Output (index, 1947–49 = 100)*

1870	23
1890	43
1910	61
1930	72
1950	100
1970	140

H) *Total Farm Employ-ment, Family Hired (millions)*

1910	13.5
1930	12.5
1950	9.9
1970	4.5

I) *Family Labor-to-Hired Ratio*

roughly constant at 3:1 1910–1970

J) *Commercial Fertilizer (short tons, thousands)*

1850	53
1870	321
1890	1,390
1910	5,547
1930	8,171
1950	18,343
1970	39,591

K) *Machinery (thousands)*

Gasoline Tractors

1910	1
1930	920
1950	3,394
1970	4,790

Combines

1910	1
1930	61
1950	714
1970	850

L) *Average Value Per Farm*

Land & Buildings

1850	$ 2,258
1870	2,799
1890	2,909
1910	5,480
1930	7,624
1950	14,005
1970	70,485

Implements & Machinery

1850	$ 105
1970	11,530

M) *Value of Real Pro-perty and Machinery Per Person (Family & Hired)*

(fixed capital to labor ratio)

1910	$ 2,621
1970	53,500

N) *Output Per Worker, 1910 vs. 1970*

increased by 770 percent

O) *Output Per Acre, 1910 vs. 1970*

increased by 185 percent

P) *Gross Farm Income vs. Expenses*

1910
7.495/3.531
billions = 2:1
1970
57.925/41.091
billions = 3:2

Source: U.S. Bureau of the Census, *Historical Statistics of the United States* (Washington, D.C.: Government Printing Office, 1975).

advantage of the situation by planting more, acquiring new lands, and so forth. The net effect is likely to be general overproduction, with the market unable to absorb expanded output without lowering the price. Even though farmers try to take their competitors and future conditions into account, their ability to plan is undercut by factors beyond their control, such as the weather. The likelihood of guessing wrong is increased by the time lag between planting and harvesting, or between calving and slaughtering. Wars, business cycles, or grain shipments to the Soviet Union may generate strong market conditions at the beginning of the production cycle which spur farmers to increase production in the expectation of higher prices. When it comes time to sell, however, market conditions may have changed, leaving farmers overcommitted.

On the other side of the ledger, farmers are bound by fixed costs. Commercial agriculture means that they must buy certain necessary inputs, such as seed, equipment, fuel, or land.[5] It is the exceptional family farmer who is not burdened with debt. Farmers go into debt to buy their farms, to buy the current season's seeds and fertilizer, to buy equipment to last for years. Credit is as basic to farming as are seeds and sunshine. Moreover, credit is the lever which allows farmers to purchase the land and capital equipment to improve their productivity. But debts bring payments that must be met, regardless of the fortunes of the harvest and the market. As a result, they also become the principal cause of financial insolvency when crops fail or prices fall.

Because the tendency to overproduction occurs in a cyclical fashion, severe cost-price crunches do also. Periods of high prices trigger new investments and new debts which cannot be met by many farmers when prices fall again. This sequence has been repeated many times. For example, the boom of World War I was followed by worsening prices in the 1920s and finally a disastrous drop in the market in the 1930s. Recently, the export boom of the early 1970s precipitated the overcommitments by farmers now joining the AAM. Each time the crunch comes, many farmers go bankrupt or are forced to sell out. Their land and equipment is bought by competitors, who consolidate their gains, waiting for demand to pick up again. Then the cycle begins anew, with fewer farmers than the last time, more equipment per farm, and higher levels of productivity. The treadmill rolls on.

The "productivity treadmill" helps explain such long-run trends in the United States as the declining number of farmers and increasing size of farms. But this dynamic has additional consequences for the nature of agricultural production and the class structure of the farm sector in the United States. To begin with, it has meant the increasing industrialization of American agriculture. With every cycle of expansion and contraction, farmers buy more machinery, apply more fertilizers, and increase the size of their operations. As they do so, the nature of farming itself undergoes fundamental changes which make it resemble in some ways industrial factory production.

The Industrialization of Farming

In areas where industrialization is most advanced, such as California, farming can be described more as a system of "factories in the field" than as one of family farms, owing to the degree of mechanization and use of hired labor. Highly industrialized tomato production in California, where specially bred varieties of bruise resistant tomatoes are harvested entirely by machine, is an example of how mechanical and genetic engineering has transformed production. This process of industrialization in U.S. agriculture has been underway for about 150 years.

Industrialization begins with the introduction of machines into the production process, where they perform the same functions previously carried out by workers.[6] Classic examples of such machines in farming are the mechanical reapers, threshers, and cultivators introduced in the mid-nineteenth century by McCormick, John Deere, and others. These machines began as imitations of the simple tools used by farmers. By increasing the number of tools in each machine, perfecting their performance, and increasing their speed (with the aid of mechanical power), the productivity of the farmer rapidly multiplied . Mechanization enormously increased the acreage that one person could plow, disc, harrow, or reap. Adding tractors as the motive force for such machines raised their capabilities still more. Not surprisingly, today's 2.7 million farms own 4.4 million tractors.[7] Yet the basic process of production on the family farm has not been as radically changed as might appear. *Individual* machines have been employed to magnify the labor power or productivity of the farmer at his or her various tasks, but the overall labor process remains much as it has for centuries: plowing, planting, harvesting, threshing. It is still caught up in the rhythms of nature.

By contrast, in true factory production, work is organized around the rhythms of machines. Such a production system means continuity of flow from raw material to finished product, automation of control, subdivision of work into detailed functions, unitary power source, and the continuous refinement of all these through the application of science.[8] Agriculture involves both mechanical and biological processes, and whereas the former have been mechanized, the latter consists of natural rhythms of growth that are not easily changed into a machine production system.[9] The problem for agriculture, then, is how to make nature step to the tune of the capitalist clock, that is, how to revolutionize the biological processes themselves, not just how to use machinery or fertilizer to augment natural processes.

Progress in agriculture in the past has, of course, involved various biological manipulations. Fertilization, crop rotation, multiple cropping, pest control, irrigation, and plant and animal breeding are all very old. Systematic efforts to control nature in these ways have sped up dramatically in the capitalist period, beginning in the eighteenth century in England. They were introduced in the mid-nineteenth century in the United States, side by side with the application of machinery. People often forget how "modern" agriculture had become even in the nineteenth century, with the use of commercial fertilizers (guano, phosphate rock), steam tractors, special cattle breeds, chemical pesticides (inorganic or plant-derived poisons), and local irrigation systems.

The twentieth century has seen further revolutions in agriculture, yielding large increases in productivity. These advances have depended on petroleum-based fertilizers and pesticides, irrigation by means of giant water projects and electric pumps, and petroleum-driven tractors and other machines. Central to the whole scheme are the so-called miracle hybrids of corn, wheat, and rice, bred to prosper under heavy applications of fertilizers, water, and pesticides, and meant to be easily harvested by machine. All of these also made possible more intensive and continuous planting, as when irrigation allows growers in mild climates to harvest three or more crops per year. Such developments bring us closer and closer to real industrial agriculture.

For most types of agricultural production in the United States (especially those where the family farm predominates), these technical advances have not yet succeeded in completely wedding mechanical and biological processes into factory type production. The one sector where significant advances in this direction have been made is in animal husbandry (livestock).

The modern feedlot, for example, bears little resemblance to the old-style cattle range. Production is no longer dependent on land and nature. Once the calves are brought to the feedlots for fattening they never see green pastures again. Thousands of head of cattle are crowded onto a few square acres where they are fed computer-monitored formula feeds. To stimulate weight gain and control diseases, massive doses of antibiotics and artificial hormones are either put in the feeds or injected into the animals. Thousands of cattle a day are run through special pens that operate with assembly-line efficiency.

Poultry production today is an even more factory-like operation. One person working on a modern chicken farm can take care of up to 75,000 chickens.[10] Some of the big food corporations, such as Ralston Purina, Cargill, and Allied Mills, run huge poultry operations that produce tens of thousands of chickens each day. As in plant production, the keys to such output are special breeding, intensive enriched feeding, and chemical stimulation (hormone) and disease control. Moreover, animals can be packed together in artificial environments, where their bodily functions can be dealt with mechanically and continuously very much like a true factory. Egg production, in particular, uses a fully automated assembly line operation. Feed passes in front of the immobile hens on one belt, while eggs and droppings are removed on other belts. Artificial lighting overcomes the natural daily cycle and keeps the hens laying continuously. Some chicken farms produce over half a million eggs a day.

Dairying too is coming under the sway of industrialization.

California and Florida dairy operations set the pace years ago by developing large-scale milking parlors capable of extracting tens of thousands of pounds of milk from a dairy herd in a matter of hours. Even the biology of the dairy cow has been altered. Special breeding combined with formula feeds—now delivered by computer in "personalized" doses to the cows' stalls—has led to the development of cows that produce 75 percent more milk than thirty years ago.[11]

Most sectors of U.S. agriculture have undergone only a limited amount of industrialization compared with livestock production, however. The ordinary American family farm is not fully industrialized, in spite of its relatively high productivity. There are no assembly lines, little detailed division of labor, no continuous flow processing, no massing of workers, except seasonally: in short, little of what one normally associates with the factory system of manufacturing. In terms of technical progress, then, American agriculture remains only semi-industrial.

There is another sense in which U.S. agriculture may be called semi-industrial: it depends on the fully industrialized economy that surrounds it for machines and other sophisticated inputs. Farmers have taken the fruits of industrialization of factory production and applied them to agriculture to revolutionize the productivity of labor there. They have also depended on the urban-industrial sectors of the economy for such things as the building of transportation systems, the marketing and processing of produce, and the overall growth of the demand for food from the urban masses. A handicraft and small manufacturing economy could never have spawned the semi-industrialized, tremendously productive agriculture of today.

In other words, the farm sector must be seen as part of the overall system of American capitalism.[12] Capitalist development in manufacturing and agricultural development based on the family farm have proceeded hand in hand in this country. Indeed, it is hard to imagine the progress of one without the other: the agricultural sector provided a major market for industrial goods, cheap food for industrial workers and a flow of surplus labor to the cities, while capitalist industry supplied inputs to raise farm productivity, purchased farm products, and absorbed the sons and daughters of farmers into its army of labor.[13]

Corporate Farms and Agrarian Capitalists

One of the burning questions in agriculture over the last decade has been whether large corporations have been moving into farming, the last American bastion of free enterprise, and driving family farmers out. The popular view is that this is so. Yet, as the *Economist* stated recently: "The idea that faceless corporations are taking over American agriculture is a myth."[14] Corporate farms account for only 1 percent of all farms, and their income for only 15 percent of total cash receipts. Contrary to public perceptions, the modern agribusiness farm is not typically owned by corporations on the Fortune 500 list. Tenneco, Del Monte, and United Brands are still anomalies as corporate farmers; most agribusiness companies are family corporations. This is even true in California, the richest farm state in the nation, and long in the forefront of agricultural mechanization.[15] Forty-five corporations own 3.7 million acres, or nearly half the state's crop land. But most of these large agribusiness outfits are family companies like the giant and wealthy DiGiorgio Corporation. A similar kind of large-scale agribusiness is also prevalent along the southern rim of the United States, from Florida to Louisiana, Texas, and Arizona.

Industrial corporations do not want to be bothered with *direct* agricultural production. Big capital, including Tenneco Corporation and Del Monte, has found it more advantageous in certain crops to contract with small farmers for their products than to invest directly in production. A Tenneco spokesman observed as the company was selling off some of its holdings acquired during an ill-considered expansion into farming, "Agriculture is a high risk business and typically shows little if any profit, especially for large corporations."[16]

Indeed, the key to why the family farm *system* has been able to survive so long while the number of *individual* family farmers has declined continuously is the inability of agriculture to make the leap to fully industrial production. This keeps the rate of profit in agriculture sufficiently low that it is not an attractive investment for corporate capital.[17] Tenneco can make better profits supplying fuel and equipment to farmers, while Del Monte can do better processing and packaging farm produce. Given the semi-industrial nature of most farming, household labor, supplemented by seasonal wage labor, has remained viable and competitive with the use of full-time wage labor by capitalist farmers.

But this is changing. A gradual expansion of corporate farming is taking place, but it is spearheaded by the larger *family* farms who are enlarging their acreage, making heavy capital investments, and relying increasingly on wage labor. The example of Pat Benedict, from Sabin, Minnesota, is illustrative.

Benedict runs a 3,500-acre "farm," on which he grows wheat and sugar beets. Besides managing a $3.5-million farm operation, he directs a regional sugar beet processing firm and owns a part of a local grain elevator company. Benedict, a true entrepreneur, spends a good part of his day in an office, handing out farm work assignments and analyzing computer printouts so he can plot his planting and marketing strategies. Every day he draws up precise operating schedules of the $.5 million in machinery he owns. Although his family does help in the farm work, Benedict also has several permanent workers, along with migrants and students hired during the peak planting and harvesting periods. Pat Benedict is part of the new farm capitalist class whose operations show, in the words of *Time* magazine, that "revolutionary changes are sweeping the crop lands, making agriculture an increasingly capital-intensive, high technology, mass production business."[18]

The rate of change in farm ownership and operation has been particularly rapid in the area of livestock raising and dairying. Concentration of ownership has taken place very rapidly in beef, poultry, and dairying over the last two decades. In 1962, almost two-thirds of the cattle slaughtered in the United States came from feedlots with less than 1,000 head; by 1973 this pattern was reversed, with two-thirds coming from lots with over 1,000 head. Over 20 percent of the beef came from feedlots of more than 32,000 head.[19] In egg production there were 1.2 million farmers in 1964; it is projected that by the early 1980s a mere 500 producers will provide almost all the eggs sold.[20]

The Changing Rural Class Structure

As industrialization has made inroads into the agricultural sector in recent years and family farming has been further eroded and modified, trends are emerging which mark a critical departure from traditional social structures in rural America. In the 1970s and 1980s, we are witnessing the development of three distinct sectors in the farmowner class. At one pole we find a semiproletarian class of small part-time farmers, at the other a true agrarian bourgeoisie. In between lie the remaining family farmers who are rapidly decreasing in number. And beneath all the owning classes can be found an increasingly permanent agricultural working class.

This polarization of farm classes grows directly out of the old system of family farming. The distribution of resources among family farms has never been equal, and some small semiproletarian and large bourgeois classes—not to mention sharecroppers and other forms of tenancy—have always existed. But in the past, divisions between social classes have been blurred, with all farmers appearing as a continuum within a broad social grouping ranging from the small family farmer through the medium-sized farmer to the large commercial farmer. Generally, all of these farmers were family owner-operators. As farms expanded and productivity rose, the tendency was for the small to medium-sized farmer to be edged out of the agricultural sector, yet family farm production was maintained overall through increases in family-labor productivity.

Government statistics have typically distinguished among three descriptive strata of farms—small, medium, and large—based on amount of sales:

Small farms	under $20,000 in sales
Medium farms	$20,000 to $100,000 in sales
Large farms	$100,000 and over in sales

While the small farm sector is the largest in terms of number of units, the telling figure is that large farms, which comprise only 6 percent of the total number of farms, produce over 50 percent of the agricultural output. Small farms, which make up 69 percent of the farm sector, only produce 11 percent of the output.[21]

Small Farms and the Semiproletariat

All indications are that the small family farm which supports the entire family is fast disappearing. In its stead comes a new type of small farm, where one or more family member combines farm work with wage labor, such as in a nearby factory or small business. The result is a rapid rise of a part-time farm class with a dual class character—as proletarians and as independent producers.

Recent figures show that small farm households now receive on the average a majority of their income from off-farm sources, and as much as 85 percent in some cases. Net income per farm from outside sources has increased by 442 percent, while net income from farm sources has increased only 165 percent. This rapid increase in off-farm earnings has occurred primarily since 1970. In 1970 the Department of Agriculture reported that nearly two of every three people living on farms made their earnings entirely from their own farms. In 1976, the figure was reduced to less than one out of two. Farm earnings were supplemented with full-time work as secretaries, factory workers, and truck drivers.[22] Farms are worked in off-hours. Vacations are planned and extra leave taken from work for the more time-consuming tasks of planting and harvesting. Unwilling to give up farming completely, small farmers are hanging on as viable producers only by putting one foot outside the farm sector to cushion the impact of competition and to avoid being eliminated from farming altogether.[23] They have been aided in this strategy in the 1970s by another significant trend in the U.S. economy—the decentralization of industrial facilities and sources of employment to small towns.[24]

Middle-sized Farms and the Squeeze on Family Owners

The middle-sized farm in the United States is the category into which the classic family farm primarily fits. The owner or manager tends to be a full-time farmer and adult family members are all engaged in work on the farm. It is this sector that is currently feeling the most intense economic pressure, which is why the middle-sized family farmer represents the most significant contingent of the American Agricultural Movement. As we will see later, the AAM's demand for higher support prices is the only course which many medium-sized farmers see left open to them. They have been forced into this sort of collective class action by their inability to seek alternative, individual solutions.

The fixed costs of middle-sized farms, particularly the debt load, have increased dramatically in recent years. To increase productivity, farmers have over the last decades assumed unprecedented debts in hopes that returns on their labor and products would increase (see Figure 2). The incredible jump in the total value of farm machinery reflects this: farmers in 1945 had $5.1 billion invested in farm machinery, a figure which had increased by 849 percent to $48.4 billion in 1974.[25] Even where the farm is in a position to earn enough income to support a family there are recurrent problems of adequate cash flow. Their deficits cannot be made up by outside income, as can those of the small part-time farm household, because the size of the operation makes it difficult to take off-farm employment and still keep up production. As a result, these families are being pinched by the decline of net yearly income per farm, down by an average of about $4,000 since 1973.[26]

Thus it is not uncommon to read about farmers such as the Nations family recently featured in *Forbes* magazine, who grow corn on 800 acres in Qulin, Missouri. They grossed a whopping $150,000, and netted only $3,400. Since 1971 they have invested $71,000 to buy new land and expand production, hoping to keep up. Added to that, they have bought $135,000 of farm equipment since 1970. The Nations participated in the tractorcade of 1979.[27]

For the smaller sized farms in this middle category who do not opt for combining family labor on the farm with wage labor in town, the solution to increased debt and low returns is to increase the exploitation of their own labor power. By increasing the working day and the intensity of labor and implicitly paying themselves less per hour, some of these farmers are able to temporarily survive a downturn in commodity prices.

For the larger middle-sized farmer, there is only one possible solution to the debt-income squeeze: increased debt combined with exploitation of a low-paid wage labor force. It is at this point that the family farm is pushed to become a capitalist unit of agricultural production.

How does this happen? Driven to increase the size of their farm, purchase the most modern machinery, and use expensive production techniques, the farmer must expand production to the point beyond the capability of family labor power. A permanent wage labor force becomes essential to maintain production levels (as in the case of Pat Benedict). In addition, migrant and student labor is hired during peak harvesting weeks. As a result, when commodity prices drop, the farmer no longer exploits family labor power but instead maintains farm income through exploitation of a wage labor force. Layoffs, wage cutting, and other devices are used to shift the burden of the falling prices from the farm entrepreneur to the farm workers.

Large Farms and the New Agrarian Bourgeoisie

Large-sized farms with sales of $100,000 or more tend to be more industrial in character. In many commodities, such as poultry, they are employing wage labor to replace family labor for most of the farm work, thus coming to resemble their capitalist counterparts in manufacturing. In some cases, family members work solely as managers. Many of these farms are fully incorporated and a few are subsidiaries of nonagricultural companies. Large-sized farms have increased rapidly in numbers in recent years, from 23,000 to 162,000 between 1960 and 1977.[28]

Consolidation of larger and larger farms should continue, fueled by two additional economic forces: (1) the skyrocketing price of land and (2) federal tax laws.

High land prices, caused in part by the desire of investors to buy farm land as a hedge against inflation, limit the entry of new farmers into the business and make it difficult for older farmers (especially in the middle-sized category) to buy more land. For instance, if an acre of farm land in Illinois were to cost $3,000 today, the cash flow resulting from its crops would not be enough to service the debt needed to buy it.[29]

The Congressional Budget Office in 1978 warned that if certain tax laws (and support programs) favoring large-sized farmers were to continue, the number of farms would drop another 41 percent by the year 2000.[30] In 1979, Secretary of Agriculture Bergland reported to a Senate committee on agriculture that "the largest tax savings apparently accrue to the largest farms and to individuals investing in agriculture to take advantage of the special provisions."[31]

As this transformation away from family farming proceeds, so does the growth of new agricultural classes. In the future we may find not only an increasingly wealthy and powerful capitalist farm class, but at the opposite pole, a much poorer class of semi-proletarian farmers and agricultural wage workers.

Agricultural Workers

For decades the ratio of family to nonfamily labor in American farming stood at approximately three to one (see Table 1). To be sure, the family farm system has always required a certain amount of supplemental wage labor owing to seasonal cycles of planting and harvesting and family life cycles (surpluses or shortages of children of working age). But the character of this labor has been unique, in that it consists largely of seasonal—frequently migrant—workers and children of other farmers.[32] Today this kind of labor force is being transformed more and more into a class of permanent, year-round wage laborers who are neither seasonal nor likely ever to move onto a farm of their own.

The development of U.S. agriculture is generating this transformation of the agricultural working class in three ways. First, as the growing size and industrialization of successful farms makes family labor insufficient, more farms are becoming capitalist, hiring permanent employees. Second, the overall decline in the number of families in rural areas makes the sharing of surplus children as temporary wage workers less feasible. Third, mechanization of harvesting and other labor-intensive tasks, as in the case of the mechanical tomato pickers in California, is lessening the demand for seasonal labor.

The size of the wage labor force in U.S. agriculture appears to be growing: between 1965 and 1974 the Lake States reported a 12 percent increase in the use of hired labor, the Pacific States a 30 percent increase.[33] But the long-run trend is hard to predict, since mechanization will continue to revolutionize the parts of farm work traditionally requiring large amounts of labor. The condition of agricultural laborers is not likely to improve markedly in the near future. Many seasonal and migrant workers will suffer as their jobs are eliminated. Furthermore, since the progress of industrialization in agriculture is slow and costly, few sectors of farming will pay good wages or maintain good working conditions. Finally, those family farmers who do hang on into the future will be hardpressed economically and therefore hungry for cheap labor and afraid of most progressive demands for unions and better working conditions. This situation should therefore provide fertile, though hard, ground for the growth of agricultural unions and labor militancy.[34]

Taking regional differences into consideration, we can begin to predict the broad outlines of a new rural class structure for the 1980s and 1990s.

1. A rapidly rising agrarian bourgeoisie in much of the South and Midwest will join an already established class of corporate farmers in California, the Southwest, and Florida. This small but powerful farm class will assume more and more control over farmer politics as the middle-sized family farmers are squeezed out.

2. An increasingly large but politically inactive semiproletarian farmer class in the South, Midwest, and Southern Plains; a slower rise of this class throughout the other regions. It may prove critical to the farm protest movement of the future that this class of farmers join its ranks. However, the combination of wage earner and independent producer status among these households seems to dampen activism in either sphere.

3. The stabilization of an agricultural wage earner class in the near future as more kinds of production are transformed to a factory-like system. It is difficult to predict the future size of this class because while mechanization increases the permanent labor force in some areas, such as livestock, the same process creates unemployment in other areas, such as vegetable crops.

4. The decline of the middle-sized family-owned and -operated farm, occurring more rapidly in the South and Midwest among cotton, corn, wheat, and livestock farmers. This group of farmers, unable or un-

interested in becoming part-time farmers or corporate capitalists, will be the most active in protesting the current changes in agriculture.[35]

This takes us back to where we started: to the American Agricultural Movement—the most visible representation of agricultural change in the United States—and to the issue of the family farm crisis.

Parity Politics: A New Populism

Many observers have argued against the AAM that farmers have nothing to complain about. During the 1979 tractorcade farmers received a significant beating from the press, which portrayed their movement with such catch phrases as "welfare tractors," "bellyaching," and "tractorcade follies of 1979." Articles in leading magazines and newspapers claimed that farmers had no grievance since 1978 had been a good year due to higher prices and a good wheat crop. Farm prices were up 20 percent from the previous year as farm income reached $28 billion, second only to the 1973 level.[36]

What this ignores, however, is that prices are not the only measure of a healthy industry. Costs must be also taken into account. And both costs and prices must be looked at over a longer term than just one year. Farmers argue that they have been receiving too little money for the commodities they produce as compared to their investment in land, capital, and labor. They have been caught in a squeeze between rising costs and falling prices for several years now: from 1973 to 1978 farm prices were down by 20 percent while costs had risen by 33 percent.[37]

For two winters in a row, farmers have camped in Washington to demand what they consider the answer to their problem: 90–100 percent parity. The term "parity" refers to the relative prices of farm products versus farm inputs (also known as the sectoral terms of trade). Full parity means restoring the price ratio that existed during the base years 1910–1914, which was very favorable to farmers. That is, it would give farmers gains in purchasing power equal to the rest of the economy over the last several decades.

Since parity as a short-run goal is beneficial to all classes of farmers, farm interests support the parity demands of the AAM (except the large livestock farmers who depend on cheap grain prices). But it is primarily the demand of the medium-sized family farmers who are representing their class interest as the interest of all classes in agriculture. As such, parity politics diverts attention from the growing division among farming classes. The agrarian bourgeoisie, with a more permanent workforce, greater access to credit and markets, and an increased ability to raise productivity levels, is in a radically different economic position from smaller farmers who exploit their family's own labor. Parity is also not a life-and-death matter for semiproletarian farmers whose debts are less and who can seek off-farm employment.

Moreover, in the long run, government-supported high prices do little to solve the structural problems of the family farmers. They simply encourage further efforts to expand output and recreate the dilemma of overproduction and overinvestment on a larger scale. Meanwhile, the initiative continues to pass to the capitalist farm operators, who stand to benefit as much or more than their smaller competitors from high prices and government payments.

Neither the AAM nor the plight of hardpressed family farmers from which it grows are unique in American history. Like previous farm movements, the AAM is rooted in the wider economic forces that shape U.S. agriculture. Many farmers have only a limited perception of those forces and the way in which they participate in their own undoing. As a result, the parity focus of the AAM touches only on the surface manifestations rather than the systemic roots of the economic woes of U.S. farmers.

While their cause is in one sense a progressive one insofar as many farmers are struggling against the encroaching power of the banks, the corporations, and the large-scale agribusiness firms, we should be under no illusions that this populist struggle can turn back the clock. The U.S. family farm cannot survive as the dominant form of agricultural production. Ultimately, the remaining family farmers, the farmworkers, and the other sectors of the U.S. working class will have to assume control of both agriculture and industry and forge a new agricultural system that takes into consideration the needs of the vast majority of the American people.

2. Exports for Empire: U.S. Agricultural Policies in the 1970s

In the past decade agriculture has become a mainstay of United States global economic power. With one out of every three acres of the country's crop land devoted to producing for the export market, agriculture has become the number one export industry. The record $30 billion in farm exports earned in 1979 have been crucial in bolstering the U.S. dollar, offsetting a now chronic trade deficit, and financing the nation's oil import bill. As ironic as it may seem for the world's foremost industrial power, farm exports are now regarded as basic to the economy, indeed, "the very bedrock" of that economy, according to Walter Mondale.[1]

The fivefold increase in the value of U.S. farm exports and doubling in volume that has occurred over the past decade has not been fortuitous. When it became clear in the late 1960s and early 1970s that the U.S. economy was in trouble, Washington policymakers—both government and corporate officials—saw agriculture as what then Secretary of Agriculture Earl Butz called the U.S. "ace in the hole." With its tremendous and not yet fully tapped productive potential, and with the prospect of growing demand for grain in the rest of the world, agriculture was slated to play a central role in a strategy to shore up the declining position of the United States in the world economy. As the following examination of U.S. agricultural policies in the 1970s reveals, the flip side of the success of U.S. strategies was a major upheaval in the world food economy and the escalation of food prices to unprecedented levels. To understand the impetus for the major shift in agricultural policies that began in the early 1970s, it is important to look briefly at the nature of the crisis that confronted the U.S. economy.

U.S. Economy in Crisis

The first sign of economic crisis was the fall of the dollar from its unchallenged position as the cornerstone of a world monetary system carefully constructed under U.S. tutelage after World War II. Dollars had been piling up overseas for years, partly as a result of massive U.S. military spending—first in postwar Europe, then in Korea, and most recently in Vietnam. By the late 1960s, the amount of dollars held abroad was far in excess of what other countries needed to purchase U.S. goods and services, and these unwanted dollars were resulting in an enormous drain on this country's gold supplies. To stem the tide, in 1968 it was announced that for the first time in two decades U.S. dollars would no longer be convertible into gold.[2]

The second dramatic manifestation of the crisis occurred in 1971, when the U.S. trade balance registered its first deficit since 1871. In contrast to the years following World War II, when the U.S. economy was the unrivaled leader in world trade, throughout the 1960s the U.S. position was slipping. Between 1960 and 1970, U.S. imports grew much faster than exports—by about 25 percent.

The underlying explanation for the declining position of the U.S. economy in world trade lies in the basic changes that occurred in the world organization of capitalist production in the postwar period. During that time the U.S. position as the foremost industrial producer has faced some serious challenges.

Initially, the main threat came from growing competition from reconstructed industries in Japan and Europe, whose new and efficient plants and cheap labor force allowed them to rapidly enlarge their share of the world market. By the 1970s, a new trend was on the horizon: the increasing growth of manufacturing production (even in basic industries like cars and steel) in developing countries, where labor costs are lower and profit margins higher.[4] As they had throughout the postwar period, U.S. transnationals also continued to expand their production facilities abroad rather than produce goods in the United States for export. This shift had a dramatic impact on the U.S. trade position. By 1975, the value of manufactured exports from the United States had dropped to one-quarter of the amount sold abroad by the foreign affiliates of U.S. companies.[5]

At the same time that U.S. industry was facing more competition, its own performance began to lag. The overall growth rate of the gross national product slipped from a yearly increase of 4.7 percent in the first half of the 1960s to only 3 percent in the last half.[6]

What all of these changes added up to was a decline in U.S. manufacturing industry relative to other capitalist countries. This deterioration was reflected in the increasingly poor performance of the United States in world trade. The U.S. share of total world manufactured exports declined from 21 percent in 1960 to 15 percent in 1976. And at the same time U.S. imports of manufactured and semi-manufactured goods rose from 44 percent of total imports in 1961 to 66.8 percent in 1971,[7] reflecting the flood of everything from foreign-made television sets to compact cars into the U.S. market.

Crisis Management

As the 1960s drew to a close, the Nixon administration began to take a long, hard look at these new international economic realities. In addition to discussions in the administration, several presidential task forces were set up to analyze the crisis and chart a course for the future. Among the most important in pointing the direction for a new agricultural policy was the Commission on International Trade and Investment Policy, known as the Williams Commission, after its chairman Albert L. Williams of IBM. Recognizing the basic changes that had taken place in the world economy, the commission's report pinpointed the two areas where the United States still maintains a competitive advantage in world production and trade: high technology manufactured goods (most notably capital equipment, armaments, computers) and agriculture (particularly grains and oil seeds like soybeans).[8]*

---

*We use the term "grain" to refer to both soybeans and cereals proper (including corn, wheat, oats, and barley). In fact, many of the "feedgrains" used in livestock production are soybean based.

Out of the Williams Commission and other high-level policy planning groups[9] came a strategy to guide the United States through a new era of crisis and instability. Central to that strategy was an aggressive drive to promote exports and reassert the U.S. position in the world economy, a drive in which agriculture was to play a crucial role.[10] It was in this context that U.S. agricultural policy was set in a new direction that has charted the course of three administrations—from Nixon to Ford to Carter—and will undoubtedly continue well into the 1980s.

The arguments made in the early 1970s to support the plan to make agriculture a cornerstone of U.S. international economic policy still echo through the halls of Congress, the Department of Agriculture, and the White House today. For one, so the thinking still goes, U.S. agriculture is the most efficient and productive in the world, and also one of the most productive sectors of the country's economy. The farm sector in the United States historically has produced more than this country's population consumes, for a variety of reasons. The climate of the midwestern farm belt is ideally suited to grain production, rarely suffering from the frost or droughts that plague other major producers like the Soviet Union. Moreover, the support infrastructure for agriculture—including education, research, transportation facilities, and the farm supply industry (chemicals, seeds, machinery)—is probably the most sophisticated and developed in the world. According to Department of Agriculture figures, output per man hour in agriculture (productivity) has risen an average of 6 percent annually since 1950, as compared to only a 2.6 percent rise in the nonfarm industries. Since 1956 agricultural productivity has tripled. The capital intensive nature of U.S. agriculture is reflected in the fact that farm production has twice the amount of capital investment per worker as does nonfarm production in the U.S.[11] By these standards of the capitalist yardstick, nowhere in the world is grain produced as efficiently as in the United States (although the costs in terms of energy use and environmental pollution call into question this measure of efficiency).

Moreover, U.S. policy planners judge the long-term prospects for expanding agricultural export markets overseas to be excellent.[12] Japan, a densely populated and agriculturally poor country which depends on imports for 90 percent of its grain, is today the largest market for U.S. agricultural exports. Yet its population is only in the early stages of what the Department of Agriculture describes as "upgrading" their diets—that is, switching to Western-style diets based largely on beef and grains. Common Market countries, while often producing a surplus of some basic grains, have what the Department of Agriculture sees as a notoriously inefficient farm sector, where production is still dominated by small-scale farmers heavily subsidized by the government. If only these government subsidies and protective trade barriers could be removed, U.S. strategists predict, there could be an enormous increase in what is already this country's largest regional market.

In the developing capitalist countries, population growth, an increasing number of middle-income consumers, and a shift to Western styles of eating all point to a growing market for U.S. food exports—provided, of course, that policies aimed at food self-sufficiency are not implemented. Indeed, since 1974 approximately one-half of world wheat imports have been by the so-called less developed countries.[13]

A final target are the vast markets of the socialist countries, where the United States was able to begin making commercial inroads after the detente initiatives of the Nixon administration. Given the continued upgrading of people's diets, the United States views the barely tapped markets of the socialist world to have spectacular growth potential.

The U.S. Food Strategy

The outlines of the U.S. agricultural policy first developed in the early 1970s flowed from these assessments. The aim was to mount an aggressive food export drive with several specific goals: (1) to impose the principle of "free trade" in agricultural products on U.S. trading partners, maximally forcing them to abandon their internal policies designed to subsidize their own domestic agricultural production, and minimally to reduce trade barriers; (2) to open the socialist markets to U.S. agriculture exports; and (3) to shift food exports to developing countries away from U.S.

government-financed sales under the Public Law 480 program described in the next chapter (which accounted for 15 percent of all U.S. agricultural exports in 1969[14]) to wholly commercial cash sales.

There was, however, one major obstacle in the way of the success of this strategy: existing U.S. farm programs. Domestic farm policy was, and still is, intimately tied to U.S international agricultural policy and has a decisive effect on the international grain market. Following is a brief glance at the outlines of this policy as it looked in the early 1970s (which was nearly identical to when it was first set up under Franklin Roosevelt's New Deal).

Most characteristic of U.S. agricultural policy was the deep involvement of the government in the farm economy on a number of fronts.[15] Starting during the Depression years in the 1930s, the federal government devised a complex set of programs to guarantee farmers' incomes. The constant tendency of farmers to produce a surplus that could not be absorbed by the market created, as we have seen in the last chapter, a recurrent downward pressure on prices. In supporting farmers' incomes, the government effectively set the price of U.S. farm products. Because this artificially set price was above world prices in most years, the federal government also had to subsidize U.S. farm exports to make them competitive on the world market. This was done by making direct payments to the handful of multibillion-dollar grain corporations that control U.S. grain exports.

This farm income support policy had the undesired side effect of further encouraging "overproduction." This in turn generated another form of government intervention: direct government control of production. The Department of Agriculture decided every year on desired production levels and then paid farmers accordingly to hold acreage out of production. But given the fluctuations in agricultural production caused by unpredictable weather conditions, surpluses continued, and the government gave farmers the option of selling directly to the Department of Agriculture's Commodity Credit Corporation (CCC) when prices fell too low. As a result, the federal government became the owner of huge reserve stocks of grain.

These policies met increasing opposition in the 1960s from a variety of sources. The grain companies wanted to cut the market loose from the fetters of government control, which prevented them from maximizing their profits by playing the ups and downs of the naturally cyclical agricultural market. Nonfarm-state congresspeople (whose representation in Congress had increased greatly since the 1930s) and U.S. taxpayers were indignant at the huge cost of subsidizing grain companies and farmers (especially since it was the largest and richest farmers who benefited the most). But the decisive impetus for change came from the impact these farm programs had on U.S. agriculture's position in world trade.

For one, the huge reserves held by the CCC had what economic planners saw as a "depressing effect" on the world grain market. Because of these surpluses, world market prices for grain were kept abnormally low, a factor which for millions of working people around the world meant a period of relatively stable and low food prices. What was good for people, however, was not good for the commercial interests of the United States, since low world market prices made U.S. farm goods too expensive to be competitive on world markets.

The government reserve system also put the United States in the position of being the world's "residual" supplier. When crops were poor in other parts of the world, buyers could always fall back on purchasing U.S. surpluses—a feature which caused policy planners to complain that the U.S. government was forced to bear the cost of world food scarcity.

And finally, the extensive involvement of the government in the farm economy and world trade directly contradicted U.S. "free trade" goals. As long as the government directly subsidized U.S. agricultural exports it would be difficult for the United States to demand that other countries abandon their protectionist policies.

Out of these contradictions came a major shift in U.S. farm policy under the Nixon administration.[16] The goals of the new policy were best articulated by Nixon-appointed Secretary of Agriculture Earl Butz, a "free-market" hardliner (who gave up seats on the boards of directors of several agribusiness corporations when he came to the Cabinet). Under the slogans of "returning to the free market" and "getting the government out of agriculture," the aim was to abolish government reserves and export subsidies, and encourage farmers to produce at full capacity to maximize export earnings with a minimum of government support. Agriculture was just another industry (Butz was fond of pointing out) and farm policy should be based on hardheaded economics, not on social welfare policies. Another objective which even the blunt secretary of agriculture could not publicly advocate (but which his department admitted to in a secret document) was to raise world grain prices to U.S. levels,[17] which would restore the competitiveness of U.S. exports.

A combination of factors, including a series of U.S. government moves on the international front (described below), the legislative revamping of the farm program, and a surge in world market demand for grain because of worldwide crop failures, helped achieve the turnaround the Nixon administration wanted: U.S. agriculture was set on a new course for the next decade. The immediate effect, however, was to send shock waves through the international economy. The result was the "food crisis" of 1973–1974. Grain prices skyrocketed (tripling in a matter of months) and food reserves fell to their lowest level in decades just as crop shortfalls threatened famine in many parts of the world. The U.S. government's role in provoking these events as a byproduct of its efforts to step up exports is important to recognize.

The International Front

The Nixon administration's first major move on the international front to implement its export drive was the devaluation of the dollar in August 1971. One month later, the Department of Agriculture explained that "a major consideration in Nixon's New Economic Policy (NEP) is the need for American agriculture to remain a growth factor and to continue expanding its markets abroad."[18] As one representative of the grain trade said in an interview, "the NEP was very important in giving U.S. agriculture an advantage due to the devaluation of the dollar."[19]

The immediate effect of the devaluation was to greatly stimulate demand for U.S. grain in Japan and Europe, whose economies were on the upswing. In the two quarters following devaluation, the quantity of U.S. wheat exports tripled and corn exports increased by about 20 percent. After the second devaluation in early 1973, the Japanese yen had appreciated 40 percent and the value of U.S. food exports to Japan doubled.[20] According to the President's 1975 Economic Report, the NEP was a significant factor in the 39 percent increase in U.S. exports between 1972 and 1974.

Third world countries, however, were hard hit by the devaluation. The rush by the more affluent countries to buy cheaper food from the United States helped create shortages on the world market which eventually contributed to higher prices. Thus third world countries were faced with a double hardship as a result of U.S. policies: first, they had to compete on the world market for scarce commodities at rising prices, and second, their financial position deteriorated as a result of devaluation. Many countries had their currencies' values pegged to the dollar, and almost all held their foreign exchange in dollars. The adverse impact on third world countries' ability to purchase food was of secondary concern, however, to U.S. policymakers, whose chief interest was the cash markets of the affluent countries. As the then assistant secretary of agriculture said at the time, "Our primary concern is commercial exports . . . . We can't subordinate our commercial exports to needy people."[21]

Opening the Socialist Market

Another crucial element in U.S. strategies that contributed to the upheaval in the world food economy in the early 1970s was the opening of the Soviet market to U.S. grain exports. Until the famous Soviet wheat deal of 1972–1973, in which the Soviet Union suddenly purchased 18 million tons of wheat, the Soviet Union (which is the world's largest wheat producer) had imported U.S. grain only in very small amounts. But the detente policies of the early Nixon-Kissinger years, which were in fact partly motivated by the economic self-interest of both countries in expanded trade relations, set the stage for a huge expansion of U.S. agricultural exports. A serious Soviet crop failure in 1971–1972, caused by unusually bad weather, was the fortuitous event that allowed U.S. plans for a major entry into the Soviet market to take hold. The Soviets' subsequent purchase of the 18 million tons of U.S. grain also played into the Nixon administration's plans by completely wiping out U.S. grain reserves and raising world grain prices to unprecedented levels.

The public outcry that followed the skyrocketing of U.S. food prices made the administration anxious to appear as an innocent bystander in the Soviet wheat deal. But in fact the evidence reveals that the administration had carefully laid the groundwork for the Soviet sales.[22] In mid-1970, Nixon announced a major policy change aimed at opening up agricultural trade with the Soviets: special export licenses would no longer be required for grain sales to the Soviet Union and the People's Republic of China. This in turn eliminated a key provision in the licensing requirement that 50 percent of exports be shipped on U.S. vessels, whose rates were far above world prices. This provision was originally enacted at the time of the first Soviet grain purchases in 1963 because of maritime union pressure, and had effectively prevented further sales to the Soviet Union. In fact, throughout the 1960s, the maritime unions were attacked by the grain companies as the chief obstacle to trading with the Soviets. Nixon's turnaround had an immediate impact: in November 1971 the Soviets purchased 3 million tons of U.S. feed grains.

Over the next several months, Earl Butz and other officials negotiated with the Soviets on the terms of a proposed U.S. credit to finance Soviet grain purchases. Even the White House was, according to one of the participants, "deeply involved." As advisor to the National Security Council, Henry Kissinger personally directed Cabinet members to develop "a recommendation on how the private transactions of the U.S. grain companies should be related to government actions including the U.S. opening a CCC credit line."[23] In July of 1972, just three days after the Continental Grain Company reported the first large sale to the Soviets, supposedly negotiated in secret without government knowledge, President Nixon announced Soviet acceptance of an offer of $750 million in CCC credits to finance their purchases over the next three years.

When the Soviets finally concluded their buying spree at the end of the summer, U.S. officials expressed surprise at the size of their purchases, which amounted to $1 billion and absorbed one-quarter of that year's wheat crop. But in fact the administration had clear indications that Soviet import needs would be tremendous. As the White House knew, the Soviet government had recently given top priority to increasing domestic meat consumption, which meant stepping up imports of the grains needed to feed its livestock. The U.S. Department of Agriculture had also received a succession of reports from its attachés in the Soviet Union and even the CIA (which closely monitors Soviet agricultural production) indicating that weather damage to the Soviet crop would be severe. Official silence was not without purpose. It served the interests of the grain companies, who were able to purchase enough grain to fill Soviet orders before news of the sales sent commodity prices skyrocketing. And it also relieved the U.S. government of any public complicity in the public outcry that followed.

Most important to administration officials, however, was the fact that the Soviet wheat deal represented a turning point in the success of their agricultural strategies. The transaction served not only as a wedge to open the Soviet market, deplete U.S. grain reserve stocks, and finally raise world market prices to U.S. levels, it also marked the beginning of expanding agricultural trade with the socialist world, which has become the fastest growing market for U.S. farm exports. By 1979, the Soviet Union, China, and Eastern Europe accounted for one out of every seven dollars in U.S. agricultural export earnings.[24] Poland now ranks first among all countries receiving CCC credits. And China, whose potentially vast market is still considered to be virgin territory by U.S. exporters, has begun to import increasing quantities of grain even though it is self-sufficient in meeting its basic food needs. Purchases of over 6 million tons of corn and wheat in 1978 put China among the top ten U.S. exports markets.[25] The current push on both sides to expand commercial relations is likely to lead to a further increase in Chinese imports, especially once the granting of "most favored nation" status gives China access to CCC credits.

The U.S. Offensive in Europe and Japan

While U.S. strategies for bolstering its trade position quickly met with success in the socialist countries, the situation in relation to the advanced capitalist countries was more problematic. When in the early 1970s the Nixon administration first set out on its export drive, the Department of Agriculture prepared a study analyzing U.S. prospects for expanding agricultural trade vis-à-vis the capitalist world. This report raised two major concerns which continue to plague U.S. policymakers. First, the Western European countries have protective trade barriers to prevent U.S. grain from selling at competitive prices in the European market: U.S. agricultural exports to Europe declined by about 15 percent between 1966 and 1969.[26] The Department of Agriculture predicted at the time that relaxation of Japanese and European trade barriers could add $8 billion to the U.S. trade balance by the end of the decade. Second, Western European governments subsidize their grain exports at prices which offer U.S. grain stiff competition on the world market. Partly because of this competition, between 1963 and 1971 the U.S. share of world trade in wheat and feed grains had dropped by 6 and 10 percent respectively.[27]

In the early 1970s government and farm industry officials found the ideal forum to launch an offensive to reshape world agricultural polices in the U.S. interest. The multilateral trade negotiations sponsored by the General Agreement on Tariffs and Trade (GATT)—the main arena in which the capitalist nations have battled out their trade interests since World War II—reconvened for its third major round of negotiations in 1973. After the previous "Kennedy Round" of negotiations in the early 1960s, U.S. farmers and grain companies had complained bitterly that their interests had been "sold down the river." But this time the scenario was different: agriculture was the key item on the agenda of U.S. negotiators, and it was here, rather than in industry, that the U.S. hoped to make its major gains. As one U.S. official put it back in 1977, some sort of breakthrough in agriculture is a "sina qua non" for any agreement.[28] Indicating agriculture's importance, the Nixon administration appointed the vice-president of Cargill (one of the world's biggest grain exporters) as special deputy trade representative.

The thrust of U.S. arguments at the talks changed little over six years of negotiating and several new faces in the White House. Why, U.S. negotiators argued, should other governments subsidize and protect their own inefficient agricultural producers when U.S. agriculture could provide them lower cost food? These negotiators claimed rational use of the world's resources made it reasonable for the United States to produce and export what it produces most efficiently and cheaply (i.e., grain), and for other countries to specialize in producing commodities where they have a comparative advantage. And they, like the Williams Commission, argued that in the case of developing countries these should be labor-intensive crops for export—crops such as fruits and vegetables (where they have a cost advantage)—thereby earning foreign exchange to import low-cost grains from the United States. And Japan should concentrate on producing cameras and electronic equipment and simply import its food from the United States. Essentially, the U.S. negotiating position amounted to an attack on policies of other countries aimed at food self-sufficiency—a position top officials at the U.S. Department of Agriculture argue explicitly.[29] This attack, of course, is not formulated in terms of national self interest. Instead, the United States invokes the principles of "free trade" and comparative advantage—both ideas developed to their fullest by apologists of the British empire to justify Britain's drive for industrial supremacy in the nineteenth century.

The U.S. Negotiating Position

One of the U.S. bargaining chips in the negotiations was a willingness to offer foreign manufacturing industries better access to U.S. markets in exchange for the removal of trade barriers against U.S. farm exports. In effect, this negotiating position recognized that certain U.S. industries which could no longer hold their own against foreign competitors—industries like steel, textiles, and footwear—would have to be sacrificed for the interests of U.S. agriculture.

By the end of the trade talks in April of 1979, negotiators were claiming that U.S. agriculture stood to gain about $3–4 billion in trade benefits as a result of Europe's and Japan's reductions in trade barriers,[30] mainly in grains, soybeans, beef, and fruit. United States negotiators saw an even more important victory in the extension of GATT's longstanding (and consistently violated) prohibition on government subsidies to foreign exports. (According to the agreement, any subsidy aimed at gaining an "undue share" of a third country's market is outlawed.) Although the United States clearly hopes to make this a blanket prohibition on export subsidies (thus curtailing competition from the European Common Market's subsidized grain exports), whether or not it will be enforced as such remains to be seen.

A major concession made by the United States was a relaxation of protective barriers against dairy imports, to the chagrin of U.S. producers. Dairy farmers claim that the U.S. promise to lower import quotas will mean a flood of European imports and bankruptcy for thousands of midwestern dairy farmers.[31] And from the rest of U.S. agriculture's point of view, as well, the negotiations fell far short of expectations. Part way through the negotiations the new Carter administration abandoned the assault on the Common Market's Common Agricultural Policy's internal farm support program, which still stands intact. The administration finally accepted, it seems, that a sudden end to the program would be politically untenable for the governments of the countries concerned, since it would mean economic ruin for Europe's farmers, who still make up 10 percent of the population.

An International Grain Reserve

An additional disappointment for the United States was the failure to include an international wheat agreement in the trade pact. Negotiations on a wheat agreement had proceeded separately since 1975, but broke down for the final time just before the trade pact was signed. The centerpiece of the wheat agreement—and the main reason the Carter administration was so interested in it—was to be an international grain reserve. Although such a reserve had often been discussed as a mechanism to safeguard against world famine, U.S. support for the reserve idea came primarily from commercial self-interest.

For exporting countries like the United States, a reserve has a dual purpose. When there is a sudden surge in world demand for grain together with a tight supply situation, a reserve stock is a form of insurance that export orders can be filled. On the other hand, when the problem is oversupply, a reserve becomes in effect a dumping ground to absorb the surplus. This second factor had a particular urgency for the Carter administration in the late 1970s at a time when several years of record harvests meant that farmers' storage bins were bulging with reserve stocks. Farmers were in effect holding the bulk of the world's reserves, and storage costs were being financed by the U.S. government. If the rest of the world would agree to share the cost burden, so much the better.

Another factor in the U.S. push for an international reserve was the desire to bring a measure of price stability to the international wheat market so as to eliminate the wild swings that characterized the market in 1972. The international reserve stocks could serve as such a buffer if they were released onto the market when supplies were low and prices rising, or built up when the opposite situation occurred.

However, when it came to the negotiating table, this interest in stability soon faded when it conflicted with other U.S. concerns. The Carter administration refused to agree to any *automatic* price mechanisms to trigger the release of stocks—the only mechanism that could guarantee avoiding another round of skyrocketing prices in the face of scarcities. Instead, U.S. negotiators maintained that price triggers should be only guidelines, and were adamant in the position that "the United States . . . will not put its grain trade in a price box."[32] They insisted that every country should control the portion of the international reserves it holds, which in the case of the United States would have been half the total, according to the U.S. proposal.

Although the United States and the European Common Market had some disagreements about the price mechanism and the size of the buffer stocks, they had apparently "agreed to agree" just in time for a wheat pact to be included in the trade package. But the final breakdown reportedly came because of the opposing interests of the United States and other grain exporting countries vis-à-vis the importing countries of the less developed world. One sticking point was the question of who should finance the world reserve. Developing countries wanted to be exempt from the obligation, but the United States indignantly insisted the reserve scheme was a commercial agreement that should not be used as a development aid mechanism.[33] Even more important was the irreconcilable conflict over the upper and lower trigger prices, which both sides recognized would effectively set a minimim and maximum price on world grain. The developing countries wanted to keep this range narrow and relatively low on the price scale so as to be able to take advantage of lower import prices when supplies were plentiful. The exporters, on the other hand, insisted on a relatively high minimum price—particularly crucial at a time when growing surpluses are threatening to drive down prices. They also wanted to allow prices to rise as high as $5.44 a bushel (almost twice the current world price) before supplies could be released from the stockpile.

Having failed to orchestrate a multilateral grain pact to suit its own likes and needs, the United States immediately began to seek an agreement with other exporting countries—what would amount to a world wheat cartel. Just a month after the collapse of the reserve talks in 1979 Secretary of Agriculture Bob Bergland said he would ask Canada (which together with the United States accounts for 75 percent of the world wheat exports) to join an agreement on setting minimum world prices to prevent market prices from falling even further.[34] He later met with the Canadians as well as representatives from the two other major exporters, Australia and Argentina, to discuss "coordination" of production and marketing policies.[35]

However, the likelihood of a grain producers' cartel succeeding are slim—partly because grain (unlike oil) is a renewable resource that can be produced in many parts of the world (especially if the international market is rigged to keep prices high). And even if the United States could weather the international political storm such a formal cartel would cause, the historical experience with cartels is that one or more members is sooner or later tempted to break ranks in pursuit of its own commercial interests. Argentina's refusal to go along with the U.S. attempt to boycott grain ship-ments to the Soviet Union in early 1980 was a typical example of the difficulty of maintaining a unified front among competitors. In any case, the mere fact that the United States has threatened to resort to a cartel arrangement points to some of the underlying weaknesses and contradictions in the country's international agricultural strategies, some of which we will now explore.

The Contradictions in U.S. Food Policies

At the beginning of the 1980s the old dilemma of overproduc tion has once again come back to haunt U.S. agricultural policy-makers, recreating a situation similar in many ways to that of 1970–1972. Farm prices had fallen (wheat was down from almost $5.00 a bushel in 1973 to $3.40 in 1979). World reserves were at their highest level since the late 1960s. A worldwide economic downturn had cut into the growth rate of world agricultural trade. There were also signs that the U.S. position in international markets is slipping. Argentina, for example, has cut into the traditional U.S. export market in Brazil. And when world agri-culture trade dropped by 6 million tons in 1976, it was the United States that absorbed the entire drop.[36] In this context U.S. talk of a cartel arrangement that could serve the purpose of dividing up world grain markets is as much indicative of weakness as it is of strength.

The return to an era of surplus—however temporary it may be given the unpredictable cycles of agricultural production—has also forced a partial return to government involvement in the domestic farm economy. The free-market purism of the Butz days is no longer a practical possibility for any administration. In 1977, after two years of record crops, the Carter administration bowed to the pressure of falling farm prices and launched a new program to hold land out of production in order to shore up prices and retard the build-up of reserves. In spite of dire warnings about the inflationary impact the policy would have on domestic food prices, the decision was made to withhold about 20 million acres of farm land from production, including 20 percent of the country's wheat lands.[37]

The government was also forced into resuming a massive subsidy program for farmers. Although the 1973 farm bill had guaranteed farmers a certain minimum "target" price for their crops, the program lay dormant as long as market prices were above the target level. But when in 1977 market prices fell below this level (which the Carter administration had raised in response to farm complaints of rising production costs) the government began making direct subsidy payments to farmers to make up the gap—at a cost of about $5 billion a year.

The domestic inflationary impact of U.S. export strategies—and particularly the destabilizing effect of large and erratic Soviet purchases on the market—presents another contradiction to agricultural policymakers. The solution has been an unprecedented level of government involvement in international trade. When the Soviets entered the U.S. market for a second round of large purchases in 1974–1975, the Ford administration felt reluctantly compelled to head off public protests against a new cycle of rising food prices. Pressured by congressional threats to step in, the White House ordered a two-month moratorium on grain sales to the Soviet Union. This last-resort measure had its own undesired consequences. It angered U.S. farmers, made other regular customers uneasy, and blatantly contradicted U.S. export goals.

Recognizing that a balance would have to be met between domestic demands for stable food prices and U.S. dependence on the Soviet market as a major commercial outlet, the administration then negotiated a five-year trade agreement with the Soviets. In exchange for guaranteed access to U.S. grain supplies, the Soviet Union committed itself to a minimum annual purchase of

6 million tons of U.S. grain, with an option of up to 8 million tons. Any purchase above that level would have to be authorized by the U.S. government.

By 1980 this effort to stabilize U.S.-Soviet trade hit upon a major snag when U.S. foreign policy considerations came into direct conflict with economic interests. In the fall of 1979, when it became clear that bad weather had caused Soviet grain production to drop far below expected levels, the Department of Agriculture gave the Soviets permission to import 25 million metric tons of corn and wheat over the next year. With record U.S. surpluses depressing farm prices, the Carter administration was delighted to allow the Soviets to compensate for the crop failure with large purchases of U.S. grain. However, when the administration decided several months later to take a hard line against the Soviet intervention in Afghanistan, diplomatic considerations took precedence. President Carter suddenly called a halt to sales to the Soviets over the 8 million ton mark.

This decision generated a new set of contradictions for U.S. agricultural policies.[38] To accommodate the grain companies, the administration decided to buy the 14 million tons of grain already purchased by the companies for shipment to the Soviets. This put the Department of Agriculture in the position of once again owning a large grain reserve—the very situation the policies of the previous decade had tried to reverse. The unsold surplus resulting from the blockage of Soviet sales was expected to force the Carter administration into still deeper and costlier involvement in the farm economy on other fronts as well. Most likely were expanded programs to hold acreage out of production and, as the surpluses pressure farm prices downward, increased subsidies to farmers. Besides the immediate loss in export revenues, this foreign policy shift is also likely to affect longer term U.S. economic interests as the Soviets seek other suppliers to reduce their vulnerability to future U.S. political pressures.

The current "problem" of U.S. surpluses is an eerie echo of a decade ago when sudden scarcities of the early 1970s assured the success of U.S. agricultural strategies. To be sure, agricultural policymakers are anxious to avoid the crisis atmosphere the sudden tripling of grain prices caused then. But a return to a tight market situation would be a boon for U.S. agricultural strategies.

Agricultural policymakers are well aware that one year's bad harvest could easily wipe out the existing surplus and create another food crisis. As one observer commented, "We are now playing roulette with the weather."[39] But given the workings of the capitalist marketplace, the logical response to a surplus is to limit production and try to reduce reserves. In the words of a White House staffer, "We have to gamble with the weather in any case, given our continuing commitment to helping support farm prices and income."[40] With the United States supplying over half the grain entering the world market, the rest of the world pays a high price for this gamble. Continuing food price inflation is the immediate price, but should the world experience another series of crop failures, hunger and famine would be the consequence for many.

At a more fundamental level, it is not just the decisions of U.S. policymakers that raise the specter of rising world food prices. The increasing costs of agricultural production in the United States is a crucial factor in the long-term trend toward food price inflation. Most arguments about the relative efficiency and low cost of U.S. production had been based on two key premises: the comparatively low cost of energy and the constant growth yields obtained on the nation's crop lands. However, since the early 1970s neither of these assumptions has held true. Skyrocketing fuel costs and declining productivity growth rates are plaguing U.S. agriculture.[41]

As the costs of fossil fuel continue to rise in the future, the extreme energy dependence of U.S. agriculture could very well threaten the success of U.S. international economic strategies.

In spite of these weaknesses and contradictions, in the short run at least agriculture has indeed proven to be the country's "ace in the hole." Without the remarkable performance of its agricultural exports throughout the 1970s, the U.S. position in the world economy would have deteriorated drastically. While U.S. hegemony in the world is clearly under challenge, it is partly due to the tremendous strength of its agricultural sector that the U.S. economy has been able to weather the economic crisis of the 1970s and still retain its position as king of the mountain in the capitalist world.

3. The U.S. Grain Arsenal: Food as a Weapon

When President Carter announced a grain boycott against the Soviet Union in early 1980 to retaliate against their intervention in Afghanistan, there could no longer be any doubt that food is a weapon in the arsenal of U.S. foreign policy. Although this action is the most dramatic instance of U.S. food diplomacy in recent years, food power has been a recurring theme in U.S. foreign policy over the past decade. Former Agriculture Secretary Earl Butz (infamous for his undiplomatic bluntness) summed up prevailing thinking in Washington when he told reporters in 1974: "Food is a tool. It is a weapon in the U.S. negotiating kit."[1]

Even though foreign policymakers in Washington are clearly committed to exploiting the rest of the world's dependence on U.S. grain for political advantage, they also face certain constraints. Probably most important is the disastrous impact food diplomacy can have on U.S. economic interests. The embargo on grain sales to the Soviet Union, for example, cost the United States several billion dollars in export earnings that are of vital importance to the health of its economy.

There is one arena, however, where food diplomacy has a virtually free rein—in the shipments financed by the government's Food for Peace program. As this chapter shows, since its inception the food aid program, under the guise of humanitarian assistance, has been an important weapon in the arsenal of U.S. foreign policy.

A History of U.S. Food Aid

The use of food aid in U.S. diplomacy dates from just after World War I. Senator Herbert Hoover (soon to be president)

The authors wish to thank Sarah Stewart for her assistance in preparing the final version of this chapter.

headed up a massive food relief program that played an important role in U.S. efforts to influence the political complexion of postwar Europe. In addition to using food relief to support anticommunist forces in Eastern Europe, Hoover attempted to use offers of food aid to the Bolsheviks as a lever to force an end to the civil war in Russia on terms favorable to the Allies. At the end of World War II, food aid again became a weapon in the U.S. fight against communism when such aid was channeled through the United Nations Relief and Rehabilitation Administration to bolster Chiang Kai-shek's troops in China. Just after the war, food relief was sent to Italy and France to stave off the social unrest the United States feared would strengthen the position of the popular communist parties in those countries, and later under the Marshall Plan, enormous shipments of food aid flowed into Europe as part of the continuing effort to strengthen noncommunist forces there.[2]

With the passage of Publc Law 480 (PL 480) in 1954, food aid was institutionalized as an arm of U.S. imperialism, and the flow of food abroad reached unprecedented proportions. In the past twenty-five years, close to $30 billion worth of agricultural commodities have been shipped overseas under the PL 480 program. It is not surprising that little of this food has reached the hungry in recipient countries, since the original legislation did not even pretend to have a humanitarian purpose. (The humanitarian intent clause was added to the law much later.) As suggested by its name—the Agricultural Trade and Development Act—PL 480 was intended primarily to develop future commercial markets for U.S. grain exports and to solve the problem of mounting U.S. farm surpluses by dumping them overseas.[3]

In line with this purpose, over three-quarters of PL 480 commodities have been shipped abroad under long-term, low-interest credits provided by Title I of the law. These credits allow foreign governments to import U.S. agricultural products for resale in their own countries, a procedure which guarantees the food does not reach the poor and needy. In Bangladesh, for example, where over 90 percent of food aid has been in the form of Title I credits since 1974, even though the government sells the food at subsidized prices through the official rationing system, 90 percent of it goes to the urban middle class.[4]

Because the sale of Title I commodities generates funds for the recipient government (known as "counterpart funds"), the United States has used the program as an important form of economic assistance to its client regimes in the third world. In many cases this budgetary support has been used by U.S. allies to finance their military expenditures—an ironic twist to the so-called Food for Peace program. In South Korea, which has become the second largest recipient of PL 480 credits, 85 percent of food aid credits were used for this purpose in the 1960s. By 1975, $6 billion worth of Title I sales proceeds had been devoted to military purposes despite a 1973 congressional ban on the use of PL 480-generated funds by the military.[5]

Title II of the program, under which the U.S. government finances food donations to "friendly" countries through private international relief agencies, is of less direct political use. But even this aspect of the program has been used to serve U.S. diplomatic interests. As one study of the political role of relief agencies pointed out, they often act as "the quiet arm of American diplomacy, living in the shadow between official policy and private charity."[6]

The repayment of PL 480 loans in local currencies—a practice allowed until 1971—created a huge pool of currencies overseas, which the U.S. government spent according to its political as well as economic interests. Once again, the military budgets of client regimes benefited when the United States simply turned the currencies back to local governments in the form of grants for "common defense." By 1971 more than $1.7 billion had been spent in this way, with two-thirds going to South Korea and South Vietnam.[7] Local currencies were also used to cover the expenses of U.S. government operations overseas, ranging from embassy costs to Department of Defense expenditures. Finally, U.S. multinationals received PL 480-generated funds to aid their expansion overseas. Under the "Cooley program," the local currencies were loaned to U.S. companies for the purpose of setting up new subsidiaries in PL 480 countries. In the seventeen years of the

Cooley program's existence, 419 subsidiaries in thirty-one countries received Cooley loans—including the Bank of America, Ralston Purina, and Cargill Corporation.[8]*

Developing New Food Markets

Judged by its original aim—to create and expand commercial markets for U.S. agricultural products overseas—the PL 480 program has been a rousing success. During the first twelve years of this program, one-quarter of all U.S. agricultural exports were financed by PL 480's easy credit terms. But by the late 1960s many of the countries which had been favored recipients of PL 480 loans—such as Japan, Taiwan, and Brazil—had "graduated" to the status of hard-cash commercial buyers. In 1969 PL 480 accounted for only 15 percent of U.S. agricultural exports, and by 1977 this figure had dropped to 4 percent.[9]

Under the guise of the food aid program, the U.S. Department of Agriculture has worked hand in glove with grain multinationals to develop these commercial markets. One of their goals has been to generate demand for U.S. agricultural products by encouraging people abroad to adopt American-style eating habits. Trade associations representing the U.S. food industry have received millions of dollars worth of PL 480 local currencies toward this end. The U.S. Feed Grains Council, for example, has used these monies to promote the development of local livestock and poultry industries which rely on imported feed grains. Another example is the Western Wheat Growers Association, which has encouraged people throughout Asia to eat wheat-based products like bread instead of locally grown rice.[10]

PL 480 has also been used as a wedge to gain a foothold in overseas markets. In many cases PL 480 credits are not given unless the recipient government agrees to expand commercial imports from the United States. In 1973 Title I shipments to the

---

*The many benefits Cargill and other U.S. grain companies have received under the PL 480 program are discussed in Chapter 13.

Dominican Republic were made conditional upon much larger cash purchases. And in 1975 loans to Egypt for wheat imports and to South Korea for rice were tied to additional commercial imports of these commodities.[11]

South Korea is often held up by Department of Agriculture officials as the PL 480 "success story." For twenty-five years the South Korean market was carefully nurtured through PL 480 shipments and related promotional activities. It has been the second largest recipient of U.S. food aid, and its livestock, poultry, and feed mill industries have been developed largely by U.S. multinationals financed through PL 480 Cooley loans. The payoff is that today South Korea ranks among the top five commercial markets for U.S. agricultural products, importing around $1 billion annually. The country has also become dependent on food imports for close to half its domestic food needs.

South Korea is not the only country where U.S. food aid has helped generate dependency on food imports. Studies show that in India, Bolivia, and Colombia—to name only a few examples—the flood of subsidized PL 480 commodities onto local markets has lowered food prices in those countries to the point where local farmers are unable to compete. In many cases this has helped to undermine local food production. And the resulting reliance on U.S. imports is, of course, precisely the effect those who conceived the program had hoped for.[12]

The success of PL 480 in enhancing the dependency of third world countries has not only expanded U.S. markets, but has also given the U.S. government considerable political leverage vis-à-vis these countries, a development which was foreseen by one of the earliest supporters of using food as a foreign policy tool, Hubert Humphrey. As the senator told Congress:

> I have heard . . . that people may become dependent on us for food. I know that was not supposed to be good news. To me that was good news, because before people can do anything they have got to eat. And if you are looking for a way to get people to lean on you and to be dependent on you, in terms of their cooperation with you, it seems to me that food dependence would be terrific.[13]

Other policymakers agreed with Humphrey. By the 1960s PL 480 had been fully incorporated into the arsenal of U.S. foreign policy, and a White House Food for Peace office was established to reflect this reality.

The Food Aid Weapon

At no time has PL 480 played a more significant role in U.S. foreign policy than in the 1970s, particularly during the Nixon-Kissinger years. The reasons for this are several. For one, the "food crisis" of the early 1970s heightened awareness in Washington of the power the United States derived from the world's dependence on U.S. grain, and in many cases materially enhanced that dependency. At the initiative of then Secretary of State Henry Kissinger, in 1973 the National Security Council undertook a comprehensive study of U.S. food policy, specifically addressing the question of the political implications of third world reliance on U.S. food supplies.[14] At about the same time, a secret CIA report was leaked in which the agency speculated that growing food shortages would mean "an increase in U.S. power and influence, especially vis-à-vis the food-deficit, poor countries."[15]

Washington's renewed focus on the notion of "food power" was also sparked by the recognition of a crisis in U.S. foreign policy. The U.S. defeat in Southeast Asia signaled a new era in which U.S. imperialism faces serious obstacles, both at home and abroad, to imposing its will in the third world. At the same time, the success of the oil producers' cartel was one of several factors galvanizing third world countries into an unprecedented united front in the fight against their disadvantaged position in the world economy. This new development represented a challenge not only to U.S. economic power, but also to its once unquestioned political hegemony.

As popular opposition to the Vietnam war grew and made itself felt in Congress, it became increasingly difficult for the White House and State Department to obtain congressional funds for economic and military aid. There was growing resistance not only to funding the Indochina war, but also to supporting repressive dictatorships around the world—the "friendly" countries that figured highest on the U.S. foreign aid priority list, from the military regime of General Augusto Pinochet in Chile to the civilian dictatorship of Park Chung Hee in South Korea. Congress annually subjected the foreign aid bill to close scrutiny, and increasingly wrote in limitations on the executive branch's use of aid funds. The White House, of course, was anxious to avoid this kind of interference with foreign policy, and sought to channel funds through mechanisms not so vulnerable to the congressional scalpel. One solution was to divert a large share of U.S. aid through the multilateral lending institutions dominated by the United States and its allies (such as the World Bank). Another was to rely more heavily on the food aid program as a channel of political support.[16]

PL 480, with its ostensibly humanitarian purpose, provided a perfect cloak for U.S. diplomacy. Few people were aware of the political dimensions of food aid (even in Congress), and it was easy to win support for a program supposedly aimed at getting food to needy people. In addition, the flexible funding procedure for PL 480 gave the executive branch an important measure of maneuverability. Although the State Department is required to submit to Congress an annual projected budget for each country slated to receive food aid, these amounts can be altered by the State Department during the course of the year without prior congressional approval. In fact, regardless of the budget submitted to Congress, the president is authorized to spend up to $1.9 billion under Title I and $660 million under Title II by borrowing from the Commodity Credit Corporation (CCC), or by drawing on previous years' unused funds.[17]

Although PL 480 is jointly administered by the departments of state and agriculture, the time was ripe in the early 1970s for foreign policy interests to take complete precedence. With sales in commercial markets booming and the government's grain reserves exhausted, the Department of Agriculture was no longer interested in PL 480 as a mechanism of surplus disposal. The amount of commodities shipped under the program dropped to an all-time low of 3.3 million tons in 1973, one-fifth the level of the mid-1960s. And for two years in a row the department made no budget requests for PL 480 expenditures. It was not long before the National Security Council and Secretary of State Kissinger became directly involved in making decisions about who would and would not receive food aid credits,[18] and PL 480 allocations became a mirror image of U.S. foreign policy priorities.

Food Power in Chile

The case of Chile is a prime example of how food aid played a central role in U.S. foreign policy strategies. In 1970 the Chilean people elected a socialist government to power under the leadership of President Salvador Allende. The White House, in a jointly coordinated effort with the CIA and U.S. multinationals, quickly moved to counter what was seen as a serious threat to U.S. political and economic interests. Hoping to create a crisis that would undermine the stability of the socialist regime, the U.S. government launched an economic blockade against Chile.[19]

Along with most private and U.S. government credits, all Title I food aid credits to Chile were suspended. Yet as the U.S. government was well aware, Chile's need for imported food had never been greater. The redistributive policies of the socialist government had boosted the purchasing power of Chilean workers to an all-time high and sent the demand for food soaring. At the same time, and not coincidentally, rightwing landowners had begun to sabotage local food production. As a result of these factors, food imports doubled in 1971 to $261 million, and rose to around $383 million in 1972. With its lines of credit cut off by the United States and its foreign exchange reserves nearly exhausted, the Allende government had great difficulty meeting the country's food import needs. Not only did the United States deny food aid credits, but shortly before the coup a request from Chile to purchase U.S. wheat *for cash* was denied "because of a political decision at the White House."[20]

When the Allende government was overthrown in 1973 by a military coup backed by the U.S. government, the State Department turned the aid spigot on full blast. Chile was immediately slated to receive the largest PL 480 credit extended in Latin

America—$35 million out of a total of $50 million—as part of the U.S. effort to prop up the new junta headed by General Augusto Pinochet.

However, revelations about the U.S. role in bringing down the Allende government created a popular protest against support for the Pinochet regime. Congressional critics managed to pass a ceiling on economic assistance to the junta of $25 million (still the second highest level of assistance in Latin America) and cut off military aid altogether. With its hands tied in other areas, the administration relied on PL 480 as the major channel of economic support. Instead of the originally programmed $35 million, by the end of the year Chile had received $52 million in food aid credits, making the Pinochet regime the sixth largest recipient of U.S. food aid for the 1975 fiscal year. In 1976 Title I allocations to Chile amounted to $55 million, or 84 percent of total food aid credits to all of Latin America.[21]

Moreover, just weeks after the coup, another little-known device in the U.S. food arsenal was called into service to rescue the junta. The Agriculture Department's Commodity Credit Corporation extended a $26 million credit to Chile for the purchase of wheat, and several weeks later another $28 million credit for the purchase of corn.[22] These credits came under the CCC's Export Credit Sales program, another program with virtually unlimited spending authority, passed out at the discretion of administration officials. Although ostensibly set up, like PL 480, to dispose of surpluses and develop markets, it has also been used to further U.S. foreign policy interests. According to one Department of Agriculture official, "word came down" from the State Department to extend the Chile credits, in spite of the fact that the program had been suspended for several months because of the tight food supply situation.[23] Butz himself commented at the time that the credits had been extended for "national security" reasons.[24]

The steady flow of food credits to Chile in the years following the coup were crucial in helping make the dictatorship viable. For one, the sale of PL 480 food locally provided a significant amount of revenue which the junta used to underwrite its budget. But even more importantly, the food credits helped alleviate the junta's desperate shortage of foreign exchange. With Chile's dependence on imported food at an all-time high every dollar they could save on food imports meant a dollar freed to finance other imports. High on the junta's international shopping list were the military equipment and arms needed to bolster its repressive apparatus. At a time when PL 480 Title I credits were accounting for 20 percent of total wheat consumption in Chile,[25] the junta was the ninth largest purchaser of U.S. arms.[26]

This barrage of food aid, however, did little to alleviate the desperate plight of the Chilean working class in the years after the coup. With unemployment at an estimated 30 percent, and purchasing power eroded by inflation rates that reached 600 percent in one year,[27] the majority of Chileans could not afford to buy the food made available under Title I. Infant mortality increased 18 percent during the first year of the military government. Two years after the coup, it was estimated that a family of five living on the industrial minimum wage had to spend 80 percent of its income on food, and suffered a caloric deficiency of 40 percent.[28]

Food for War

Perhaps even more dramatic than the Chilean case was the use of the "Food for Peace" program to subsidize the U.S.-sponsored war to contain communism in Southeast Asia.

As opposition to the Vietnam war grew and made large-scale aid programs increasingly vulnerable to criticism, PL 480 was used to channel dollars to U.S. allies in Indochina. In the early 1970s, the Thieu regime in South Vietnam received well over $100 million in PL 480 credits each year, and by 1974 the Lon Nol government in Cambodia was also high on the food aid list. For that fiscal year the Nixon administration budgeted a total of $207 million in food aid credits to the two countries. Later that year when Congress cut more than 20 percent out of the administration's economic aid request for Indochina, the White House more than doubled Title I allocations to Cambodia and South Vietnam to $499 million.[29] This meant that these two countries received three-quarters of total U.S. food aid credits that year.

In addition, special provision was made for both countries to maximize the availability of PL 480 funds for military use. Whereas other countries were required as of 1971 to repay food aid credits in dollars, both Cambodia and South Vietnam were excepted from this provision. Moreover, both countries were allowed to use 100 percent of PL 480 counterpart funds for military purposes—a waiver of the 80 percent limitation that applied to other countries.[30] Although in 1973 Congress passed a new amendment altogether prohibiting the use of PL 480 sales proceeds for military purposes, this provision had little effect in Indochina or elsewhere. Since all sales proceeds go into the general budgets of recipient countries, specifications as to their use are virtually meaningless.

Another important channel of support to the war effort that was in practice immune from congressional scrutiny was a little-known provision of PL 480, the Title III "barter program." Originally set up as a scheme to barter U.S. surplus agricultural commodities in exchange for strategic materials, by the 1960s the program was used almost exclusively to finance the overseas operations of the Department of Defense and the Agency for International Development. Under this program, food was sold in overseas markets by private exporters, who then either turned the sales proceeds over to the U.S. government agencies, or used the money to purchase goods and services on behalf of the agencies for use overseas. The Department of Agriculture now claims that records about how the money was used are unavailable, but officials admit that AID used the program extensively to procure supplies for its operations in Vietnam.[31] The budget for the barter program increased dramatically in the early 1970s, just as the Nixon-Kissinger administration was searching for ways to support the Indochina war effort. In 1973, in spite of the fact that the commercial surpluses the program was designed to dispose of no longer existed, barter sales reached an all-time high of $1.1 billion, four times the average level of spending in the 1960s.[32]*

As the war drew to a close, however, the State Department's

---

*Defunct after 1975, the barter program was revived in 1977 under Title III of PL 480. So far it has not been used.

free-handed use of food aid to fund the Indochina war machine began to backfire. Public disclosures about the use of PL 480 to finance and feed the Nguyen Van Thieu and Lon Nol armies gave the lie to the claim that food aid was serving humanitarian purposes in Indochina and caused a public outcry. Under pressure from antiwar groups, Congress began to take a more critical look at the total foreign aid package, including PL 480. Revelations about the political use of food aid in Indochina were especially embarrassing at a time when the U.S. government was simultaneously refusing to grant international pleas for an overall increase in its emergency food aid budget.

When the administration budgeted half of all PL 480 credits for fiscal year 1975 to South Vietnam and Cambodia, Congress finally took a decisive step: an amendment to PL 480 was passed requiring that 70 percent of food aid go to countries on the United Nations list of countries "most seriously affected" by food shortages. Neither Cambodia nor South Vietnam were on the list. The State Department, however, quickly mobilized to get around this new constraint. Administration officials argued that the limitation applied only to food, not to other commodities shipped abroad under PL 480, such as cotton and tobacco. Secretary of State Kissinger lobbied to have South Vietnam placed on the most seriously affected list, a suggestion rejected by the UN.[33] Ultimately, the White House circumvented Congress by simply increasing the total PL 480 budget from $1 billion originally programmed to $1.6 billion, thereby complying with percentage limitations on aid to Indochina without reducing the absolute levels of aid.

The Human Rights Refrain

In the years since the Vietnam war, politicians in Washington have been forced to respond to the ground swell of disaffection with the excesses of U.S.-supported dictatorships. One result has been the introduction of a new refrain in U.S. foreign policy— that of "human rights." Both Congress and the Carter White

House have begun to voice concern for human rights violations in the third world, and Congress has taken a number of additional steps to limit the use of food aid for political purposes. But Congress also has graciously left some large loopholes in these restrictions, and has continued to play the restriction-circumvention game with the White House.[34]

In 1975, for example, Congress stipulated that three-quarters of Title I credits must be channeled to "poor" countries, as defined by the World Bank's poverty line of an annual per capita GNP of less than $300. In other words, only 25 percent of PL 480 credits could be used for political purposes. The year the amendment was passed several devices were used to get around the restrictions. The total program was expanded, thus increasing the amount available for political use. There was also a small loophole in the 25 percent restriction: it did not apply to nonfood commodities, which account for 10 percent of the program. To take advantage of this loophole, 83 percent of all nonfood commodities were programmed to countries above the poverty line, and 80 percent of this amount went to two of the State Department's favored dictators in Asia, the Park Chung Hee regime in South Korea and the government of Ferdinand Marcos in the Philippines.[35]

The Carter administration's vows not to use food for political purposes also have amounted to empty promises. When in 1977 Congress began a major redrafting of the PL 480 legislation, the State Department made clear its dissatisfaction with the political use limitations. Of particular concern was the fact that important U.S. allies were above or about to surpass the $300 per capita GNP line. In Senate hearings on the bill the State Department argued for a change in the law partially on the grounds that Egypt was about to cross the poverty line.[36] Congress responded to administration pressure for a loosening of restrictions by lifting the "poverty line" to $520, and allowing this level to rise with inflation. With the level raised, only thirty-three countries are put above the poverty line. At the same time, Congress added another amendment giving the president the right to waive the poverty line restriction for particular countries—a provision the Carter administration used to channel aid to Lebanon in 1977.[37]

The new law also stipulates that food may not be sent to those governments determined by a special executive committee to be human rights violators. Congress, however, left a gaping hole in this restriction: a government labeled as a human rights violator can receive food aid if it merely promises that the food, or proceeds from the food sales, will go directly to needy people.[38] (Congress never addressed the contradiction in supposing that such a government would carry out a pledge of concern for the needy.) Furthermore, Title II donations are exempt from the human rights review process on the grounds that Title II by definition contributes to the well-being of the poor. The usefulness of this provision was apparent in the case of the Philippines in 1977, when the Marcos regime received three times as much money under Title II as under Title I.[39]

Thus, the application of the human rights provision by the Carter administration did nothing to alter the fundamentally political thrust of the food aid program. The one move toward sanctioning human rights violators under the provisions was short lived. In late 1977 the State Department announced that food aid to eleven countries was being suspended while their human rights records were reviewed. After seven short weeks the administration ordered that the aid shipments be renewed to all eleven countries, even though the State Department still classified three of them—South Korea, Indonesia, and Bangladesh—as having "troublesome" policies in the area of human rights. The continued flow of food aid to these countries was justified under the "food to the needy" loophole.[40] In fact, credits to oil-rich Indonesia were almost doubled by the end of the year, even though that country continued to hold an estimated 5,000 political prisoners in its jails.

While food aid flowed to U.S.-supported dictatorships that disregarded both the rights and needs of their people, the Carter administration immediately cut off all food aid to the new communist government in South Vietnam. When the South Vietnamese rice crop fell short by 20 percent in 1978, the U.S. government refused to send any food assistance in spite of the pressing need and the commitment of the government there to providing an adequate diet for the entire population. When private church groups sent relief shipments, the U.S. government refused to carry out its normal practice of paying for transportation costs.[41]

New Strategic Priorities

When the Carter-appointed Special Task Force on PL 480 came out with its report in 1978,[42] it contained what must have been an embarrassing admission for the administration. The report extolled the "unique flexibility" of the program in serving U.S. interests, and went on to list eight countries which in its estimation were receiving food for purely political reasons. Not surprisingly, half of the countries listed were in the Middle East, the oil-rich region that has become a primary focus of U.S. strategic interests in the post-Vietnam era. These four countries—Egypt, Israel, Jordan, and Syria—were not only high on the list of U.S. food aid recipients in 1979, they were also receiving over $1.2 billion (in addition to regular economic aid) from the Economic Support Fund, a program used to channel "security" assistance to countries of particular importance to the U.S. "national interest."[43]

Egypt in particular has become a favored recipient of U.S. food aid ever since Kissinger launched his Middle East *tour de force* to woo the Sadat government away from its Arab neighbors and into the U.S. camp. From the outset, PL 480 played a central role in this diplomatic effort. During its years of militant support for the Palestinian cause, Egypt had been entirely excluded from the PL 480 program. Egypt's extreme dependence on food imports (half of the country's total imports are agricultural commodities and one-third of these come from the United States) gave the United States a powerful bargaining chip. Recognizing this, Kissinger promised Sadat significant amounts of food in the course of his Middle East visit in late 1974. This was one reason the State Department argued so strongly at the time against the restrictions on food aid to countries not on the UN's most seriously affected list.[44] Although Egypt was not on the list at the time the law passed, the UN suddenly added its name, thus paving the way for a massive inflow of PL 480 credits.

In 1975, true to Kissinger's promise, Title I credits to Egypt jumped from zero to $120 million, and the level of credits never dropped below $100 million over the next five years. Today, the Sadat government is the world's largest recipient of PL 480 credits, receiving twice as much as all of Latin America combined for a total of $206 million in fiscal year 1979. The flow of food aid credits to Egypt is a clear reflection of overall U.S. foreign policy priorities: today the Sadat government is receiving more U.S. economic aid per capita than Western Europe did under the Marshall Plan.[45]

Another of the countries listed by the Task Force as a purely political recipient, South Korea, unlike Egypt, has been a long-time frontrunner for PL 480 credits. Back in 1969, Nixon used the promise of hundreds of millions of dollars in PL 480 credits to coax the Koreans into limiting their textile exports to the United States—a concession the president delivered to southern textile interests as a payoff for their political support. (It was later revealed that South Korea's lobbyist in Washington was paid in the form of commissions on every ton of PL 480 he delivered to the Park regime.)[46]

The political importance of food credits to South Korea was heightened when the fall of U.S. client regimes in Southeast Asia made South Korea a lynchpin in U.S. strategies for holding the line against communism in Asia. When in 1975 Congress threatened to reduce and eventually phase out all military aid to South Korea, the U.S. commitment to help finance a $.5 billion plan to modernize the South Korean army was put in jeopardy. To help fill the potential gap, PL 480 credits were raised to $150 million that year, twice the level of the previous year. In 1976, South Korea received a $140 million credit, more than any other country in the 25 percent political use quota. That year the Park regime also received $304 million in credits from the Commodity Credit Corporation, more than any other country.

In spite of this profoundly negative balance sheet on PL 480, it is tempting to reason—as the sometimes well-intentioned humanitarians in Congress obviously have done—that the United States should have a humanitarian food aid program to share its agricultural abundance with the world's poor and needy. Although the distribution of aid to the needy in times of famine must be supported, future attempts to transform U.S. food aid into a humanitarian program are not likely to meet with any more success than they have in the past. The problem is not with loopholes left in the food aid legislation but rather with the fundamental priorities and aims of U.S. foreign policy. As long as food aid is part of the U.S. policy apparatus, it will be used to support U.S. economic and political interests. In many cases that means supporting dictators, and bypassing or even subverting popular governments. And only rarely does it mean feeding hungry people, as revealed most recently in the case of U.S. food aid policies in Cambodia, where people's needs were sacrificed for the sake of political goals. It is not a change in the food aid program that is required, but rather a fundamental change in the objectives of U.S. foreign policy.

PART TWO:
AGRIBUSINESS IN LATIN AMERICA

4. Modernization Capitalist Style: An Introduction

For decades, international agriculture and hunger experts have been analyzing Latin America's "agrarian crisis." Why is it, they ask, that this vast and fertile continent—with more arable land than any other and a low population density, blessed with expansive valleys, rich water resources, and climates capable of growing almost every known crop—cannot feed its own people? Agricultural production is barely keeping pace with population growth, most countries of the region import vast quantities of staple foods, and one in five Latin Americans is the victim of severe malnutrition.[1] And why is it that the vast majority of the 100 million people who live in the countryside—an estimated 40 percent of the region's population—are underemployed and desperately poor?

Most experts of the prestige funding institutions of the capitalist world (such as the World Bank and the U.S. Agency for International Development) have diagnosed the root of the problem as agricultural backwardness. The solution, they argue, is extensive modernization of Latin America's agrarian sector: modern farming practices and technology (like tractors, fertilizers, and pesticides) and—some would add—a change in the outmoded land tenure system dominated by a traditional landed oligarchy.[2] In short, what Latin America's agrarian sector needs is a thoroughgoing transformation that would set its agriculture on the path traveled by the advanced capitalist countries. A revolution in agricultural production would spell the end of poverty and hunger.

Today, Latin America's agrarian reality is testimony to the bankruptcy of this modernization strategy. Latin American agriculture *is* undergoing a capitalist revolution, but this has meant only a deepening crisis of hunger and poverty for the vast majority of rural Latin Americans.

Revolution Capitalist Style

For any visitor to Latin America today, the surface signs of the agricultural revolution are in some regions both impressive and dramatic. Driving through the rich Cauca Valley of south-western Colombia, for example, one passes through mile after mile of lush new sugar and sorghum fields, punctuated by billboards advertising the latest in tractors and pesticides. In Mexico's northwest the fast-growing fruit and vegetable industry has transformed the fertile river valleys into a vast patchwork of irrigated fields and packing sheds resembling those of California's Imperial Valley. In southern Brazil, more than a dozen multimillion-dollar soybean processing plants owned by U.S. multinationals are scattered through the region, surrounded by large-scale mechanized soybean farms, none of which existed two decades ago. While a few countries—such as Brazil, Colombia, Mexico, and Argentina—are clearly in the forefront of the agricultural revolution, no part of the countryside has been left untouched by capitalist development.

In some regions once-traditional estates have been transformed into modern farms or ranches; in others, new lands have been opened up by entrepreneurs who view farming as a lucrative field of investment. Although traditional forms of agriculture still persist, modern farming enterprises, run much like the large agribusiness farms in the United States, are becoming increasingly common. They are directed by accountants and managers who organize production according to scientific principles; they employ a wage labor force; and they utilize modern technology to increase productivity. In short, these farms operate as capitalist enterprises, intent on maximizing profit and accumulating capital for reinvestment.

Although Latin American agriculture still lags behind that of the advanced capitalist countries in level of technological development, the use of capital inputs has increased dramatically in the post–World War II era. Between 1965 and 1975, fertilizer consumption more than tripled and the number of tractors increased by roughly 75 percent.[3] If one looks at the countries where modern agriculture is most advanced, the change is even more marked. Mexico's fertilizer consumption jumped from 3,500 tons in 1950 to 700,000 tons in 1972.[4]

These changes in the organization of agricultural production along capitalist lines have begun to unleash the tremendous productive potential of Latin America's land. Behind the aggregate data that shows lagging growth rates of only 3.3 percent lies another reality.[5] Some crops, particularly export commodities, have experienced spectacular growth rates. In Brazil, for example, soybean production has been growing at the rate of about 8–12 percent a year over the past decade. The accompanying surge in Brazil's soybean exports has made that country one of the world's largest exporters of agricultural commodities, second only to the United States.[6]

At the same time, most staple food production has been left virtually untouched by the technological innovations that have transformed export crops. In the majority of Latin American countries staple food production has stagnated in relation to population growth, giving rise to shortages, rising prices, and increased dependency on imported food—all part of the social crisis of contemporary Latin America.

The root of the crisis, however, lies not in *what* is produced, but rather in *how* it is produced. For capitalist development means more than technological change. It also means the shaping of a new system of social relations and labor exploitation that profoundly transforms people's means of livelihood and the very fabric of their lives.

From one end of the continent to the other there are millions who can testify to the grim consequences of capitalist development. For the most part, these are peasants who have been evicted from their lands and have no other means of survival but the sale of their labor power—often to the very landowners that were responsible for their dispossession. There is the Mexican (one of that country's 8 million migrant farmworkers) who lives on the road during the six months of the year he is able to work, earning only 50¢ a day for harvesting tomatoes that will be sold to a U.S. supermarket; or the family in El Salvador (one of that country's many landless families) living in a miserable makeshift shack along the roadside, near a new cotton plantation that absorbed the land they once farmed for subsistence; or the Brazilian squatter, who has tried to escape the seething poverty of his life as a canecutter in the northeast by clearing a small patch of land in the Amazonian jungle frontier, only to be evicted the next year by a landowner who hopes to make a handsome profit raising cattle.

While the situation of those who till the land is worsening as they are expelled from their own land and enter the ranks of the proletariat in growing numbers, at the other end of the social ladder wealth, income, and land are becoming increasingly concentrated in the hands of a new agrarian capitalist class. This growing inequality and polarization in the countryside—and the human suffering it entails—are part and parcel of the new social order being created by capitalist development.

In spite of the tremendous diversity and uneven pace of change from country to country, it is possible to identify some common forces that have combined to bring about the growing predominance of capitalism throughout the Latin American countryside. Chief among these are (1) the expansion of industrial capitalism as it developed in Europe, the United States, and finally in the urban centers of Latin America, (2) investments by foreign capital in Latin American countries, (3) support for capitalist modernization provided by international agencies and the governments of those countries, and (4) the transformation of class structures within each of those countries.

While the particular convergence of these factors in the last three decades has made this a decisive period, the capitalist transformation of agriculture must also be seen as the outcome of a long process of social and economic change that began with the Spanish Conquest. This chapter begins therefore, by looking at some of the key features of the agrarian structures that arose during the colonial era, and then goes on to explore later developments during the nineteenth century and finally the era of industrial capitalism. It should be pointed out that however decisive the outward expansion of capitalism from the so-called metropolitan countries of Western Europe and North America, this impact by itself was not sufficient to spark the capitalist transformation of Latin America. Rather, it required a particular evolution of internal social forces before capitalist production became the predominant feature in the countryside.[7]

Land and Labor Exploitation After the Conquest

Although there were many variations in the social structures that evolved in different regions after the Conquest, it is possible to generalize two predominant systems of land and labor exploitation: (1) the hacienda system, characterized by semifeudal or precapitalist land and labor relations, and (2) the plantation system, originally based on slave labor.[8] Which of these forms of social organization developed varied from region to region depending on a number of factors that shaped the possibility for exploiting local resources—the existence of mineral deposits or land suitable for cultivation, the access to export markets, and the nature of the indigenous societies encountered by the Spanish at the time of the Conquest.

The hacienda system gradually became dominant in those areas of the continent—such as the Andean highlands of Peru, Bolivia, and Ecuador and in north and central Mexico—where the colonialists found highly developed civilizations, with large populations and sophisticated systems of agricultural production.[9] In spite of many instances of valiant resistance, these Indian societies were forceably subjugated by the Europeans, whose main interest was in exploiting the tremendous mineral wealth of the colonies. The Spanish then quickly devised a method to coerce the Indian population to do the perilous job of extracting the precious metals from the mines. In most places, this was accomplished through the "repartimiento," a form of forced labor service. Elsewhere Indians were made to work for the Spanish by means of the "encomienda," under which Spanish conquerors were granted Indian towns, with the right to assess tribute, in the form of both labor and agricultural goods. Under such arrangements, both of which expropriated labor rather than land, tens of thousands of Indians worked and perished—on the land or in the gold and silver mines—while the goods and precious metals that were the fruits of their labor served to enrich the Spanish Crown and its loyal servants.

The tribute required by the encomienda also enabled the Spaniards to supply the new population centers with food and other basic necessities during the first years of the Conquest. Without taking direct control of agricultural production, they either appropriated most of the surplus produced by indigenous agriculture or required the Indians to produce new food crops to feed the urban populations.

However, by the seventeenth century, the Spanish settlers preferred to take control of vast tracts of agricultural land. In part this was due to a growing colonialist demand for food to feed an expanding population at the same time that a declining Indian population meant that less food was produced. "Haciendas"— large colonial estates—were consolidated on landholdings obtained by the Spaniards in a variety of ways, and usually legalized by the Crown only after they had been acquired. They became the basis of a new social order in the countryside. As virtually self-contained social and economic units the haciendas generally combined cattle raising with agricultural production. Sometimes handicrafts were produced also. In general, production tended to be labor-intensive, involving only minimal capital investment, and was geared to internal consumption. Many haciendas also began to engage in commercial production of wheat, cattle meat, and hides to supply these basic necessities to the growing populations in the urban and mining centers.

The exploitation of Indian labor was still a fundamental feature of the hacienda system. Although the encomienda provided an early source of labor to the haciendas, the need to protect themselves against labor shortages at a time of declining Indian population spurred the Spanish hacendados to introduce new forms of labor exploitation that would make the Indians completely dependent on the hacienda. Various systems of "usufruct" were developed (known variously as "peonage," "colonaje," "inquilinaje") whereby Indians were granted use of a small plot of hacienda land for subsistence farming. In exchange, the Indian families were required to put their labor power at the service of the hacienda for a given period of time. Another device used to exploit Indian labor was the system of debt peonage, under which the landowner extended credits for goods and services. These credits quickly mounted into what were enormous debts for the impoverished Indian laborers, who were forced by colonial authorities to repay the debts with the only commodity of value they possessed—their labor power. In some places this took a particularly brutal form: under the "repartimiento de efectos," money or goods were forcibly distributed by a local authority to make an Indian a debtor—and hence a "peon."[10] Strict enforcement of debt repayment meant that many Indians spent their lives working as peons in virtual bondage to the hacienda owner.

In spite of important commercial ties to outside markets, the hacienda system remained essentially precapitalist in nature.[11] In other words, labor was exploited mainly through coercive methods like those described above rather than through the purchase of free wage labor on the market. Moreover, the money earned from commercial transactions was used by the hacendados primarily for items like personal consumption or the purchase of more land rather than for investment in improved production techniques that would have maximized the haciendas' profit-making possibilities. As we will see, in most countries it was not until well into the twentieth century that conditions were ripe for the transformation of haciendas into capitalist enterprises.

New World Plantations

In other parts of Latin America, such as Brazil and the Caribbean region, a somewhat different social system evolved. When the European conquerors arrived they encountered dispersed indigenous populations, with less developed societies than in the Andean region or Mexico. Although there was very little mineral wealth to be extracted, the land and climate were ideally suited to growing a commodity that was much in demand in Europe: sugar. By the end of the seventeenth century English, Portuguese, French, Dutch, and Spanish colonists had set up sugar plantations in the Caribbean and in Northern Brazil, using slash-and-burn cultivation.[12]

Initially the planters attempted to force the native population to work on their plantations. But a combination of disease, brutal exploitation, and warfare decimated the indigenous people who came in contact with the white settlers. The planters then turned to a new source of labor power—the African slave trade. Over the next several centuries millions of Africans were uprooted from their homelands and transported to the New World. In the triangular trade that developed, European merchants used the money from the sale of slaves to purchase sugar from the colonies, which they then sold in Europe, using the profits to return to Africa for another human cargo.

The plantation systems took their toll in both Africa and the New World. As European demand for sugar and other tropical commodities increased with the growth of urban centers in the late eighteenth and nineteenth centuries, the slave trade was stepped up considerably. The slaves were not only subject to labor exploitation on the New World plantations, but millions lost their lives at sea, and many African societies were disrupted by this plunder of their human resources. In the Caribbean, the intensification of sugar production meant the serious depletion of soils when the periods of fallowing of the land required in slash-and-burn cultivation were shortened or abandoned. As a result, many sugar producing regions were suddenly abandoned and went into decline as new areas of cultivation were opened up.[13]

Throughout this period the Western European countries were undergoing profound internal changes. The feudal structures of the countryside gave way to capitalist forms of production, and the Industrial Revolution created a modern manufacturing industry, first in Europe and later in the United States. Through trade and financial channels European capitalism had a strong influence on Latin American plantation agriculture. The flowering of European capitalism in the nineteenth century generated a new and growing demand for raw materials and food, and this demand greatly stimulated the production of the tropical commodities that still dominate Latin American agriculture—such as coffee, sugar, and cocoa. Frequently, European merchants and bankers financed both the production and trade of these agricultural commodities, thus developing strong ties with the Latin American landowning and merchant classes. Yet it required more than this close integration with European capitalism through commercial channels to bring about a transformation of production and to change the social relations on the plantations.

The Foundations of Capitalism Are Laid

The late nineteenth century brought some important changes that helped lay the basis for future capitalist development in the regions where plantation agriculture predominated. One was the abolition of slavery. Not only was this a progressive change in human terms. It also created the free labor force that is the precondition for capitalist production. The end of slavery opened the possibility of a more rational system of labor exploitation whereby plantation owners could purchase labor power when needed rather than incurring the cost of buying slaves as well as feeding and housing entire slave families.[14]

The change to a capitalist-type wage labor force was not, however, immediate and automatic wherever slavery was abolished. In Brazil's northeast, for example, the semifeudal traditions of the large sugar estates remained strong, and for the former slaves the new legal status as "free" laborers was more formal than real. In fact, most of the slaves became "moradores," resident workers who were given a plot of land on the sugar estates in exchange for regular labor service. Their continuing ties to the estate were partly ensured by the fact that they had no other options (with most of the land in the region already monopolized by the large landowners), and partly by the successful efforts of the estate owners to enmesh the former slaves in debt obligations.[15]

In Cuba, on the other hand, the major sugar producing area of the Caribbean, the end of slavery opened the way for rapid capitalist development. By contrast to Brazil's northeast, Cuba was a relatively new sugar producer; its social system was not encumbered by the strong feudal heritage that characterized Brazil. The Cuban planter class adopted the most modern technical innovations and organization of labor, and their drive to increase productivity was greatly stimulated by the expanding North American market only ninety miles away.[16]

Another important development in the late nineteenth century was the introduction of large-scale coffee production in Central America and in the south of Brazil. Stimulated by an expanding European market for a drink that had once been a luxury, coffee production was controlled by a modernizing planter class with extensive political and economic influence. In both Brazil and the Central American countries, the coffee planters had close links to the new national states that had emerged with independence from Spain and Portugal. These links, as well as the state's interest in generating export income to finance investment in other sectors, led to state-backed modernization programs that greatly aided the interests of the coffee planters. In Central America, a succession of governments sponsored projects to establish transportation, communication, and credit facilities, all of which helped pave the way for later capitalist development.[17]

The state also gave legal sanction to the massive takeover by the coffee planters of most of the remaining Indian communal landholdings in the coffee-producing regions of Central America. In Mexico the Porfiro Diaz regime eliminated Indian land tenure in order to pave the way for commercial production of such export crops as cotton, sugarcane, and henequen.[18]

In spite of its modernizing impact, coffee production did not signal the immediate advent of typically capitalist forms of labor exploitation in Central America. Most of the workforce on the plantations continued to have a semiservile relationship to the landowners reminiscent of the old colonial forms. With the help of the state, however, new forms of coercion were developed, such as the law in Guatemala requiring the Indians to work a minimum of 100 days each year for the large landowners.[19]

In the case of the Brazilian coffee plantations in the state of São Paulo, the particular historical conditions gave rise to a different labor system, one which more closely approximated a capitalist free wage labor force. Since the Brazilian planters had no available supply of Indian labor, they turned instead to immigrant workers brought over from Europe. Although these immigrants were often enticed to the coffee plantations by the offer of a free plot of land to grow their own subsistence crops, many relied primarily on the wages paid to them by the plantation owners.[20]

Probably the most fully developed capitalist production system in this period evolved in Argentina and Paraguay. In contrast to other parts of Latin America, the sparsely populated River Plate region was largely ignored by the Europeans until the eighteenth century, when it began to develop as a major trading center.

When in the late nineteenth century the pampas of the interior were opened up for wheat and cattle production to supply the European market, conditions were ripe for capitalist development. Unlike the Andean region, there was no legacy of colonial social structures that acted as an obstacle to rapid modernization. The one obstacle to the settlement of the interior—the dispersed Indian population—was eliminated in a series of genocidal wars similar to those fought against the natives of North America. As entrepreneurs from the port towns and from Europe carved up the pampas into large wheat farms and cattle ranches, they adopted the most modern machinery and technology (most of it imported from the United States and Europe). These new estate owners employed a wage labor force of European immigrants, many of whom became migrant farmworkers without any ties to the land.[21]

The Age of Imperialism

The continuing development of industrial capitalism in the United States and Europe in the late nineteenth century also came to have a profound impact on parts of the Latin American countryside. Until that time, Europe's influence had been felt mainly through the stimulus an expanding market offered to Latin American agricultural exports. While European capitalists did have close trading and financial relationships with Latin American producers, these had virtually no impact on the internal organization of production.

This began to change with the development of a new stage of "monopoly capitalism" in the United States and Europe, characterized by the increasing concentration of industry and finance in the hands of a few powerful monopoly corporations. These monopolies ushered in the age of imperialism as they began to make large-scale direct investments in production facilities in the former colonies. In Latin America, United States corporations were in the forefront of this trend, reflecting the United States' new role as the dominant political and economic power in the region.

Agriculture, along with mining, became the principal field of these early investments by foreign capital. Food processing companies like Hersheys Chocolate and the American Sugar Refining Company, anxious to control the source of their principal raw material, bought up millions of acres of sugar lands in Cuba. United States financiers, in need of lucrative new outlets for their capital, formed enterprises like the South Puerto Rico Sugar Company and the Cuba Company to invest in sugar plantations on the Caribbean islands. In Peru, the giant U.S.-owned shipping firm, W. R. Grace & Co., began large-scale sugar production in the rich coastal plains. Banana production was dominated by another newly formed enterprise, the United Fruit Company, which acquired a vast network of plantations throughout the region—in Cuba, Jamaica, the Dominican Republic, Panama, Honduras, Nicaragua, Guatemala, and Colombia.[22]

These U.S.-owned plantations were thoroughly capitalist production units, different in many respects from the traditional plantations of the Caribbean and Brazil. They employed a wage labor force, as contrasted to earlier labor systems of slavery or debt peonage. In order to increase productivity and profits, they used scientific methods of cultivation and modern technology and machinery (although still relying on intensive use of cheap labor). They created a strict division of labor on the plantation, bringing the workforce under the discipline of the capitalist drive to maximize the amount each worker produced.

The extent of the impact of foreign capital penetration varied from country to country. On the small islands of Cuba and Puerto Rico capitalist sugar production had a pervasive effect on the whole economy and society. The best land fell to the control of U.S. companies, the local planter class was superseded, and the entire economy became subordinated to the needs of North American capital.[23] As capitalism came to dominate Cuba and Puerto Rico, the people in these countries also became some of the most impoverished in the hemisphere.

In the Central American countries, U.S.-owned banana plantations became "enclaves" of capitalism. These companies built irrigation systems on their plantations, imported machinery and fertilizer, constructed railways, ports, and road systems. But they had no interest in developing the rest of the economy. United Fruit's operations in Guatemala were typical. The company controlled a network of modern railways (the only one in the country) which ran from the plantations straight to the company port, while most areas of the country remained backward and without any infrastructure.

This is not to say that the banana companies did not have a profound impact. United Fruit monopolized vast tracts of the most fertile lands throughout Central America, owning close to half a million acres in Guatemala alone. The companies and their railways often employed thousands of workers, the core of an incipient working class that was to become a militant political force in the 1940s and 1950s. So pervasive was the political influence of the banana companies—based on a close alliance with the ruling elites and the strong arm of the U.S. government and marines—that the Central American countries came to be known as the "banana republics."[24]

Twentieth-Century Industrialization

In spite of the persistence of the traditional social and economic structures inherited from the Conquest, by the first decades of the twentieth century the seeds of capitalist development had been planted in most Latin American countries. But it was not until the post–World War II period that capitalist relations became the dominant trend throughout the countryside. In spite of particular variations in each country, the same general set of social, political, and economic forces spurred capitalist development throughout the continent.

One of the most crucial factors affecting the agrarian sector was the development of capitalist industry, accompanied by the rise of an industrial bourgeoisie and the emergence of a modern state under its influence. In countries like Brazil, Argentina, Mexico, and Colombia where light manufacturing industries had already started up in the early part of the century, the international economic crisis of the 1930s gave a tremendous boost to industrialization. The decline in export earnings and Latin America's inability to pay for manufactured imports—both byproducts of contracting world markets—created favorable conditions for a spurt of industrial development. Many governments revamped their economic policies to encourage "import substitution"—local production of items like textiles, footwear, light chemicals, and processed foods, most of which previously had been imported.[25]

This pattern of import substitution industrialization, which was repeated throughout different Latin American countries in the next several decades, had far-reaching repercussions. It succeeded in creating a manufacturing base; it spurred the formation of an industrial working class, and it laid the basis for a small but growing internal consumer market in the expanding urban centers. It also attracted investments by foreign monopolies, which gradually extended their control over many of the most dynamic industries.

The consolidation of industry greatly strengthened the material basis for capitalism in the countryside. The whole network of support systems that grew up along with industry—a national transportation network, a banking and credit system, educational and research institutions—all these facilitated the growth of capitalist agriculture. And just as happened in the United States decades earlier, the development of industry placed at the disposal of agricultural producers a variety of machines and inputs (like agrichemicals) that until the 1950s and 1960s had been available only through costly importation.

The Role of the National State in Capitalist Development

In addition to its role in encouraging the growth of capitalist industry, the national state has also been an important force behind the modernization of agriculture in Latin America in the post–World War II period. In most centers of dynamic capitalist growth in the countryside, government financed infrastructure, support services, and investment credit have played a crucial role.

In Mexico, for example, what are today the lush irrigated

fields of the northwest were dry and unproductive lands until the Mexican government spent millions of dollars to finance dams, irrigation canals, and road systems in the 1940s.[26] Similarly in Nicaragua, some of the country's most modern and productive agricultural lands along the Pacific coast were grazing pastures until the government opened the region to cotton production in the 1950s with a massive program of road and infrastructure construction.[27]

In the post–World War II period many governments set up a whole institutional network to administer financial and technical support for commercial agriculture. Typical examples are the National Agrarian Development Bank (BANDESA) in Guatemala, the channel for most state financing of agriculture; the National Federation of Coffee Growers (FEDERCAFE) in Colombia (founded in the late 1920s but greatly expanded later), which coordinates a whole series of technical and financial assistance programs to coffee growers, as well as acting as a state export board; and the Brazilian Association for Credit and Rural Assistance (ABCAR), later superseded by the more comprehensive Brazilian Enterprise for Technical Assistance and Rural Extension (EMBRATER).

Since 1950 the amount of money flowing from these institutions to finance commercial agriculture has reached massive proportions. In Colombia, for instance, public spending in agriculture (including such programs as investment credit, technical assistance, infrastructure development, etc.) increased fifty times between 1950 and 1972, from 48.7 to 2,467.6 million pesos.[28] Probably the most dramatic example of the national state's role in stimulating capitalist development is provided by Brazil. Since 1963–1964, agriculture has received between one-fourth and one-third of total state credit, at an interest rate of about half what industry pays.[29] In 1978, Brazilian agriculture benefited from roughly $18 billion in credit and loans (the bulk coming from the state), and the state-owned Banco do Brasil is reportedly the largest agricultural lender in the capitalist world.[30]

The Brazilian government has also stimulated capitalist development by granting tax concessions to encourage mechanization in agriculture, and has guaranteed a minimum price for crops like soybeans (which is, not coincidentally, the country's fastest growing and most mechanized sector of agriculture).[31] These policies have helped transform Brazil's southern states into one of the most modern agricultural regions in the hemisphere.

Although in no way matching the volume of lending provided by national governments, such international financial institutions as the World Bank and the Inter-American Development Bank have sometimes stepped in to play a strategic role in getting modernization projects off the ground. The World Bank, for example, helped finance the dams and irrigation projects in Mexico's northwest. Since the late 1960s, when it began to down-play infrastructure development and emphasize projects which directly generate export income, the World Bank has channeled 70 percent of all loans in Latin America's agrarian sector to export oriented livestock production—one of the fastest growing sectors of capitalist agriculture.[32]

A New Class Structure

The national state has also played an important role in modernizing social relations in the countryside and in helping to spur the growth of a wage labor force that is essential for capitalist development. Laws abolishing debt peonage—such as that enacted in Mexico under the modernizing Cárdenas regime in the 1930s[33]—were passed in many countries and helped create the "free" labor market required for capitalism to operate. The extension of protective labor legislation to the countryside was another "progressive" reform that helped erode precapitalist labor systems and swell the ranks of the wage labor force. An example of this process was the Rural Labor Law passed in Brazil in 1963 in reaction to the demands of the militant and powerful peasant movement which had emerged in the northeast. In both the sugar producing region of the northeast and the coffee region of the south, the response of landowners was to expel their resident workforce of "colonos" from the estates rather than incur the expenses of the numerous benefits extended to permanent workers—social security payments, a minimum wage, ownership rights to property improvements, and so on.[34] A similar process has taken place in many Central American countries, where progressive social legislation has given impetus to the breakdown of semiservile labor systems.[35]

Land and population pressures have also fed the growth of the wage labor force necessary for capitalism. The concentration of land in the hands of a relatively few large landowners ("latifundistas") over the centuries had condemned the vast majority of Latin America's rural inhabitants to eking out a subsistence living on tiny plots of land known as "minifundios." By the 1950s the minifundio system, which had never sustained the rural masses at a decent standard of living, entered into crisis. Average population growth rates of about 2.8 percent annually (higher in some countries) placed a tremendous pressure on the scarce land resources available to the minifundio population. The continual subdivision of minifundio plots through inheritance meant that they were not only growing in number, but also shrinking in size. To cite a few examples of these trends in the minifundio sector:

1. In Brazil's northeast, the number of farms under 10 hectares more than doubled between 1940 and 1960 (a trend which continued in the 1960s) and the average size of the minifundio fell from 4 hectares in 1940 to 2.7 hectares during the 1970s.[36]
2. In Ecuador, the number of farms under 5 hectares doubled from 1954 to 1968, and the average size of the minifundio also declined from 1.7 to 1.5 hectares.[37]
3. In El Salvador, the number of farms of less than 1 hectare nearly doubled from 1950 to 1970 (from around 70,400 to 132,900).[38] Moreover, the proportion of the rural population with less than 1 hectare or without any land at all increased from 53 percent in 1961 to 75 percent in 1975.[39]

With the minifundio lands increasingly incapable of supporting the rural population, growing numbers of minifundistas are being increasingly or even totally marginalized from the land, forced to become part of a new class of wage laborers. As the final chapter in this section examines in more detail, the ranks of this new proletariat are continually swollen by peasants dispossessed from their land by the expansion of capitalist agriculture.

The combative response of an increasingly marginalized peasantry has pushed many Latin American governments to undertake agrarian reform programs over the decades in order to quell class struggle. Although purportedly designed to satisfy the peasants' hunger for land, few of these reforms have resulted in any significant redistribution.[40] Indeed, in many cases—such as Mexico in the 1930s and Chile and Peru in the 1960s—they have accelerated capitalist development in the countryside.[41] Modernizing regimes have used land reform programs to force the old latifundistas to modernize their large and inefficient holdings under threat of expropriation, to abolish precapitalist labor relations, and in some cases to finally dissolve the power of the landed oligarchy. By so doing they have turned agrarian reform into an important factor in the emergence of a modern agrarian bourgeoisie in Latin America.

The New Agrarian Bourgeoisie

Like all other aspects of capitalist development, the formation of a modern agrarian bourgeoisie has been a gradual and uneven process, which takes different forms. In some regions, as indicated above, the old latifundios have been transformed into commercial enterprises, and the landed oligarchy has become part of a modern capitalist class. Such has been the case, for example, in the Peruvian highlands. Responding to the growing demand for milk in nearby urban centers, many of the haciendas in Cajamarca province have become modern dairy farms over the last thirty years. In some cases the hacienda owners were stimulated to modernize their operations by the threat of agrarian reform. In others, it was the arrival of a new heir to manage the estate which sparked the transition.[42]

In many regions, however, the latifundia have given way to a new class of capitalist entrepreneurs—such as the cotton and sugar growers of Colombia and Central America, the fruit and vegetable growers of Mexico, and the soybean and sugar growers of southern Brazil. Some of these large commercial operations are actually run by wealthy tenant farmers, an increasingly important sector of the agrarian bourgeoisie in some areas. Central American cotton production is one example. Data for Nicaragua and El Salvador show that in the early 1970s 60 percent of all cotton was grown on rented land.[43] The situation is similar in parts of Colombia, where 50 percent of the cotton in coastal regions was grown on rented lands, as well as a large proportion of sugar in the Cauca Valley.[44] In the Mexican state of Sonora about 70 percent of communal-owned lands known as "ejidos" are rented to large commercial farmers.[45]

The largest and wealthiest of this new group are not just growers but also agro-industrialists who process and market commodities. They may own and operate integrated agribusiness complexes. They frequently have ties with foreign capital. And they often wield considerable political influence among the national bourgeoisie.[46] One such example is the Atalla family in Brazil, which immigrated from Lebanon to Brazil in the 1920s to take up coffee farming. Today they operate a vast agro-industrial complex, which includes sugar and coffee plantations and the largest sugar mill in the world. The parent company, Copersucer, is one of the largest corporations in Brazil. It has recently gone multinational by purchasing a U.S. coffee company, Hills Brothers. The Atalla empire, valued by *Fortune* magazine at $1.3 billion, also includes significant manufacturing investments. The head of Copersucer, Jorge Wolney Atalla, is known as a powerful figure on the Brazilian political scene. He was once an executive with Petrobras (the state oil monopoly), where one of his fellow executives and confidants was former president of Brazil, Ernesto Geisel.[47]

Another example of this new bourgeoisie is the large growers who dominate northwestern Mexico's fruit and vegetable industry (described in depth in another NACLA study).[48] Many of these growers, who had a relatively modest start when the vegetable export industry was in its infancy during World War II, are today millionaires who live in country mansions and exercise considerable clout on the national political scene. In addition to their irrigated production and packing complexes, they have diversified investments in the region's industry, commerce, and banking. They own distributorships for U.S. farm equipment, automobiles, fertilizers, and pesticides. They have close ties with U.S. agribusiness interests across the border (sometimes even partnerships) and are frequently financed by U.S. distributors, banks, and supermarket chains. For growers with the largest spreads (such as the eighty-five who control one-fourth of the irrigated land in the state of Sinaloa) their invested capital may be in the millions of dollars.

Transnational Capital

This raises the more general question of the role foreign capital has played in this recent period of intense capitalist development. In comparison with the turn of the century, when they played a crucial role in reorganizing production and modernizing social relations, foreign investors are no longer the main force behind capitalist development in the countryside.

For one thing, foreign corporations have been forced to lower their profiles in response to a wave of nationalization by Latin American governments (themselves responding to popular resentment against years of political intervention and economic exploitation by foreign capital). The plantation lands of foreign-owned sugar companies have been nationalized in recent years in one country after another—Cuba in the early 1960s, Peru in 1969, and Trinidad, Belize, Jamaica, and Guyana in the 1970s. Gulf and Western, a huge conglomerate which owns one-fourth of all arable land in the Dominican Republic, is virtually the only major foreign sugar producer in Latin America today.

Although the U.S.-owned banana companies still have vast plantations, their landholdings have also shrunk in recent years. United Fruit was forced to abandon its Colombian plantations in the 1950s, and in the wake of the 1954 agrarian reform in Guatemala it sold off tens of thousands of acres. More recently, the Panamanian government of Omar Torrijos took over some land belonging to foreign-owned banana plantations. In all the countries where the banana multinationals still run plantations, the companies have sought to accommodate nationalist sentiment by working increasingly with associate producers—local growers who produce on their own lands under contract to the multinationals.[49] (For a fuller description of the associate producer program see the case study of Del Monte in Guatemala, Chapter 11.)

For economic reasons as well, agribusiness transnationals are no longer as interested in controlling production directly. Profit margins in agriculture are always a risky business, given the inevitable and unpredictable swings in the market. With the advance of capitalist agriculture it has become possible for foreign corporations to rely on local growers for agricultural commodities. Meanwhile, the transnationals increasingly have invested their capital where profit margins are larger—in processing and distribution. Castle & Cooke, to name only one example, has diversified its holdings in Central America to include breweries, a margarine plant, a bottling factory, and a cottonseed oil mill, in addition to its plantation lands.

Although foreign capital is no longer in the forefront of revolutionizing production, its key role in other spheres still gives it a decisive influence in the process of capitalist development in the countryside. Food processing companies based in the United States, for example, have a far-reaching impact on agricultural production through their financing, technical assistance, and purchase contracts with local growers (see Chapter 9). In the case of Mexican vegetable production, financing by U.S. capital is a crucial force in the industry. Yet another example is provided by the beef industry in Costa Rica, where a consortium of multinational corporations is a major (if little known) investor in the country's largest privately owned beef export company.[50]

The Contradictions of Capitalist Development

By the 1980s, the effect of decades of capitalist development adds up to a dramatic and qualitative change in the Latin American countryside. Although the process is still uneven and incomplete, the trends are clear. A new class structure is emerging in the countryside: on the one hand, a powerful and influential agrarian bourgeoisie and, on the other, a growing number of wage labor-ers who must sell their labor power to survive. The growing use of modern technology, a more scientific management of the pro-duction process, and a more intense exploitation of labor—all mechanisms to "modernize" by increased productivity—are the hallmarks of modern agriculture in Latin America.

What this capitalist revolution has meant for the majority of Latin Americans, however, is impoverishment and misery. For one thing, agricultural modernization has taken place at the ex-pense of the food needs of the local population. With the fastest growing and most profitable markets for agricultural commodities located in the advanced capitalist countries, the most dynamic sector of capital accumulation is in export production. For the most part, this is the sector where modernization has taken place. At the same time, staple food production for the local market remains the most backward sector in many countries. It is left for the most part to small peasants and subsistence farmers, those with the least fertile lands who have virtually no access to the credit and government programs that have transformed the rest of agriculture. In Guatemala, for example, 87 percent of all government credit between 1964 and 1973 went to finance ex-port production, while rice, corn, and beans (produced primarily on small plots) received only 3 percent.[51] In Brazil where rural credit is reportedly reaching only 28 percent of all producers,[52] the small farmers who produce an estimated three-quarters of the country's basic staples receive only 5 percent of all agricultural loans.[53] Three of Brazil's major staple crops (black beans, manioc, and maize) received only 13 percent of government-subsidized credit from 1970 to 1977, while huge amounts of credit were channeled to export production.[54]

The monopolization of modern inputs by large farms in the export sector reflects this credit distribution pattern. In Brazil, 80 percent of all tractors are in the southern states of Parana, São Paulo, and Rio Grande do Sul, the center of production for export crops like soybeans and coffee. São Paulo state alone has 42 percent of tractors and consumes one-third of all fertilizer.[55] In Mexico the distribution of capital inputs reflects a similar pattern: 73 percent of all farm machinery was owned by large landholders in 1970.[56]

In most countries, moreover, the small producers who grow staple crops are fighting a losing battle for control of their lands in the face of expanding export production. Land that once produced blackbeans in Brazil is now being used to grow the soybeans that are turned into animal feed to fatten cattle for the Japanese market. In the country as a whole the area devoted to export crops has increased at an average of 5.4 percent a year for the last decade, while the growth rate for area devoted primarily to domestic consumption was only 2.9 percent.[57]

In some of the countries where capitalism has penetrated most deeply into the countryside the food situation has reached crisis proportions. Mexico is a case in point. Since 1970 agricultural production grew at an average annual rate of only .7 percent (with production actually dropping in 1973 and 1976, by 2.5 percent and 2 percent respectively). Most of this decline occurred in production for the internal market.[58]

What this pattern adds up to is a common trend throughout Latin America toward shortages of basic foods, a growing dependence on increasingly expensive imported staples, and rising food prices. In Mexico, for example, food prices have gone up between 25 and 30 percent a year since 1973, and by the late 1970s the country was importing record amounts of grain.

This situation has had disastrous consequences for poor and working people in both the cities and the countryside. Rising food prices have been a major factor behind the drop in purchasing power and decline in the standard of living experienced by millions of Latin Americans over the past decade. Today in Brazil, for example, 43 percent of the labor force earns the minimum wage ($92 a month) or less, yet a basic food basket costs three times that much.[59] It is no coincidence that 40 percent of the Brazilian population suffers from malnutrition. And the statistics are equally grim for other countries: four out of five children in Guatemala suffer from malnutrition[60] and 80 percent of the rural population of Mexico is malnourished.[61]

This situation has fueled general social unrest in Latin America. Recently people have also taken to the streets specifically to protest rising food prices. Large street demonstrations followed steep food price hikes in Peru in 1978, and mass protests have been carried out by the "Cost of Living Movement" in Brazil. The social contradictions generated by capitalist development are even more starkly illustrated by the plight of the millions of dispossessed peasants and agricultural workers in the countryside. Before looking at their situation, the chapters that follow will examine in greater depth two factors that are crucially linked to the capitalist transformation of the countryside: first, the role of transnational agribusiness corporations, and second, Latin America's role in the world market.

5. The Grim Reapers: Transnationals and Their Impact

Today the tentacles of the transnational agribusiness corporations extend deep into Latin America. Old-time banana companies such as United Fruit have been joined by an array of modern agribusiness enterprises intent on penetrating the most dynamic and profitable sectors of Latin America's emerging agribusiness system. Food processors such as Pillsbury, Standard Brands, and General Foods, agrichemical producers such as DuPont and W. R. Grace, and farm equipment manufacturers such as International Harvester and John Deere now number among the biggest transnational agribusiness investors in Latin America. And these corporate giants are far more active in Latin America than in any other third world region—over three-fourths of all U.S. agribusiness subsidiaries in the third world are now located in Latin American countries.

Although the total dollar amount of U.S. agribusiness investments in Latin America is not available, a NACLA survey shows rapid expansion in recent decades, especially in the food processing industry; there the number of subsidiaries more than tripled between 1960 and 1975.[1] And in the last ten years, the pace of investment seems to have quickened: U.S. grain companies have invested more than $50 million in soybean processing facilities in Brazil since 1973, and the farm implement companies, which prior to 1960 dominated the market mainly through exports, have opened a number of production facilities. Ford, for example, has made a $100-million investment in a Brazilian tractor plant. And as any visitor to Latin America can attest, fast-food chains like Kentucky Fried Chicken and McDonalds are springing up in cities throughout the region.

Why has Latin America become the center of this feverish investment activity by transnational agribusiness corporations? The surge in foreign investments reflects an inexorable economic process at work in the Latin American agricultural sector. Just as it does in the advanced industrial countries, capitalist agriculture in Latin America means the growing integration of agriculture and industry. The new agrarian bourgeoisies, in their drive to increase agricultural productivity, turn increasingly to the manufacturing sector for fertilizers, farm implements, and other capital goods, or "agricultural inputs" as they are called. At the same time more and more agricultural commodities are purchased by the manufacturing and service industries that cater to the growing urban populations.[2] The spread of processed foods, fast-food chains, and supermarkets in Latin America shows that agriculture is increasingly linked to the commercial and industrial sectors.

Latin America's rapid economic growth in recent years has also facilitated agribusiness expansion. Between 1965 and 1980, the Latin American economies grew by an annual average growth rate of over 6 percent.[3] Much of this growth occurred in agricultural production and agriculture-related industries, creating new opportunities for transnational capital.

But the surge in transnational investments cannot be explained solely in terms of the dynamics at work within Latin America. The transnationals themselves are powerful entities that impose their economic needs and interests on third world countries. The corporations use their control of technology, financial resources, manufacturing facilities, and marketing to penetrate and dominate key economic sectors in the third world. In terms of sheer size, the big transnationals often overwhelm third world countries. The sales of each of the top ten U.S. agribusiness corporations exceed the Gross Domestic Product (GDP) of twenty-one of the twenty-eight republics in Latin America and the Caribbean.

The flow of foreign capital to Latin America is shaped by the global investment strategies of the transnationals. Since the end of World War II, the transnationals have focused increasingly on setting up manufacturing facilities abroad and have paid less attention to mining and the extraction of raw materials. Agribusiness expansion in Latin America reflects this global pattern. Few new transnational investments now go into direct agricultural production. Instead the transnationals focus almost exclusively on the manufacturing end of the emerging agro-industrial complex in Latin America. Even the old banana companies are following this pattern as they channel many of their new investments into the food processing industry.[4]

The expansion of foreign investments in Latin America's agro-industry is also facilitated by the concentration and centralization of capital that is taking place on an international scale. Acquisitions and mergers now occur with increasing frequency among big agribusiness corporations. Nestlé, a Swiss-based firm and one of the world's largest food processors, recently bought Libby, McNeill, Libby, a big U.S. canning company. United Brands represents the merger of the John Morrell meat processing firm and United Fruit, while the Swift meatpacking company is now owned by Esmark, a conglomerate involved in fertilizer production as well as food processing. These general linkages within monopoly capitalism form the international context for understanding the growth of agribusiness investments in Latin America.

To more fully understand the forces at work in the expansion of the agribusiness transnationals, we will highlight the role of U.S. corporate capital in three key areas: (1) the chemical fertilizer industry, (2) the mechanized farm equipment industry, and (3) the food processing industry. The bulk of U.S. agribusiness' new investments in Latin America are in these three sectors. The latter, the food processing industry, will be looked at in depth in the next chapter. Here we will analyze the first two—the fertilizer and mechanized farm equipment industries—which together constitute what is known as the agricultural input industries.

Agricultural Input Industries

Of all the areas of agribusiness, the mechanized farm implements industry is the most highly concentrated. Four U.S. companies—John Deere, International Harvester, Ford, and J. I. Case (a Tenneco subsidiary)—along with a Canadian firm, Massey Ferguson, dominate the international production of tractors and market most of the farm equipment sold in Latin America. With the exception of Ford, which began as an automotive company, these firms are some of the oldest agribusiness corporations, having consolidated their positions in the North American market in the first quarter of the twentieth century.[5]

The fertilizer industry is not so tighly controlled by U.S. companies, and international competition from Western European and Japanese firms is intense. However, in the United States a relatively small group of firms dominates the industry. W. R. Grace, Monsanto, International Minerals & Chemicals, Williams Companies, Beker Industries, Exxon, and Allied Chemical number among the largest producers.

The fertilizer and farm implement companies made their first direct investments in Latin America much later than the food processing companies. Until the late 1950s they controlled the Latin American market almost totally through exports, with production located in large, capital-intensive manufacturing facilities in the United States. Even today, approximately half of Latin America's fertilizers are imported and many countries still rely totally on imports for their mechanized farm equipment.[6]

Besides creating a severe drain on Latin America's foreign exchange reserves, the reliance on imported farm inputs has subjected the region's agriculture to the economic cycles of the monopoly industries. The economic dislocations caused by the boom-and-bust cycle of the fertilizer industry over the past fifteen years illustrates the adverse repercussions that arise when third world countries are dependent on transnational corporations for vital industrial commodities.

The cycle began in the early part of the 1960s, when technological advances cut the production costs of petroleum-based fertilizers in half. As companies rushed to take advantage of new profit possibilities, there was a rapid expansion of production facilities in both the advanced countries and the third world,[7] especially Asia and Latin America. The result of this expanded production was a worldwide glut of fertilizers. The U.S. government stepped in to help the companies solve the overproduction problem by extending Agency for International Development (AID) loans to finance fertilizer exports to many third world countries, significantly expanding the market in Latin America. One W. R. Grace executive noted that "thanks to AID financing, Chile and Brazil became important fertilizer markets."[8]

But this growing import dependency soon took its toll. In response to the overproduction crisis, some of the oil companies pulled out of fertilizer production, both in the United States and Latin America. These reductions in investments led to a fertilizer shortage just as the world food crisis occurred in 1973–1974. When fertilizer prices more than doubled, many countries were forced to cut back on fertilizer imports. The UN Food and Agriculture Organization calculated that in the forty-three poorest countries the resulting loss in agricultural production was equal to 2.7 million tons of grain, the margin between subsistence and starvation in many countries.[9]

The U.S. fertilizer industry profited handsomely from the rise in prices—especially firms like W. R. Grace, Williams Companies, and Beker Industries, which had bought some of the facilities sold by the oil firms. These fertilizer companies made annual returns on invested capital that ranged as high as 65 percent. An executive of Beker Industries admitted, "You might say we're gouging the poor."[10]

Investment Strategies

While still relying heavily on exports to penetrate the Latin American markets, the farm equipment and fertilizer companies are expanding their direct investments in the region. The new investment sites are chosen carefully by the companies: capital requirements for tractor and fertilizer production are enormous, usually in the tens of millions of dollars. Corporations consequently look not only for countries where the political situation guarantees a favorable investment climate, but also for locations where they will be assured a large market. Thus, most of the foreign-owned tractor and fertilizer facilities are located in the countries where large-scale capitalist agriculture is most developed—namely Brazil, Argentina, and Mexico.

Currently, the farm equipment manufacturers are especially interested in gaining direct access to the rapidly expanding Bra-

Table 5.1
*Major North American Farm Machinery Investments
in Latin America*

Country	Entry year	Percent ownership
Ford Motor Co.		
Mexico	1967	Min.
Brazil	1974	100
International Harvester		
Mexico	1947	100
Argentina	1963	—
Venezuela	1976	JV
J. I. Case (Tenneco)		
Brazil	1971	
John Deere		
Argentina	1957	100
Mexico	1957	40
Venezuela	1977	20
Massey Ferguson		
Brazil (two facilities)	1961	50
Mexico	1967	—
Argentina	1969	—
Peru	1971	51
Peru	1976	JV

Sources: M. Herold, "Multinational Enterprise Data Base," University of New Hampshire, Dover.
JV = Joint Venture

zilian market where growth rates are much higher than in the United States. According to a J. I. Case executive, the U.S. tractor market is growing by "maybe 2 to 3 percent per year," but if "you put the same amount of investment into Brazil you get a market growing at 10 percent to 15 percent per year."[11] J. I. Case, Massey Ferguson, and Ford all have subsidiaries in Brazil, with Ford's new $100 million plant the largest.

The advantages to foreign investors of production in Brazil—a cheap and controlled labor force and government incentives—also make the country an attractive export platform for supplying

Table 5.2
Current U.S. Fertilizer Investments in Latin America

Country	Entry year	Percent ownership
Beker Industries		
Brazil[1]	1974	JV
Exxon		
Colombia[2]	1961	—
W. R. Grace		
Trinidad[1]	1958	100
Puerto Rico[2]	1959	100
Dominican Republic[2]	1969	100
Jamaica[2]	1969	100
St. Lucia[2]	1969	100
Trinidad[1]	1974	49
International Minerals & Chemicals		
Colombia[1]	1970s	25
Occidental Petroleum		
Nicaragua[2]	1964	JV
Standard Oil Indiana		
Trinidad[1]	1978	49
Williams Companies		
Brazil[1]	1973	40
Argentina[1]	1975	49

Sources: M. Herold, "Multinational Enterprise Data Base."
1. Production plant
2. Mixing facility
JV = Joint Venture

other third world countries. J. I. Case has already begun to export tractors from its Brazilian subsidiary and plans to nearly double its sales abroad in 1978.[12]

Latin American investments also play an important role in the global strategies of the fertilizer companies. Like the implement manufacturers, the fertilizer companies are most interested in penetrating the more developed markets in the region. Because of the large capital outlays required for new production facilities, the industry is relying on the participation of both international lending agencies and local governments. In both Argentina and Brazil, the Inter-American Development Bank and the U.S. Export-Import Bank have helped finance fertilizer facilities. Williams Companies, which already owns plants in Brazil and Argentina, is contemplating a new $38-million facility in Brazil if it can find "acceptable financing arrangements" for $23 million of the total investment.[13] While production facilities are concentrated in the largest markets, the fertilizer companies have penetrated the smaller markets in Latin America by setting up plants to mix and bag fertilizer produced in other countries.*

An important new trend in the fertilizer industry is the establishment of plants in Latin America to take advantage of low production costs to supply the U.S. market. The Caribbean, with its access to cheap natural gas (one of the principal materials used in making fertilizers), plus its lack of strong antipollution regulations, is becoming especially attractive to U.S. companies. W. R. Grace is currently building an $80-million facility in Trinidad, and when completed 90 percent of its production will be shipped to the United States.

Inappropriate Technologies

A basic issue raised by these transnational investments concerns the social impact they have in the Latin American countryside. Modern agricultural inputs do have a tremendous potential for increasing agricultural production in Latin America. Fertilizers consistently raise crop yields and can lead to increased staple food production, while mechanized farm equipment increases pro-

---

*In some cases Latin American governments operate fertilizer facilities without the direct participation of foreign companies. In Mexico, most fertilizers are produced by the state-owned enterprise, Guanomex, while in Brazil the government took over direct control of a fertilizer subsidiary of Phillips Petroleum in the early 1970s. However, in setting up a new fertilizer facility, the governments are almost always dependent on international financing from such organizations as the World Bank and the Inter-American Development Bank, and they rely on the technology produced by such foreign construction firms as M. W. Kellogg and Fluor.

ductivity and eliminates some of the most grueling and arduous agricultural work. But the impact of these technologies depends on the social structures and economic conditions that exist in the countries that adopt them. The main impact of mechanization in Latin America has been to increase the profits of the large land-owners who are able to acquire mechanized equipment. And as we see in Chapter 7, mechanization also means the loss of jobs for tens of thousands of farmworkers.

The centrality of local conditions in determining the impact of new technologies is illustrated in the state of Sonora, Mexico, the birthplace of the "green revolution." There in the late 1940s, Nelson Borlaug (the "father" of the green revolution), with the backing of the Rockefeller Foundation and other international agencies, began developing the hybrid seeds that are the basis of the green revolution. While hybrid seeds developed for wheat production dramatically increased yields in Sonora, only a rela-tively small group of agricultural producers benefited. The spe-cially bred varieties could be planted only on irrigated lands and required the intensive use of pesticides, chemical fertilizers, and mechanized farm equipment. The cost of these inputs, and the limited resources of small farmers, meant that green revolution technology was controlled and utilized principally by the large landowners in Sonora.

Attempts to introduce the high-yield seeds to the "ejidatarios"— small peasant farmers who worked communal lands—ended in complete failure. In general, the ejidatarios had neither the tech-nical assistance nor the financial credit necessary to adopt the new agricultural techniques that went with the hybrid seed varieties. In fact, in some instances production on the ejidos actually de-clined, because fertilizers and other inputs required by the hybrid seeds were not available in sufficient quantities. As a result, the ejidatarios became even more impoverished.[14]

The transnational corporations are never neutral observers in this process of social and economic dislocation. Over the years they have foisted agricultural technologies on the third world that have had devastating consequences. In the 1960s the fertilizer companies numbered among the main propagators of the myth that the hunger and malnutrition problems of the third world could be solved by applying the technologies of the green revolution. The corporations' motives for pushing this approach were not based on a concern for world hunger, but on the need to get rid of the supplies of excess fertilizer that were depressing world market prices. Questions of adverse social and economic effects were not even considered as the fertilizer companies pressured the Agency for International Development, the World Bank, and other agencies to finance the use of green revolution technologies throughout the third world.

The technologies favored by green revolution seeds and promoted by transnational corporations frequently are those that can be used effectively only on large-scale capitalist farms. For example, the tractors manufactured by the transnationals abroad are generally costly machines with high horsepower ratings that are both too expensive and unsuitable for use by small farmers. In Brazil, where U.S. transnationals dominate the mechanized farm equipment industry, the production of heavy duty tractors quadrupled between 1970 and 1978, while the output of medium and small tractors grew by less than one-third. And the production of micro-tractors and motorized cultivators, more appropriate for small producers, was stagnant from 1973 to 1978.[15] The U.S. companies were simply not interested in mass producing mechanized farm equipment for the small agricultural producers.

The Impact of Pesticides

Transnational corporations also export agricultural technologies that have a devastating impact on the environment and human life. Such U.S. firms as Dow Chemical, Eli Lilly, Dupont, Monsanto, and Chevron manufacture an array of pesticides that are known to be carcenogenic.[16] Some of these pesticides are banned in the United States, but this does not prevent the companies from exporting and manufacturing them abroad. Indeed, it encourages this practice, since otherwise there would be no markets. DDT, for example, is sold in Latin America today, even though its use in the United States has been illegal since 1972.

The fact that pesticide production facilities require far less capital outlay than fertilizers or tractors has encouraged a proliferation of pesticide production throughout Latin America. In the richest agricultural regions huge billboards often crowd the highways, advertising fungicides, herbicides, and other pest killers. Few controls are placed on the sale or use of pesticides: the standard labeling on bags and containers usually says only "not for internal consumption." The labels give little or no warning about the impact of pesticides on the environment or the specific dangers involved in their application.

Before the overthrow of the Somoza regime in Nicaragua billboards advertising pesticides were particularly noticeable. Under the Somoza government, Nicaragua had been designated the main pesticide producer for the Central American Common Market and was known as the "pesticide capital" of Central America. The transnational corporations, through licensing agreements and direct investments, came to dominate Nicaraguan pesticide production.

The growing criticism of pesticide use in both the United States and Latin America has not deterred the transnationals from expanding their investments. A trade journal survey of the leading pesticide firms revealed that the companies foresee continued growth in the Latin American markets, with all but one of them planning to expand production in the region.[17] Their expansion and prosperity as well as that of the other agricultural input manufacturers, is part and parcel of capitalist development.

The Food Processing Industry

Transnational food processing corporations are far more prolific in their investments abroad than the agricultural input industries. Brand names like Quaker Oats, Del Monte, and Pillsbury are household words not only in the United States and Western Europe, but also in many parts of the third world. Some food processors, such as International Multifoods and Coca-Cola, draw over 50 percent of their profits and close to half of their revenue from international operations. Increasingly, the companies regard their marketplace as global rather than national. As the chairman of Coca-Cola recently said, "Instead of there being an offshore business and a domestic business, there is a world market."[18]

Spanning both the urban and rural areas, the foreign food

processors in Latin America form the core of the region's new agro-industry. Although locally owned companies still produce much of Latin America's processed food using traditional small-scale production techniques, there is also a highly modern sector that utilizes the most sophisticated imported equipment and the most advanced marketing strategies. This sector is dominated by the transnational corporations.

Early Expansion

Although the expansion of the transnational food processors in Latin America has been especially intense since 1960, a handful of U.S. processors first became interested in the region's market in the 1930s. To penetrate the trade barriers that many countries had erected to protect their economies during the Depression, the U.S. companies set up direct manufacturing subsidiaries. The bulk of the investments were made by five enterprises—the Corn Products Company (CPC), Fleischman's (Standard Brands), Anderson Clayton, Pet Milk, and Carnation.[19] They produced vegetable oils, corn meal, yeast, and canned milk, all of which are staple food commodities in urbanizing societies.

During this early phase, the transnationals held certain advantages over local competitors. With greater capital resources and the ability to purchase and install the latest processing equipment, the foreign companies could manufacture processed food much more cheaply than local producers. At the same time, Pet and Carnation eliminated competition among themselves by forming a single enterprise, the General Milk Company, which made investments in Jamaica, Panama, and Cuba. Thus, the transnationals quickly gained ascendancy in their respective markets, a position that some of these same firms still hold.

Post–World War II: Testing the Markets

After World War II, the expansion of the food processors received a new impetus with the development of import substitution industrialization. The decision of most Latin American governments to push local industry had a double effect on the foreign food processors: (1) it encouraged them to take advantage of the incentives offered to companies that produced for the domestic market; and (2) it stimulated urban growth in the region, thereby creating new markets for processed foods.

As in the 1930s, many transnationals went into producing staple foods needed by the growing urban populations. Cargill and International Multifoods milled wheat flour, while Borden and Kraft produced dairy byproducts. And the leading banana exporters, United Fruit and Standard Fruit, diversified into the production of vegetable oils and margarine.

During the period from 1945 to 1960 U.S. food companies introduced their snack and convenience foods to Latin America: Quaker Oats began producing its puffed wheat and rolled oats in Brazil and Colombia, while Kellogg made breakfast cereals in Mexico, and Nabisco manufactured crackers in Venezuela. The two giants of the soft drink industry, Coca-Cola and Pepsi-Cola, licensed local bottlers in a number of countries, and set up six subsidiary plants under their direct control.

In this period U.S. food processors invested more in Mexico than in any other third world country. For Mexico the period was one of sustained capitalist growth in both industry and agriculture. The middle class grew rapidly, and some of the food processors moved quickly to establish their brand names in the households of the new urban groups. For the agribusiness companies, Mexico was both a testing ground and a harbinger of what would occur in other Latin American countries.

The Processing Boom

The real boom in U.S. food processing in Latin America began in the 1960s, facilitated by conditions in both the United States and Latin America. In the United States, some food processors became concerned with what they called "industry maturity," i.e., the limited potential for domestic expansion. Faced with saturated U.S. markets in most standard lines of processed foods, the companies could expand their sales and profits in only two ways: (1) by increasing advertising expenditures to sell more snack and convenience foods to domestic consumers, and (2) by pushing aggressively into new markets abroad.[20] The larger food processors followed both strategies.

Already heavily involved in Western Europe and Canada, many firms looked toward the third world, where virtually un-tapped markets offered unlimited growth possibilities. And Latin America, with its growing urban population and its relatively small but numerically significant middle class, proved especially enticing. Between 1960 and 1975, 33 of the leading U.S. food processors made 335 new investments in the third world, four-fifths of them in Latin America.[21]

The canning industry figured prominently in the new rush abroad, with companies such as Del Monte, Heinz, Campbell, and W. R. Grace setting up canning facilities in a number of countries. Some of the processors which had been operating in Latin America since the 1930s diversified into new areas of produc-tion, thereby becoming vast food complexes. CPC (formerly known as Corn Products Company) opened up nine new sub-sidiaries in the region, producing an array of products ranging from ketchup, bouillon, and mayonnaise to biscuits, cheeses, and starches. Anderson Clayton grew rapidly in Mexico and Brazil; by the early 1970s its subsidiaries figured among the largest enterprises in both countries and were listed on the local stock exchanges.[22]

The most notable expansion in the last two decades, how-ever, has occurred in the production of snack and convenience foods, the "junk foods" that have become a virtual staple in the United States.

The list of expensive, highly processed, low-nutrition foods that the U.S. companies manufactured in Latin America became almost limitless. A few examples are Kool-aid (General Foods), candies (Beatrice Foods), gum (Wrigley and Warner Lambert), pizza mixes (Anderson Clayton), imitation cheese (Kraft), gelatin mixes (Pillsbury), puddings (Standard Brands), and instant tortilla mix (General Mills). Between 1960 and 1975, U.S. food processors set up at least seventy-five new subsidiaries in Latin America to produce these products while many established firms expanded their product lines to include "junk" foods.

Although most of these processed foods are designed for the

elite urban markets, some, like candies, gum, and soft drinks, are sold to poorer sectors of the population. In Mexico, 14 billion bottles of soft drinks are consumed every year, or nearly five bottles each week for every man, woman, and child. Due to extensive advertising, the vast majority of the country's people have come to adopt soft drinks as an integral part of their diets. Foreign brands control three-quarters of the market and Coca-Cola alone, through its various brand names, accounts for 42 percent of the soft drink sales in Mexico.[23]

While no nation in the region has been untouched by the assault of the U.S. food processors, the companies concentrate their investments in certain countries. Mexico continued to attract large numbers of investors throughout the sixties, and today it has more transnational food processors than any other Latin American country. But the most rapid expansion occurred in Central America. Even though the five countries of the region have a combined population of only approximately 15 million people, the emergence of the Central American Common Market, combined with special financial incentives offered by both the U.S. and local governments, made the region especially appealing to foreign investors.[24]

In the seventies, however, the booming markets for food processors were in Venezuela and Brazil, both countries with rapidly growing middle and upper classes that are prime consumers of snack and convenience foods. In Brazil, where the government provides special incentives to agro-industry and maintains tight control over the labor force, the food processing industry is growing very rapidly. An executive of Adela Securities, a firm that advises potential foreign investors in Brazil, summarized this trend: "Of every ten visits we get from potential investors, four or five are in the food processing area. I think every single company in the business in the U.S. is down in Brazil looking at projects for the internal market or exports."[25]

Marketing Strategies and Advertising

Many people in the United States are becoming increasingly aware of the detrimental effects of the food processing industry on people's health. Companies like Kellogg, General Mills, and Pillsbury spend millions of dollars advertising processed foods of limited nutritional value. Studies show that these advertisements can create lifelong dietary habits that have adverse health effects.[26]

In the dependent countries of Latin America, the impact of the transnational food processors is even more harmful. They encourage people to consume Heinz ketchup, Pillsbury cookies, and Pepsi-Cola, all products that provide calories rather than protein. For the millions of people on subsistence incomes, every cent spent on these products leads to the further deterioration of their already meager diets. And when the companies do produce nutritional foods, the costs are often so high that only the affluent can afford them. Ralston Purina, for example, runs large-scale egg and poultry operations in Colombia, but the cost of a dozen eggs and a kilo of poultry meat is equal to a week's earnings for over a quarter of the country's population.[27]

To penetrate both the affluent and the mass markets, the food processors use the same business tactic they employ at home—advertising. Many companies bring in their own advertising experts, while others work through transnational agencies like J. Walter Thompson and McCann-Erickson. As a Quaker Oats executive in Colombia commented: "Advertising is a capitalist tool and we won't go into a country that doesn't allow us to advertise."[28]

The Food Processors and Agriculture

In many regions of Latin America, the expansion of U.S. food processing companies has spurred the process of capitalist development in the countryside. Their plants require a constant supply of high quality agricultural produce, a demand that increasingly integrates the rural areas into the web of modern agro-industry. Their impact varies depending on the commodities they need and on the economic and social conditions in the regions where they operate. As the study of Del Monte in Mexico (Chapter 9) shows, the food processors' impact tends to marginalize peasants from their lands. But in other instances they are able to exploit small agricultural producers without depriving them of their property. This is the case in southern Peru.

Peru: Carnation's Peasant Producers

Arequipa, a colonial city in southern Peru, is the location of one of the subsidiaries of Carnation Milk. The city is centered in a fertile agricultural oasis surrounded by volcanic mountains. Every day, Carnation's agents collect milk from some 7,000 dairy producers in the outlying areas, about 85 percent of whom are small peasant landowners with only a few head of dairy cattle. The milk plant, one of the biggest industries in the region, produces almost 90 percent of Peru's canned evaporated milk.[29]

Ever since it set up its plant in 1942, Carnation has incorporated more and more small peasant producers as suppliers. Initially, the company competed with traditional local cheese makers for the region's milk supply, but it soon drove these small cottage industries out of business by offering slightly higher prices to the local milk producers. Many other peasants, in need of a cash income to purchase simple necessities, shifted from staple subsistence crops like corn and potatoes to producing milk for Carnation. Today, most of these peasants grow only pasture and forage crops for their cattle and are completely dependent on Carnation for their livelihood.

But their commercial relationship with Carnation has done little to improve their standard of living. Most of the peasants earn less than the minimum wage from their milk sales, live in small adobe dwellings with their cattle tethered nearby in open stables, and rely on their wives and children to help tend the cattle and deliver the milk to the collection points.

The example of Carnation's Arequipa operations illustrates one facet of capitalism's penetration into the countryside. Instead of formally breaking down the existing social structures and marginalizing peasants, food processors are able to work with the small peasant producers. But, as an extensive study of the company's operations in the region concluded, "the peasant cannot freely choose what to produce, how to produce it, nor who to sell it to. His autonomy as an independent producer has disappeared completely, and he is formally subordinated to the control of transnational capital."[30]

Agricultural Factories

At the other extreme from Carnation are transnational firms that are setting up factory-like units for producing agricultural commodities. Companies like Ralston Purina and International Multifoods have established large-scale poultry and egg production facilities in many Latin American countries that are run on a factory-like basis. Using techniques developed in the United States, the companies set up breeding stock farms, feed milling plants, assembly-line techniques for collecting eggs, and poultry slaughtering houses that process thousands of chickens in a day. In recent years, local capitalist entrepreneurs have also adopted these techniques.

Such large-scale enterprises are gaining control of the poultry market in the larger Latin American countries like Mexico, Brazil, and Argentina. In the São Paulo region of Brazil, 70 percent of the eggs consumed now come from large-scale poultry operations.[31] As a result the traditional small-scale peasant who raised a few chickens for the market is fast disappearing.

Colombia: Valley of the Transnationals

In the fertile Cauca Valley in southern Colombia, nine transnational food processing plants have had a significant impact on the valley's economic development. As capitalist farms expand their operations to supply the food processing companies and the export market, tens of thousands of peasants have been expelled from the land. The transnational corporations and their apologists claim that the new agro-industries in the cities create jobs for those who leave the countryside. But this has not happened in the Cauca Valley. The nine foreign-owned plants, which number among the valley's largest enterprises, employ less than 2,000 workers.[32] Their plants use the most modern imported machinery, and therefore require relatively few employees.

For those who do find work in the processing plants, the conditions are highly exploitative. Many of the workers are employed for only fifty-nine days and then laid off so the company does not have to register them as permanent workers and pay them social security benefits. And as in other Latin American countries, the food processors take advantage of the large pool of unemployed workers by paying only the minimum wage required by law. As one woman said who was waiting to be hired at the gates of the CPC plant: "We have to work for the minimum wage here because there are no other jobs."[33] Such is the reality of the new "opportunities" at the bottom.

Whether they set up milk processing plants in traditional peasant areas or canning factories near major urban centers, the transnationals have a decisive impact on Latin America's development. Together with the local agrarian bourgeoisies, they exercise increasing control over local agricultural resources, thereby depriving millions of peasants and workers of the means to make a decent living. The result is increasing class polarization, and for those at the bottom, malnutrition and hunger.

6. Latin America in the World Market: The Ties that Bind

The agricultural revolution in Latin America is changing the region's role in the world market. Export agriculture is no longer synonymous with one-crop economies. The old export mainstays—bananas, sugar, and coffee—are declining in importance as the export of such commodities as soybeans, fresh vegetables, orange juice, beef, and cotton are stepped up. These commodities now account for over half of Latin America's agricultural exports. Furthermore, the sheer volume of the region's exports is expanding: after a period of relatively slow export growth in the 1950s and early 1960s, Latin America's agricultural exports have almost tripled over the last decade, from $6 billion in 1967 to $17.9 billion in 1976.[1]

What accounts for this shift? Why, after centuries as an exporter primarily of tropical commodities, is Latin America now altering its role in the international division of labor? Basically, the change is rooted in the general advance of capitalism. Latin America's productive capacity has now developed to the point where it can produce a wide array of commodities for the world market.

The change in the international division of labor is illustrated by the growth of soybean production in Latin America. Until the early 1970s, the United States was practically the world's only exporter of soybeans. But then Brazil's rising class of agricultural entrepreneurs turned to soybeans. Using mechanized farm equipment and moving onto some of the old coffee producing lands, they began to challenge U.S. hegemony in the world soybean market. Today, much of Japan's and Western Europe's supply of soybeans and of the soya byproducts (oil and meal) now come from Brazil. Furthermore, two of the Rio de la Plata countries—Argentina and Paraguay—are also becoming a major factor in the world soybean market.[2]

The capitalist transformation of agriculture in Latin America means that now more than ever the dominant classes are able to use the region's cheap labor supply to compete in the world market. For example, the new agrarian bourgeoisie in north-western Mexico uses that country's low-paid, nonunion labor force to compete in the fresh fruit and vegetable market in the United States. And in Central America, large-scale commercial cotton farmers take advantage of the large unemployed army of labor by growing special handpicked varieties of cotton for the Western European market.

Imperialism and Latin American Agriculture

Cheap labor and the development of capitalist agriculture are not the only factors that explain Latin America's changing role in the world market. The economic needs of the imperialist countries also have an impact on Latin American agriculture.

Feeding Industrial Capitalism

While the worldwide food crisis of the early 1970s caused most observers to focus on the strategic role the United States held in world agriculture because of its large grain reserves, few noticed that the United States and other industrialized countries were actually stepping up their food imports from the third world.

Next to petroleum, food accounts for the largest single item in U.S. imports. In 1978 the United States imported over $17 billion in agricultural commodities, of which more than 40 percent came from Latin America. Japan and Western Europe, which do not possess the agricultural resources of the United States, are even larger importers of agricultural commodities. Altogether over 75 percent of Latin America's food exports go to the industrialized capitalist nations.[3]

The role of the dominant capitalist countries in world agricultural production is also changing. As the first section of this book points out, the world's largest food producer, the United States, has been increasingly specializing in wheat production while relying more and more on imports of dairy, beef, and vegetable products. Furthermore, a recent study of the National Academy of Sciences reveals that rising production costs make it highly improbable that the United States will continue to expand its agricultural production as rapidly as it has in the past. The expanding use of marginal lands, the diminishing returns from heavier applications of chemical fertilizers, and the rising costs of a petroleum-based agricultural system—all these factors mean that U.S. agricultural production will become increasingly costly.[4] And there is another factor which the Academy of Sciences study failed to mention: increasing labor costs, as farm laborers become organized in the United States and demand a larger share of the wealth they produce. All these factors mean that the third world will play an expanding role in the production of food for the world market.

The Impact on Latin America

What do these changes in agriculture portend for Latin America's future development as a whole? Is it possible that the leading countries of Latin America—Brazil, Mexico, and Argentina—will soon be able to compete on a viable basis with the advanced industrial countries in the world's commodity markets?

There is no doubt that fundamental shifts have occurred in the world economy in recent years. Latin America now competes with the advanced industrial countries in an array of commodities, industrial as well as agricultural. Brazil exports automobiles and steel as well as soybeans and orange juice; Mexico ships television sets, electronic components, and fresh vegetables to the United States; and Uruguay is becoming a major exporter of shoes and finished leather goods while expanding its beef exports.

These changes, however, while increasing Latin America's participation in the world market, have profound social and economic consequences. As export production expands in Latin America, the region becomes more tightly integrated into the economies of the advanced industrialized countries. While Latin America exports more soybeans, shoes, and automobiles, it also imports more plant equipment, computers, and heavy industrial machinery.

For Latin America's workers, this arrangement has devastating consequences. The bourgeoisies of Latin America, to remain competitive on the world market, must repress the working classes and keep wages at a bare minimum. It is no accident that the Brazilian military government, an aggressive competitor in the world market, has driven down the real wages of Brazilian workers during the past decade and a half. The military regimes in the countries of the area known as the Southern Cone—Argentina, Chile, and Uruguay—have also reduced real wages so that their exports are more competitive on the world market.[5] Chile is now exporting large quantities of fresh grapes to the United States, while Argentina and Uruguay have stepped up their agricultural exports and are pushing light manufactured exports on the world market.

But the intensified exploitation of the workforce, while increasing the profits of the bourgeoisies, has not enabled them to gain control of the channels of international trade,nor has it allowed them to compete on an equal footing with producers in the imperialist countries. To understand the position of the local bourgeoisies, we will first look at the role that U.S. capital plays in international trade, and at how it uses its political and economic power to manipulate the world market.

Modern Merchant Capitalists

Until the end of the nineteenth century, foreign involvement in Latin American agriculture occurred primarily through merchant capitalists who financed local planters and controlled the export trade. Then as mercantilism gave way to a new stage of imperialism, foreign capital assumed direct control of plantations, mines, and factories in Latin America. But foreign capital by no means abandoned the realm of international trade. In fact, its role in the region's trade grew along with the increase in direct foreign investments. New transnationals, such as United Fruit and the Swift and Armour meatpacking firms, established facilities abroad and assumed direct control of the international marketing of the commodities they produced. And as the twentieth century unfolded, U.S. banks, including Morgan Guaranty Trust and Chase Manhattan, became deeply involved in financing international trade.

Today, an array of foreign enterprises and financial institutions have taken over the old role of the merchant capitalists. Banks, transnational corporations, commodity brokers, state trading enterprises, and private commercial firms are active in the international commodity trade and provide the financial grease necessary to move goods from one country to another.

The organization of the trade in coffee and sugar provides an insight into how international trade is conducted. In the case of these two commodities, transnational corporations involved in processing and refining in the United States are also an important force in international trade. The leading coffee processor, General Foods (with one-sixth of the U.S. market), and the biggest sugar refiner, Amstar (which controls one-fourth of the U.S. sugar market) are among the largest international traders in their respective commodities. Amstar, for example, negotiated a long-term contract in 1976 for buying most of the Dominican Republic's sugar,[6] while General Foods bought one-fifth of Brazil's coffee crop in 1977.

Along with the international commodity brokers (who are also major traders of sugar and coffee on the world market), the transnationals often speculate by buying and selling futures contracts—contracts for future deliveries—on the London and New York commodity exchanges. Three-fourths of all raw sugar traded internationally represents speculative trading, and speculation accounts for at least 25 percent of coffee futures contracts.[7]

Latin American financiers and merchants also participate in the coffee and sugar trade. During the 1977–1978 coffee shortage, business interests from Brazil and Colombia were very active in the coffee market as they tried to cash in on the high prices and volatile market. One of Brazil's most powerful financial groups, the Atalla family, moved to expand its position in the coffee trade by acquiring control of Hills Brothers, a U.S.-based coffee processing firm involved in international trading.

But the transnationals remain the ascendant force in both the coffee and sugar trades. Their marketing intelligence networks, their control of processing facilities, and their enormous financial power allows them to buy heavily when the market price is low, to stockpile, and then to reap windfall profits when the price goes up. When sugar prices skyrocketed in 1974 for example, Amstar's profits rose by 420 percent.[8]

U.S. capital, in this case transnational corporations and some of the biggest U.S. banks, has been involved in the growth of Brazilian soybean exports also. Chase Manhattan, through its Brazilian branch banks, has extended over $100 million in loans for soybean production.[9] Cargill and Continental Grain, the world's two largest grain traders, are major exporters of Brazilian soybeans and have set up multimillion-dollar plants in Brazil that process soybeans for the export market.

In some commodities, regional commercial enterprises rather than transnational corporations play a central role in trade by financing agricultural producers. The trade in Mexican vegetables, for example, is dominated not by big transnational capital but by commercial enterprises and financial institutions based primarily in the southwestern United States. Banks such as the Valley National Bank of Arizona, supermarket chains such as Lucky's (based in Oakland), and California agribusiness enterprises such as Deardorff-Jackson are all heavily involved in the fresh vegetable trade between Mexico and the United States. These firms not only buy and distribute the produce in the United States, they also provide financing for the growers at planting time in exchange for guaranteed delivery of the crops. In the vegetable producing state of Sinaloa, 20 to 40 percent of the agricultural credit comes directly from foreign sources.[10]

Thus foreign capital adapts quickly to the demands of international trade and assumes a variety of organizational forms as it strives to control the commercial arteries of the world capitalist system. Whatever form it takes, however, foreign capital's primary function is to break down national boundaries and to help deepen the international division of labor. By following the old merchant's dictum of buying as cheap as possible and selling dear, the modern merchant firms encourage agricultural producers around the world to specialize in the areas of production where they are most efficient. If Brazil produces soybeans cheaper than the United

States, the giant trading firms move quickly into the Brazilian market and promote its exports around the world. It makes no difference to the corporations if their sales adversely affect soybean producers in other parts of the world, or if millions of inhabitants in Brazil suffer from hunger and malnutrition. What does matter for the companies is that they purchase commodities from the cheapest producers and sell to the highest bidder in the world market.

At the same time, the predominance of foreign capital in Latin America's agricultural trade reveals that the region's bourgeoisies are still relatively weak. Brazil is the world's second largest agricultural exporter (after the United States) but its national capitalists play a marginal role in world trade. Anderson Clayton is a major exporter of Brazilian cotton, a Coca-Cola subsidiary, Minute Maid, markets Brazilian orange juice abroad, Cargill is a leading exporter of Brazilian soybeans and soya oil, while General Foods buys a large share of Brazil's coffee beans.[11] In sum, Brazil and Latin America are stepping up their exports, but foreign capitalists reap increasing profits from the region's expanding trade.

The Terms of Trade for Latin America

Although the Latin American bourgeoisies do not control the channels of international trade, they are striving to raise agricultural prices by forming producers' associations and drawing up special commodity agreements. Over the years, the prices of Latin America's main exports (agricultural commodities and raw materials) have either stagnated or risen much more slowly than the costs of industrial imports from the advanced countries. For Latin America this has resulted in what is called a decline in the terms of trade. Today Latin America has to sell a much larger quantity of commodities abroad just to import the same amount of manufactured goods. Where it took 160 bags of coffee to purchase a tractor in 1960, it took 400 bags to buy the same tractor in 1970.[12]

As shortages arise in many primary commodities, the Latin

American bourgeoisies are supporting moves by their goverments to change the terms of trade. In 1975 the Union of Banana Exporting Nations (UPEB) was formed, in 1977 the International Sugar Agreement was drawn up, and in 1977 and 1978 the major coffee producers of Latin America and Africa met to try to set minimum coffee prices. These steps are part of the efforts by third world governments to establish what is being called a "New International Economic Order." The third world is pressuring the industrialized countries for higher prices for their raw materials and agricultural exports, arguing that "trade, not aid" is the key to economic development.

As American consumers know, the prices of some imported agricultural commodities have risen in recent years. The price of a pound of sugar jumped from 11¢ to 66¢ in 1974, and that of a pound of coffee more than quintupled from 1975 to 1978, going from 65¢ to $3.40. But these dramatic price increases were not caused by producers' associations or special commodity agreements, and did not signal a permanent improvement in the terms of trade to producers. Rather, they reflected the general instability in commodity prices that has hit the capitalist world in recent years. As the world capitalist system becomes more integrated, a crop failure or a drop in exports by a particular country has profound consequences for commodity prices around the world. Moreover, the onset of the world economic crisis in the late 1960s and 1970s has fueled both inflation and speculation, not only within the United States but also in the rest of the capitalist world and in international commodity markets. This is why the prices of wheat, beef, coffee, sugar, and cocoa as well as those of copper, aluminum, and petroleum, have fluctuated wildly in recent years.

Even the leaders of the major capitalist countries have declared that they want to stabilize international commodity prices—not so much because unstable prices adversely affect third world countries, but because the price fluctuations provoke economic distortions and consumer protests in the advanced industrial societies. In 1976 a special task force of the Trilateral Commission (comprised of representatives of the leading capitalist industrial nations) concluded that the interests of Trilateral nations would be served by "attempts to devise stabilization measures that have a chance of working."[13] President Carter in the early days of his administration also called for negotiations to stabilize prices.

But while the developed capitalist countries are interested in stable prices, it is clear that they are determined to stabilize prices for the commodities they import at the lowest possible level. Efforts to forge international trade agreements for Latin America's two main exports—coffee and sugar—reveal that the Latin American bourgeoisies have been unsuccessful in their efforts to drive up prices. The imperialist countries have tremendous leverage and flexibility within the world capitalist system, and they often use it to hold down the prices of imported agricultural commodities and to jettison efforts of the third world countries to draw up special commodity agreements.

Freezing Coffee Prices

In the case of coffee the United States has traditionally used its clout in the International Coffee Organization (ICO) to keep prices low. Formed in the early 1960s, the ICO, which is comprised of both coffee producing and coffee consuming nations, periodically draws up agreements to regulate the international coffee trade. The United States government, through its control of one-third of the votes, has virtual veto power in the ICO. And U.S. coffee processors have traditionally played a strong role in negotiations through their advisory role to the U.S. government.

In 1976, after a long and bitter fight which almost led to the collapse of the ICO, a new agreement was drawn up which called for a minimum price of 77¢ per lb.[14] Then early frosts in Brazil drastically curtailed that country's production, depleted international coffee stocks, and sent the price soaring to $3.40 per lb. At this point the major coffee producers of Latin America sought to use their newly won leverage in the coffee trade by agreeing to limit their future coffee exports, thus making sure the price would not drop below $2.00 per lb. In early 1978 Mexico and the leading Central American coffee exporters even threatened to halt the export of coffee completely unless the United States and other importing countries agreed to this new minimum price.[15]

However, as total coffee production rose again, it proved impossible for the third world countries to control their exports.

The coffee processors and the international brokers continued to buy and sell on the world market, thereby pitting one exporting country against another. Over forty-one nations export coffee, and many of them, because of their desperate need for foreign exchange earnings, found it impossible to resist selling as much coffee as possible on the open market. As a result, efforts to form a coffee producers' cartel collapsed, and less than a year after coffee exporters had called for a minimum price of $2.00 per lb., the price was $1.20 per lb.[16]

In the case of sugar U.S. actions have virtually destroyed the International Sugar Agreement (ISA) that was drawn up in late 1977. The U.S. government was an initial signatory of the agreement, which called for a minimum price of 11¢ per lb. But Congress has refused to ratify the pact, and the Carter administration did not push the agreement aggressively, claiming that it has other foreign policy priorities.[17]

The dispute in the United States was not over the price of 11¢ (the Latin American nations had already withdrawn their early demand of 15¢), but over how much protection U.S. domestic sugar producers should have against foreign imports. Currently U.S. producers are protected by import quotas and by a 5.5¢ per lb. import tax.[18] The International Sugar Agreement called for a reduction in these protectionist measures, but the U.S. growers used their political clout in Washington to prevent any significant changes in their protected status.

A New Economic Order for Whom?

In sum, the efforts of Latin American bourgeoisies and their governments to obtain higher prices for their agricultural commodities have been largely unsuccessful. Agricultural commodities, unlike petroleum supplies, are renewable resources and thus there are no natural limits on their output. The free market of capitalism drives third world countries to compete with each other to increase their agricultural production and their exports, thereby leading to excess supplies and falling prices.

At the same time, the governments of the dominant countries

use their enormous economic and political power to intervene in the marketplace: they protect their own agricultural producers, while at the same time they maneuver to undermine efforts by third world governments to form producers' associations that would raise agricultural prices. This is why the quest for the New International Economic Order is doomed to failure. As long as trade in the world market is based on an international hierarchy of capitalist economies, third world countries will often succumb to the needs of the dominant capitalist countries. The less developed countries simply do not have the economic clout to drive up international agricultural prices through the formation of cartels or producers' associations.

In the final analysis, the Latin American bourgeoisies have only one means of strengthening their position in the world market—by intensifying their exploitation of the labor force and the peasantry. As the next chapter shows, rural workers throughout Latin America are compelled to sell their labor power for subsistence or starvation wages. This enables the bourgeoisies to compete effectively in the world market, not only in the production of such traditional export commodities as bananas, sugar, and coffee, but also in the development of such new agricultural exports as soybeans and vegetables. Modern methods of agricultural production (mechanized farm equipment, fertilizers, etc.) are used, but they are as costly for the Latin American bourgeoisies as they are for producers in the advanced capitalist countries. Only by harnessing a cheap labor force to these new production methods can the agrarian bourgeoisies gain a competitive edge in the world market.

It is not the local bourgeoisies that will create a new international economic order, but the workers and peasants who bear the brunt of the present system of exploitation. Ultimately, the Latin American bourgeoisie can only go so far in challenging the structure of the world market. Although they are anxious for a bigger share of the capitalist pie, their basic interest is in maintaining the system of exploitation that makes their profits possible. Far from wanting a genuine change in the international economic order, they have a fundamental shared interest with foreign capital in maintaining the world capitalist system intact.

7. The Agricultural Workforce: From Peasant to Proletarian

When world coffee prices hit an all-time high of $3.40 per lb. in 1977 the profits of General Foods Corporation (the largest coffee maker in the United States) soared, Brazil registered record coffee export earnings of $4 billion, and some Brazilian coffee plantation owners became overnight millionaires. But for Sebastian Maura, one of Brazil's 5 million coffee workers, the situation was as bleak that year as any other. Along with his wife and three of his six children, Sebastian set out at dawn every morning from his family's miserable wooden and tin shack for one of the nearby coffee plantations. After ten hours of backbreaking work under the scorching sun, the Mauras would earn only about a penny for each $3.00 pound of coffee they picked. To make matters worse, the plantation owner would not pay them for their labor until the end of the month-long harvest. And then they would be without a job.[1]

The Maura family's situation is similar to that of tens of millions of other agricultural workers in Brazil and throughout Latin America. It is their labor that produces the agricultural wealth that swells the profits of corporations like General Foods and builds the fortunes of Latin America's thriving agricultural bourgeoisie. But regardless of whether international prices are high or low, Sebastian Maura and his fellow workers face the same grim conditions year after year. They work for subsistence wages, often without rights or benefits. They are constantly at the mercy of the landowners' seasonal needs for labor, working from dawn to dusk one month and without a job the next. Reflecting their status as the lowest paid sector of the labor force, rural workers and their families also have the lowest standard of living, the highest illiteracy rate, and the least access to such basic services as decent housing and health care.

One of the most important trends in the Latin American countryside over the past three decades has been the mushrooming size of this agricultural proletariat, made up of men and women like Sebastian Maura who are forced to sell their labor power to survive. The increase in the number of rural wage workers has been most dramatic in those regions where capitalist agriculture has expanded most rapidly. In São Paulo, for example—one of the southern states where Brazil's "agricultural miracle" is centered—the number of agricultural day workers swelled by almost 175,000 in the last half of the 1960s to reach 350,000.[2] In the Mexican state of Sinaloa, capital of that country's booming fruit and vegetable export industry, the number of farmworkers nearly doubled between 1960 and 1970, from 66,000 to 126,000.[3]

Although the trend toward proletarianization is uneven both from region to region and from country to country, it shapes the lives of growing numbers of men, women, and children. It also marks a profound change in the class structure of rural Latin America. Moreover, with around 40 percent of the population still living in rural areas, the agricultural proletariat is an increasingly important part of the working class as a whole, a fact which is bound to have profound political repercussions for Latin America's future.

From Peasant to Proletariat

If one were to ask a canecutter in Colombia, a cotton picker in El Salvador, or a coffee worker in Brazil how they became agricultural workers, chances are that each would have a different story. For some proletarianization may have been sudden and violent, for others gradual and peaceful. But for all it has been a story of dispossession and the wrenching transformation of their lives.

Prior to the 1950s, the majority of rural inhabitants in most of Latin America were "peasants," a catch-all grouping that included anyone from minifundistas (small farmers who possessed their own plots of land), to sharecroppers (tenants who paid rent in crops), to colonos (resident estate workers alloted a piece of land for subsistence farming), to ejiditarios (indigenous small holders who farmed their communal lands). What all these people had in common was that they relied largely on farming their small plots for subsistence.[4]

Today, due to the development of capitalist agriculture, it has become impossible for many of these people to subsist on the land. Some must turn to wage labor for part of the year to supplement their meager income from the land. But, as we will see, increasing numbers have been completely dispossessed from the land. Before describing the conditions of exploitation faced by this new agricultural proletariat, we will examine some of the many ways in which this process of marginalization and dispossession occurs, focusing on two different sectors of the peasantry: colonos and minifundistas.

The Dispossession of Colonos

As we saw in Chapter 4, resident workers (sometimes known as "colonos") date back to colonial times, when the owners of vast landed estates sought to assure themselves of a constant source of highly exploitable labor at a time when labor was in scarce supply. In an arrangement reminiscent of the European feudal system, the estate owners alloted resident workers and their families small plots of land in usufruct for housing as well as for subsistence farming. In exchange the colonos were required to spend a substantial part of every year working the lands of the estate owner. While they sometimes received a small salary payment, the colonos subsisted mainly on what they could produce on their own small plots.

With the transformation of many traditional estates into modern commercial farms, colonos have become victims of the merciless rationality of capitalism. A modern plantation owner finds it is far cheaper to hire laborers on the open market only at planting or harvest time than to carry the responsibility and cost of maintaining both workers and families on a year-round basis. This is particularly true when there is no scarcity of unemployed people in the countryside. Moreover, in regions where modern agriculture is a dynamic center of capital accumulation, land has become an increasingly valuable and scarce commodity. From the perspective of maximizing profits, subsistence farming by resident workers is a waste of land that could be used to grow lucrative commercial crops.

It is not surprising, then, that millions of colonos have been expelled from once-traditional estates over the past several decades. The small and densely populated country of El Salvador is a dramatic example. During the first half of the 1960s favorable prices for cotton on the international market sparked a boom in cotton production throughout Central America. In those years El Salvador's production tripled[5]—an increase that was made possible partially by the expansion of cotton onto much of the land once used by colonos to grow subsistence crops. To accomplish this expansion the landowners carried out a massive expulsion of colono families. One study shows that between 1961 and 1971 there was a 77 percent decrease in the amount of land farmed by colonos, and the number of colono plots declined by 70 percent.[6] Today many of these dispossessed peasants live in the makeshift mud and straw huts scattered along the dusty roads and barren mountainsides of the Salvadorean countryside.

In some parts of the continent the colono system is fast on its way to disappearing. But in other areas the proletarianization of the colono has been a more gradual process, reflecting a slower pace of capitalist development. Guatemala is one such case. The story told by one resident worker on a sugar plantation in the province of Escuinlita is typical of the process occurring throughout the Guatemalan countryside.[7] Over a period of more than half a century, the colonos on this plantation experienced a slow but steady change in their relationship to the plantation owner and the land. As the owner began to modernize and invest more and more capital in production, the colono families were given progressively smaller and less fertile plots of land for subsistence farming. At first the reduction in subsistence plots was compensated for by food rations from the owner, but gradually the colonos came to rely increasingly on salary payments to survive. By the early 1970s the situation of resident workers had changed drastically. Even though they were still allowed to live on the estate, the owner demanded money payment for the use of subsistence plots and no longer provided housing or guaranteed work. Although some of the older workers still received food rations, children were completely deprived of this right. Many were forced to leave the estate permanently to seach for work elsewhere. Even those who remained as regular workers had been almost completely proletarianized.

Small Farmers: Expropriation and Competition

Small peasant farmers, in spite of their apparent independence, are no less vulnerable to the forces of capitalist development. Latin America is replete with stories of the violent expropriation of small farmers who have fought to hold on to their lands in the face of expanding capitalist enterprises. One example comes from Nicaragua, where thousands of peasants in the rich coastal province of Chinandega lost their lands during the Somoza dictatorship. Many of these peasants had farmed the land for decades without any formal title, a common situation in Latin America. But when the cotton boom began in the early 1960s enterprising capitalists (many of them linked to Somoza) suddenly registered ownership papers for the lands. When the peasants refused to abandon their lands, they were forcibly evicted by Somoza's National Guard.[8]

Some of Nicaragua's dispossessed peasants tried to make a new start by migrating to the frontier province of Zeyala. But once again the encroachment of large-scale capitalist enterprises meant brutal and violent expropriation for many. This time it was the expansion of cattle production that drove them from the land. Nicaragua's new-found role as a major exporter of meat coincided with the construction of a new road system linking Zeyala with export markets for the first time. Large ranchers soon moved in to snatch up the prime lands for cattle production. The peasants once again resisted. When the National Guard was sent in, not only were people evicted from the land, but many were murdered for their alleged ties to the local Sandinista resistance—then leading the struggle of rural and urban people in an ultimately triumphant movement to overthrow Somoza.[9]

But it is not only blatant force that pushes peasant farmers into the ranks of the proletariat. In a pattern more similar to what has unfolded in the United States, tens of thousands of small farmers in Latin America have also lost their lands in the ruthless competitive struggle that characterizes capitalism. As other chapters in this book point out, the larger and wealthier farmers have all the advantages in this struggle. They usually monopolize the best lands, and they have the capital and credit to finance expensive machinery and other inputs. Small farmers, on the other hand, often possess the least fertile lands, without irrigation facilities; and they have neither the collateral nor political clout to qualify for credits to finance modern inputs. Many small farmers are driven out of production because they cannot even attempt to compete with large growers. Others face ruin when they try to play by the rules of the capitalist game that is stacked against them.

The story of the peasant farmers of the Cauca Valley in Colombia is only one example of the losing battle small farmers are fighting throughout Latin America in the face of expanding capitalism. Since colonial times this semitropical river valley was known as one of the richest agricultural regions in the continent. In those days the valley was dominated by vast cattle-producing haciendas which provided meat to the population in the nearby silver mines. During the nineteenth century most of the large estates converted to sugar production. Living on the edges of these still traditional estates were thousands of relatively prosperous small peasants, some of them engaged in subsistence farming and others in commercial cacao and coffee production.[10]

Beginning in the early 1960s the lives of these peasants were transformed by two simultaneous developments in the valley: the modernization of the sugar plantations and the arrival of a number of U.S. food processing corporations. Ralston Purina, among the first of the multinationals to arrive on the scene, set up a plant to manufacture animal feed concentrate made from sorghum and soybeans, neither of which were grown extensively in the valley. To obtain the needed raw materials, the company bypassed the small peasant producers and began to contract for crops with an emerging group of agricultural entrepreneurs, many of whom had come from other regions to invest in the valley's booming agriculture. These commercial enterprises had access to ample credits from both private banks and state agencies, and used the most modern agricultural techniques. At the same time, the Corn Products Company (CPC) and Quaker Oats, both of which manufacture a variety of expensively canned and packaged corn-based products, contracted with these large growers to produce a special varietal corn. Once again, the small peasants who traditionally produced corn for local consumption were ignored by the companies. By the late 1960s these flourishing large-scale commercial farms had encroached onto both hacienda and peasant holdings, renting or purchasing land as they expanded.

Then in the early 1970s the peasants found themselves further squeezed by a new source of competition for increasingly scarce lands—the expansion of the thriving sugar industry. Vast areas of land were turned over to sugar production to meet growing demand from the mills. The peasants were caught between the large growers who had wanted more land for sugar and those who wanted to continue producing crops for the food processors. Some were forced to sell their land to expanding commercial operations. Others lost their lands as a result of renting their plots to large producers who at the expiration of the rental agreement demanded to be paid for the improvements they had made on the land. Most small peasants could not afford the exorbitant charges, and were forced to forfeit their lands. Still other peasants were pushed into bankruptcy when their crops were purposely destroyed by chemical sprays and their irrigation waters polluted.[11]

As peasant organizations developed and land invasions were threatened, the situation in the valley came to the exploding point. The U.S. Agency for International Development, along with the Colombian government, tried to alleviate the social unrest with a program ostensibly designed to assist the small peasant producers. The subsequent agricultural assistance program only sealed the fate of the peasants and further facilitated the expansion of large-scale farming. It provided peasants with financial and technical aid so that they could switch to producing for the food processing companies. By participating in the program, however, many peasants became heavily indebted, and when they could not repay loans they were compelled to sell their lands.[12]

Today small-scale peasant agriculture in the valley has been virtually destroyed. Many of the region's once prosperous peas-

ants are now landless, obliged to seek work on the sugar plantations or in the factories of the U.S. companies. In one of the
peasant communities ironically called Villarica (or "rich village")
the older generation remembers the days when they could at least
survive from the land. But now an estimated one-half of the
children in the village suffer from malnutrition.[13]

The Dispossessed

Each of the above examples, multiplied by thousands of such
occurrences from one end of the continent to another, adds up to
an astounding increase in the number of landless people in the
countryside. In the case of Mexico alone, the number of landless
is estimated to have increased almost ten times since 1950, from
1.5 million to approximately 14 million, well over half the rural
population.[14] Figures for El Salvador show that the proportion of
the rural population without land soared from 12 percent in 1961
to 29 percent in 1971, and by 1975 it had reached 41 percent.[15]

The options for those millions of peasants who have been
forced from the land in recent decades are usually few and bleak.
Many are drawn to the larger towns and cities in the hopes of
finding jobs there—only to discover their hopes were illusory.
Even in the most developed industrial centers like São Paulo or
Mexico City, industry is growing at a much slower pace than the
rapidly expanding labor force, and jobs for unskilled workers
from the countryside are few and far between in the new capital
intensive industries. The city of São Paulo, for example, has over
500,000 new arrivals every year.[16] Once in the cities the majority
of these migrants are faced with the prospect of living in crowded
slums without services, and finding occasional jobs as street vendors, maids, or prostitutes. For many, the only option is to stay in
the countryside and try to find work as agricultural laborers.

In spite of the accelerating trend toward landlessness, there are
still countless numbers of small independent peasants who continue to farm their own plots.[17] However, for the majority of these
minifundistas, their position as independent producers is pre-

carious. Their plots are too small, their land is too poor, and their resources inadequate to provide even minimal subsistence for their families. In El Salvador, for example, 34 percent of the rural population (in addition to the 41 percent who are landless) have one hectare or less of land.[18] Many of these marginal peasants have already taken the first steps toward proletarianization by leaving their land for weeks or months at a time to find work as wage laborers in agriculture. For decades the small coffee farmers of Colombia regularly worked as wage laborers on the larger plantations of their wealthier neighbors. But in recent years many have become fully proletarianized as the number of coffee mini-fundias drastically declined.[19]

For a growing number of these part-time workers, part-time peasants, wages are now their main source of income, even though desperately low wages mean continued subsistence farming is still necessary for survival. One recent study in Guatemala, where semiproletarians make up a large portion of the agricultural labor force, found that cotton workers there obtain 74 percent of their total income from wages, sugar workers 70 percent, and coffee workers 60 percent.[20] The growing reliance on wages is also evident in Mexico. Whereas in 1950 about 84 percent of Mexico's ejido peasants earned over half their income from farming, by 1960 this was true of only 66 percent of ejido families. As a result, many ejidarios now rent their lands to large growers and work as day laborers in the fields. In the state of Sonora, an estimated 70 percent of ejido families are in this position.[21]

A Climate for Exploitation

The intolerable living and working conditions faced by growing millions of farmworkers in Latin America are fundamentally shaped by the drive of agricultural capitalists for expansion and profit. But there are a number of other contextual factors that affect the desperate situation in the countryside, including (1) the large pool of unemployed, (2) the seasonal nature of the work, and (3) the lack of effective worker or peasant organizations that accompanies the repressive political climate.

Structural Unemployment

In most capitalist societies there is a pool of unemployed workers who function as a "reserve army of labor": they are hired by employers when needed, and then laid off when the rhythm of capital accumulation renders them expendable. The growing number of landless and impoverished peasants and the inability of agriculture or industry to provide them jobs has swollen this reserve army to massive proportions. Unemployment rates of 20 to 30 percent are common throughout the continent, and always highest in the countryside. This large reserve of impoverished and unemployed is a major factor in keeping wages in agriculture low. People who desperately need work are forced to accept rock-bottom wages and inhumane conditions when for most the option would be starvation.

Seasonal Unemployment

Since seasonality is characteristic of all agricultural production, the vast majority of agricultural workers are able to find work only during the relatively short periods of time required for harvesting. During the month-long coffee harvest, for example, hundreds of thousands of workers will suddenly be needed to harvest the delicate beans from the trees. Then, just as suddenly, they will be without a job. This fact has a disastrous impact on the standard of living of agricultural workers.

In Mexico, there are an estimated 5 million farmworkers who find employment less than ninety days a year. Those who work in the modern vegetable industry of the northwest—among the best paid seasonal workers in Mexico—earn only about $2.50 to $3.00 a day.[22] Spread out over the year, this comes to an annual income of only $270. In Nicaragua, the 200,000 cotton workers who received a daily salary of about $2.40 a day in the mid-seventies worked an average of seventy-six days a year—amounting to an income of about 80¢ a day when spread out over the year.[23]

To earn enough to survive many agricultural workers are forced to become migrants for part of the year. Following the seasonal rhythm of different crops they travel from one harvest to another, often crossing into neighboring countries. Men sometimes leave their families behind, but often women and children join the migrant stream as workers. In Brazil's northeast thousands of small peasants who try to eke out a living on the parched lands of the interior migrate to the coast each year for the sugar harvest. In the southern Brazilian state of Parana an estimated one-third of the rural population are migrants.[24] In Mexico some 600,000 migrant farmworkers follow the harvest of five major crops— cotton, sugar, coffee, tobacco, and tomatoes. Seventy percent of these migrants are on the road for seven months of the year, many of them traveling as far as the lettuce fields of California's Imperial Valley.[25] In other parts of Latin America, thousands of Nicaraguans cross into Costa Rica to pick cotton each year, Guatemalans stream into Mexico for the coffee harvest, and Salvadoreans flock to Guatemala looking for work in the fields.

Unions and Peasant Organizations

Another set of factors play a crucial role in stacking the cards against farmworkers and in favor of employers. Only a tiny percentage of agricultural workers belong to unions or peasant organizations. In Guatemala for example, out of an agricultural workforce of over 300,000 only slightly over 12,000 workers were formally members of unions in 1975.[26] Those organizations that do exist are for the most part either not committed to protecting workers' interests, or are limited in their ability to do so by government and employer repression.

Without effective unions, farmworkers have no lever to bargain for better wages and working conditions, for job security, or for a work day of reasonable length. Farmworkers are often hired on the basis of an oral contract that leaves wages and the length of employment openended. Even when wage rates are agreed upon, workers are routinely cheated by employers, for example by short-weighting the amount of produce picked by workers paid according to piece rate. Arbitrary dismissal by employers without payment for prior work is not uncommon. In countries where minimum wage laws apply to rural workers, such legal niceties are almost uniformly ignored by employers, even where unions do exist.[27] In general, however, farmworkers have been accorded few legal rights and in fact may be discriminated against by the law. In Guatemala, for example, the labor code prohibits strikes during harvest season—the only time a farmworkers' strike can be effective.[28] In El Salvador rural unions have no legal status whatsoever.

The obstacle to organizing rural unions stems partly from the seasonal and migratory nature of the work. When the bulk of the workforce is together only for a brief period it is difficult to build a permanent organization that depends for its effectiveness on unity and cohesion. It is no accident that the bulk of unionized farmworkers work in foreign-owned banana plantations and the sugar mills—both areas where the workforce is permanently employed and concentrated in large numbers.

Historically there has been a long tradition of militant rural organizations in Latin America. But in recent decades many of these organizations have been either destroyed or severely weakened by a combination of repression and cooptation. In Central America, for example, the large and powerful banana workers' unions became a militant force in the postwar period in defending not only their own interests but in the forefront of the entire labor movement. However, by the end of the 1950s, rightwing governments (such as the one installed by the U.S.-backed coup in Guatemala in 1954) had smashed both militant leaders and members. With the help of the American Institute for Free Labor Development (an organization linked to the AFL-CIO which has received CIA funding) a new and docile leadership was installed at the head of most banana workers' unions in Central America.[29]

Another example were the powerful and militant peasant leagues that arose in the early 1960s among sugar workers in Brazil's impoverished northeast. In the wake of the 1964 military coup there—a coup which received crucial backing from the landowners of the northeast—the peasant leagues were virtually destroyed.[30]

More recent efforts to build militant union organizations among Latin America's fast-growing rural proletariat have made some small advances, but have also met with setbacks. In El Salvador, for instance, two important union and peasant organizations— the UTC and the FECCAS—have emerged in the last several years. With a membership numbering in the thousands and a much broader base of support, they have carried out activities ranging from land invasions to militant demonstrations in the capital demanding improved conditions for their members, as well as an end to general repression. Their combativeness has led to brutal attacks by the army and paramilitary groups, which break up union meetings and otherwise attempt to terrorize members by murder or kidnappings.

Another example comes from the Dominican Republic, where the U.S.-based Gulf and Western Corporation—the country's largest sugar producer—has waged a battle of over ten years with militant workers on its La Romana plantations. Shortly after Gulf and Western first moved to take over the La Romana operations in 1966, the militant sugar workers' union there was smashed, with strong evidence of company complicity. Police occupied the mill, dozens of leaders were fired, and others killed or arrested. As a result of government pressure and the efforts of a labor organizer connected with the American Institute for Free Labor Development, a new union whose leadership was sympathetic to the company was started—the same union still recognized by Gulf and Western today. Efforts since 1975 to organize another union that would stand up to the company have met with continuing repression. Workers involved in the organizing effort have been fired by the company and arrested; thugs have been paid to identify and beat up participating workers; and the main organizer at the mill was found dead at the La Romana police station—a supposed "suicide victim."[31]

These are not isolated cases of repression. Military-backed dictatorships with strong antilabor policies are in control of governments from the Southern Cone to Central America. Even in countries where "democratic" governments exist, such as Mexico or Colombia, the state has consistently used its repressive force to protect the interests of large landowners and agribusiness enterprises. This political situation puts rural workers at a serious disadvantage in defending themselves against exploitation by agricultural employers.

The Conditions of Exploitation

The particular conditions of exploitation faced by different sectors of the agricultural workforce ultimately are determined by the logic of capitalist rationality: the maximization of profit. In addition to keeping labor costs to a minimum, competition drives capitalists to try to maximize profits by forcing workers to be as productive as possible. Unless costs can be lowered, it is only by increasing the amount each worker produces that employers can increase profits. There are several methods employers can use to make workers more productive. They may push the labor force to work longer and harder work days, a commonly used mechanism in the early stages of capitalist development. Or when production techniques become more advanced, they may turn to more sophisticated methods of boosting productivity: organizing the production process in a more efficient and scientific way, or increasing the use of technological inputs like machinery.

In Latin America today, even in the most modern agricultural enterprises, long days of hard work that drive workers to the limits of physical endurance are still common. This is true in part because workers have little protection against this blatant form of exploitation, but also because of other factors that discourage or limit employers' ability to use more sophisticated techniques of exploitation. For one, the organization of production with factory-like precision comes up against certain natural limits in agriculture that do not exist in industry, as we have seen in the case of U.S. agriculture. Even the most sophisticated technology cannot completely control the growing season of a crop or regulate the weather. In addition, the relatively high cost of machines in Latin America's capital-scarce economies combined with the existence of a huge pool of low-cost and unorganized labor makes the use of available labor-saving machines like harvesters or tractors a less attractive alternative. Moreover, in some cases there are no existing machines that can perform the delicate and meticulous tasks (such as picking coffee beans or trimming banana plants) required for the production of many of the crops in which Latin American countries specialize. For all of these reasons, even highly modern enterprises still rely heavily on labor intensive techniques, particularly in the harvest. Because labor costs represent such a huge chunk of the total cost of production, agricultural employers have a strong incentive to keep wages to bare subsistence levels.

Regardless of which combinations of methods agricultural capitalists use to exploit the workforce, the drive for profits translates into a daily onslaught on the lives and working conditions of agricultural laborers. To illustrate what this means for the workers, we have taken some examples from three different sectors of the agricultural proletariat: (1) part-time agricultural workers in Guatemala, (2) landless day laborers in Brazil, and (3) plantation workers in Central America.

Guatemala: Part-Time Proletarians

"In this country," remarked a character in a Latin American novel, "they treat cattle better than people." For the hundreds of thousands of Guatemalan migrants who harvest coffee, sugarcane, and cotton in the coastal plantations every year the truth of this statement reverberates through their tired bodies and half-empty stomachs.

The vast majority of these migrant workers are impoverished minifundistas from the western and central highlands.[32] Typical are the man and woman who have eight children to feed and only one and a half hectares of land. Every year beginning with the coffee harvest in September the husband sets off on the long and difficult trip to the coast, the first of two or three month-long trips he will make that year. Many times not just the men but women and children as well travel to the coast to sell their labor.

Most of those who make the annual trek to the coast are recruited in the highlands by labor contractors who act as agents for the plantation owners. From the moment they sign up with a contractor the workers are harnessed to the brutal yoke of exploitation. They are given a cash advance by the contractor to pay for the journey, and they must work until they can repay the debt regardless of the conditions they find on the plantation. Since contractors are paid by plantation owners according to the number of workers they provide, it is not uncommon for them to deceive workers by promising wages or working conditions that have little resemblance to reality.

Workers are herded like cattle into crowded and often unsafe open trucks for the journey to the coast. During the harvest season Guatemala City newspapers carry reports of these trucks careening off the road leaving countless numbers of injured and dead. Once on the coast the workers face miserable conditions. They are housed in barrack-like dormitories, most of which have dirt floors and are without walls or lighting. The constant buzz of flies and insects is a reminder of the lack of hygienic facilities and the generally unsanitary conditions in the camps.

Most workers spend few hours in these camps. They often rise as early as three o'clock in the morning in order to have time to travel to the fields before work starts at six. After an average of nine hours of backbreaking work, picking cotton perhaps, they must stand in line for their sacks of cotton to be weighed. Like most agricultural workers in Latin America, they are paid by the piecerate system—according to how much they pick. This system becomes an arena of daily conflict between workers and employers. It is commonplace for owners to cheat workers by short-weighting their bags, and workers are kept under constant scrutiny to keep them from responding by adding rocks to increase the weight of their sacks. Depending on how far the weighing station and how long the wait in line, workers may not return to camp until eight or nine o'clock at night. There they can expect a dinner of beans and tortillas, rations given out by the plantation owner and deducted from their salary. At the end of the typical thirty-day contract, most of these men and women have earned a daily salary below what they need to supply their families with minimal daily nutrition. After repaying the contractor, most return home to the highlands with only a meager supplement to their incomes.

Brazil: Temporary Workers

During the harvest season in southern Brazil, every morning before dawn trucks rumble toward the fields laden with their human cargo of workers.

In contrast to the migrants of Guatemala, for most of these

workers—men and women like Sebastian Maura—wage labor is not a seasonal occupation but a permanent condition. This does not mean they are permanently employed, however, nor does it mean that they are part of a *rural* proletariat. An increasing number of Brazil's farmworkers are actually urban residents who live in the mushrooming slums that have grown up around the edges of major towns and cities of southern Brazil.[33] Some are recently arrived migrants from rural areas, dispossessed colonos or sharecroppers; others are long-time urban dwellers. Desperation forces these people to find jobs wherever and however they can—as street vendors, gardeners, construction workers, domestic servants, or as agricultural day laborers on the vast sugar, coffee, and soybean plantations that stretch across southern Brazil. Especially for women, children, and older men—those for whom other employment opportunities are most limited—laboring in the fields during harvest season is their best hope for regular work.

These urban dwellers who work as agricultural day laborers are known in some parts of Brazil as "boias frias," so-named because of the "cold snack" they bring with them to the fields every day. Like all so-called casual laborers, most boias frias have no legal rights since they are not registered workers, and the plantation owners are anxious to keep it that way. Rather than enter into a direct contract with workers that would make them subject to rural labor legislation, the employers use labor contractors (known in Brazil as "gatos" or cats) as intermediaries. In some cases a contractor hires a work gang to complete a specific job on a plantation. But most often workers are hired on a daily basis, never knowing from one day to the next whether they will be rehired.

A typical day for the boias frias begins long before sunrise. The workers leave their shacks by dark to gather on streetcorners known as the points where gatos pass each morning looking for laborers to hire for the day. Those lucky enough to be hired are hauled to the fields in cattle trucks, in a journey that sometimes takes several hours. They work in the fields an average of ten to twelve hours (including a half hour for lunch and a fifteen minute break), but it is common to spend a total of eighteen hours away from home on a work day. Most can afford to bring only a meager lunch of rice and manioc to the fields, and it is not unusual for malnourished workers to faint in the middle of a day of back-breaking work under the hot sun.

After the contractor deducts anywhere from 20 to 50 percent from the worker's wages for his "services," most boias frias receive no more than 50¢ to $1 after a long day of work. This is far below the minimum wage of $60 a month, which is itself insufficient to provide a family with an adequate diet. And even worse, most boias frias are able to find work in the fields only an average of three months out of the year.

Banana Workers: Permanent Proletariat

Although the year-round workforce on most plantations is a small fraction of the numbers hired during harvest, there are many tasks—such as pruning, weeding, and planting—that must be carried on throughout the year. Those hired as permanent workers to carry out these tasks are the "lucky" ones: they can at least count on a regular income, and they may receive social security and other benefits. They are more likely to belong to a union than migrant or day workers, and as a result they may have won reluctant concessions from their employers, such as higher wages or slightly improved living and working conditions. But the relative well-being of some permanent workers is more than anything a commentary on the miserable situation of the rest of the rural population.

The situation of banana workers on U.S.-owned corporate plantations in Central America is a case in point. They enjoy a higher standard of living than any other sector of the agricultural proletariat—the outcome of years of militant struggle. Yet a study done recently in Guatemala reveals that the incomes of 17 percent of the families who work on banana plantations are not adequate to meet the minimal nutritional needs of a family of four.[34]

Even more revealing is a study of the situation of banana workers on the Costa Rican plantations owned by one of the world's three largest banana companies, Castle & Cooke.[35] Instead of the blatantly inhumane exploitation described above, the company relies heavily on more modern techniques to increase productivity by intensifying the work process. For one, work on the plantation is organized according to a strictly defined division of labor in which company efficiency experts have broken down the harvesting process into forty-eight well-defined steps—from cutting the massive banana stem, to attaching it to the cable for transportation to the packing house, to weighing, sorting, washing, and so on. The purpose of imposing this factory-like precision is to maximize the output of every worker by making sure that no movements are wasted.

About 70 percent of the workforce is also paid according to the familiar piecerate system, which gives workers an incentive to push themselves as hard as physically possible. Those who do the work of cutting are further driven to accelerate their work pace by the fact that each worker is paid according to the productivity of the whole work team, usually consisting of five men. This device engenders intense pressure within the teams, an ingenious company strategy for imposing a system of self-discipline on the workforce.

This style of rational and efficient exploitation of labor has paid off for the United States banana companies throughout the region, and these have registered productivity increases of about 400 percent over the past twenty years in four Central American countries. Since technical innovations in banana production have been limited, most of these increases have been borne on the backs of workers.[36] While workers have seen token benefits in the form of higher wages, they actually realize an even smaller *portion* of the value of the commodities they produce, since the lion's share of the increase goes into company coffers in the form of higher profits. In other words, productivity gains make possible an even higher level of exploitation of the workforce.

The intensification of the work process has a significant impact on health and safety conditions on the banana plantations. Each worker has an average of one accident a year, with most accidents occurring during the cutting process. Many also suffer chronic health problems. Those who stand in the packing sheds all day are commonly afflicted with circulatory diseases, and many who wash and spray the fruit with chemicals suffer a persistent fungus on their hands. During harvest days (which can be anywhere from three to six days out of each week) those who do cutting and packing often work twelve-hour days, from five o'clock in the morning to five o'clock at night. For the workers who cut and carry the 100- to 150-pound banana stems laden with fruit, the result is often permanent muscular disorders, not to speak of constant exhaustion. It is no wonder that these workers have a useful plantation work life of about twelve years.

The Adverse Impact of Modern Technology on the Workforce

It is not only intensification of the work process but also the growing use of technology associated with modern agriculture that has an adverse impact on agricultural workers. Two examples of this impact are the increased use of agrichemicals and machines.

The devastating impact of chemicals on the health of farm-workers—a familiar problem in U.S. agriculture—is even more serious in Latin America, where restrictions on their use are extremely limited and seldom enforced. Latin America cotton production is a particularly dramatic illustration. Because of problems with insect infestation, cotton production is character-ized by a relatively heavy use of pesticides. In an effort to raise yields in recent years, cotton growers now apply dangerous pesti-cides like DDT thirty, forty, or even fifty times a year, as com-pared to an average of seven times a year in the past. Such heavy doses of potentially lethal chemicals create a health hazard not only for workers (who are often forced to enter the fields before the medically prescribed waiting period of seventy-two hours), but also for local inhabitants. Crop-dusting planes often apply the pesticides indiscriminately, contaminating nearby fields, rivers and lakes, and dwellings. A United Nations study revealed that in the cotton producing regions of Guatemala and Nicaragua the average DDT content in human blood is 520 parts per billion (compared with 46 in Dade County, Florida).[37] In Central America as a whole, between 1972 and 1975 there were 40 reported deaths attributable to the use of pesticides, and 14,133 DDT-related illnesses. Doctors, priests, and peasants in the area, however, say there are many additional unreported deaths attributable to pesticides. A planter in the region summed up the attitude of the growers: "More pesticides means more cotton, fewer insects mean higher profits."[38]

While job loss due to mechanization is not as much of a problem for Latin American farmworkers as it is for those in the United States, where the process has gone much further, it is beginning to have a significant impact on the availability of jobs in some parts of the countryside. The International Labor Organization estimates that for Latin America as a whole the current pool of tractors displaces a minimum of 2.5 million workers.[39] Even though most harvesting of such traditional crops as sugar, cotton, and coffee is still done manually, mechanical harvesters have been introduced in some areas. Some Brazilian sugar plantations use harvesting machines and in Mexico the use of harvesters in sugar and cotton is increasing. In areas where new commercial crops (particularly grains) have been introduced in recent decades—soybeans in southern Brazil or wheat in northwestern Mexico—production is almost completely mechanized. The massive shift of Brazilian coffee growers from labor-intensive coffee production to capital-intensive soybean production drove tens of thousands of workers into the ranks of the unemployed in the early sixties.[40] In Mexico, the government estimates that mechanization is displacing workers at the rate of 30,000 a year.[41]

The adverse impact of mechanization, however, stems not principally from the technology itself, but rather from the fact that it is employed in the service of capital for the sole purpose of increasing profits. The potential exists to use agricultural machinery for socially beneficial purposes: to increase the supply and lower the costs of food, and to relieve workers of the difficult and backbreaking tasks involved in agricultural production. However, within the context of capitalist production, technology becomes not only an instrument for increasing profits, but, like the rationalization of the labor process discussed above, also a means by which capital controls and disciplines the workforce. One of many illustrations is the mechanization of sugar harvesting in Peru. During the 1960s workers on the W. R. Grace Company plantations, because they belonged to a strong labor union, earned wages that were significantly higher than those paid to other workers in the area. In a move designed both to undermine the union and cut labor costs, the company began a massive program to mechanize the harvest. Over 75 percent of the workers were fired and forced onto a labor market already swollen with large numbers of unemployed.[42]

Resistance in the Countryside

As capitalism continues to penetrate into the countryside, the contradictions it engenders can only deepen. Although this chapter has focused on the forces that shape the desperate situation of rural workers, there is another side of the story to be told by the workers themselves—not in words but in deeds. Dispossession and intensified exploitation are meeting with resistance and a new upsurge of militancy in the countryside. In the last several years rural workers and landless peasants in El Salvador have risked their lives occupying government buildings and churches to demand an improvement in their working and living conditions. In Mexico there have been literally hundreds of land occupations since 1975 in which tens of thousands of rural workers and landless peasants have participated, as well as a burst of activity by rural unions.[43] In Nicaragua, the rural workers and peasants organized into the Sandinista Rural Workers Association during the last year of the anti-Somoza struggle there were an important force in the overthrow of the dictatorship.

One of the most significant developments of recent years occurred in Guatemala in early 1980 when over 50,000 workers on the coastal plantations carried out a two-week strike. Led by the recently formed Committee of Campesino Unity and the affiliated National Committee of Trade Union Unity (which groups together urban workers' unions) the strike completely closed down over fifty plantations and won more than a doubling of wages for all agricultural workers. The unprecedented defiance and unified action of the plantation workers (a majority of whom were Indians from the highlands) signaled to the alarmed plantation owners as well as the rest of the bourgeoisie that things are changing in the Guatemalan countryside. As an editorial in a Guatemala City newspaper wrote, "We are witnessing a new scenario with different actors from the Indian who takes off his hat and meekly places it over his chest asking the boss, by the grace of God, for a few cents more."

These and other actions reflect not only an upsurge of organization in the countryside, but also a change in the consciousness of those who have experienced proletarianization. In the past, political mobilizations and movements in the countryside have tended to focus on demands for land redistribution and agrarian reform, reflecting the peasant desire for access to land. While this is still an important issue in the countryside, the trend toward proletarianization has raised a new set of demands put forward by rural worker movements that are growing up in some countries like Mexico and El Salvador—demands for higher wages, for shorter working days and better working conditions, and for recognition of rural unions. These demands directly challenge the interests of the agrarian bourgeoisie and corporate capital and signify a new level of class struggle in the countryside. They are also demands that for the first time unite the concerns and interests of the rural poor with those of the urban working class in opposition to the existing social order. This potential unity could become a powerful force for revolutionary change in Latin American societies.

PART THREE:
THE CORPORATE CONNECTION

8. The Del Monte Corporation: Planting the Seeds of Empire

The Del Monte Corporation is one of the world's agribusiness giants. With sales of over $1 billion and subsidiaries in more than twenty countries, it is the world's largest producer of canned fruits and vegetables. Its vast plantation holdings span three continents—from South America to Asia to Africa. This California-based corporation is one of the agribusiness transnationals that have integrated the industrialized and less developed capitalist countries into a global system of food production and distribution. Both in California and overseas its operations have reinforced the power of larger and richer growers at the expense of small farmers, and its profits have come from the exploitation of poorly paid agricultural workers.

In many ways the history of Del Monte reflects the forces that have shaped American capitalism in the twentieth century. This chapter chronicles the early history of Del Monte on the West Coast, and then goes on to see how the company used its California base to build a worldwide empire and eventually merge with another corporate giant, R. J. Reynolds Industries. The chapters that follow analyze the impact of Del Monte's operations in Mexico, Guatemala, and the Pacific.

The Agricultural Setting

At the time of Del Monte's birth in 1916, the California countryside was dominated by extremes of wealth and poverty. Unlike the midwestern and eastern states where family farms predominated, California's fertile lands were owned by a relatively small group of growers who lived in lavish ranch houses and ran modern agricultural enterprises. To till the land, the growers employed a huge army of itinerant field workers drawn from the four corners of the globe. Every year droves of migrants born in Japan, China, Mexico, India, Portugal, and Armenia roamed from valley to valley in search of agricultural work that paid subsistence wages.[1]

This system of agriculture had its roots in the latter part of the nineteenth century when railroad barons, land speculators, and successful gold mining entrepreneurs seized control of many of the large estates that had been carved out by the earlier settlers, the Spaniards and the Mexicans. California was an ideal setting for the rapid growth of agribusiness. Here, the small family farmer would never gain ascendancy. Already in 1880, Karl Marx, in a letter to an American correspondent, noted the tendencies at work:

> I should be very much pleased if you could find me something good (meaty) on economic conditions in California. California is very important for me because nowhere else has the upheaval most shamelessly caused by capitalist centralization taken place with such speed.[2]

The rise of fruit farming in California in the 1870s and 1880s contributed mightily to the upheaval occurring in the state's economy and set the stage for the emergence of Del Monte. Fruit farming required irrigation, which in turn meant heavy capital outlays. Since only the state's larger growers, in alliance with big banks and business interests, had the capital necessary to finance the vast irrigation projects, their role in the development of the region's agriculture increased significantly. The new orchards also needed a large, seasonal body of laborers, and the insatiable quest of California agribusiness for a cheap exploitable pool of labor began with fruit farming in the late nineteenth century.

In the 1870s the Chinese were the first field workers brought into the orchards. By this time, many of the Chinese who had been brought over earlier to build railroads and work the gold mines were without work, and San Francisco and other cities passed racist legislation that barred the Chinese from many urban jobs.[3] Here was the ideal labor force for the growers. Aside from being a cheap source of labor, the Chinese were also highly skilled farmworkers, since many had been involved in agriculture in China.

But when the worldwide depression of the 1890s struck, causing widespread unemployment in California's cities and fields, a furor of anti-Chinese violence erupted and the Chinese were driven from the agricultural valleys of California. The saga of the Chinese was repeated many times by other immigrant groups in subsequent decades: a cheap, migrant labor force would be lured into the fields during periods of agricultural expansion, only to be driven out and labeled "undesirable" whenever a downturn occurred in the business cycle.

Monopolizing the Canning Industry

The growth of capitalist agriculture in California led to the emergence of another factor in modern agribusiness—the canning industry. Stimulated by the demand for California fruit, a number of small canneries and dried fruit processing firms emerged in the late 1870s and 1880s. However, their ranks were soon thinned out by the downturn of the business cycle in the 1890s. Seeking a way to weather these economic shocks, the canning industry, like other sectors of U.S. manufacturing, began to consolidate. In 1899, eleven companies merged to form the largest canning firm in the world, the California Fruit Canners Association (CFCA).[4]

In this era of trusts and corporate mergers some San Francisco-based capitalists pushed for an even greater consolidation of the California canning industry. George N. Armsby, who would later move to New York and become one of Wall Street's leading financiers, proposed a merger of (1) his own distributing house which served the canneries, the J. K. Armsby Company, (2) the newly formed California Fruit Canners Association, (3) its nearest competitor, the Central California Canneries, and (4) a large dried fruit processing and canning firm, Griffin & Skelley.

For nearly a decade Armsby argued with and badgered the firms involved to consolidate. To finance the consolidation he arranged for Wall Street to put up $16 million. The final push for the merger came from the Bank of California. Worried about the viability of some of the canning companies it had helped finance, the bank used its clout to force the more reluctant firms to approve the merger.[5] Finally, in 1916, the companies consolidated to form Del Monte, legally registering the new enterprise under the name of the California Packing Corporation.*

With this merger Del Monte joined the ranks of the large corporations that were opening up the era of monopoly capitalism in the United States. The company's holdings extended beyond the borders of California: of its sixty-one plants, four were in Washington, three in Oregon, one in Idaho, and one in Hawaii. The new company also owned 70 percent of Alaska Packers, a large salmon fishing and canning operation.

Early Expansion

Although Del Monte was the biggest canning corporation in the world, its large volume did not give it significant per unit cost advantages over its smaller competitors. The same manufacturing techniques were used by large and small canners. Basically, a firm with one cannery and a hundred workers could turn out a can of peaches as cheaply as could Del Monte. Thus the new corporation, like many of the other emerging giants of the food processing industry, seized the initiative in the one area where they could outdo the smaller firms—marketing and brand advertising.[6]

In 1917, the company embarked upon the first national advertising campaign ever undertaken by a fruit canning company. Using the expertise of McCann Erickson, one of the new advertising agencies that played an important role in developing national consumer tastes, Del Monte first placed ads in the *Saturday Evening Post* and then in a number of the leading women's magazines.[7] From the beginning Del Monte boasted that its brand name was synonymous with "quality" and a modern style of living.

To expand its national market, Del Monte linked up with the largest food chain in the country, the Great Atlantic and Pacific Tea Company (A & P). In exchange for paying part of the advertising costs and granting special wholesale price discounts, A & P

---

*Although the new company's principal brand name was Del Monte, it was known as the California Packing Corporation until 1967 when it officially became Del Monte. For simplicity's sake, we will use the name Del Monte.

pushed the Del Monte brand name in its regional and local advertising campaigns. With its food chain network concentrated in the midwestern and eastern states, A & P provided Del Monte with a marketing system in those areas where its sales were weakest.

To diversify its line of canned goods, Del Monte purchased or set up plants across the country. By 1926, canning facilities in Illinois, Wisconsin, Minnesota, and Florida turned out canned produce ranging from peas and sweet corn to grapefruit and sauerkraut. Del Monte even went into midwestern farming; in northern Illinois alone it leased 17,000 acres.[8] The drive for special canning fruits in the 1920s also led the company into the ranks of the emerging multinational corporations, when it began growing pineapples in Haiti and the Philippines.

Del Monte did not neglect its interests in California in the midst of this national and international expansion. In 1920, the company bought the Fancher Ranch, a 4,000-acre spread in the San Joaquin Valley. The ranch soon became the world's largest peach orchard and supplied one-fourth to one-third of the peaches marketed under the Del Monte label. Del Monte also purchased 9,000 acres on Union Island in the Sacramento and San Joaquin river delta. There, Del Monte operated one of California's largest asparagus farms, employing hundreds of Filipino and Hindu workers to harvest the delicate asparagus shoots for its canneries.

Del Monte's Labor Imperatives

The canning industry was different from most sectors of monopoly capital in that it did not rely heavily on major technological advances. Over the years, outlays for research by leading canners such as Del Monte, Libby, McNeill, Libby, Green Giant, and Stokley-Van Camp have been minimal.[9] Major innovations in canning have been few and far between, and the basic technology that goes into producing a can of peaches today is little different from that employed in 1916.

The relatively low technological base of the canning industry directly affected the companies' labor policies. The industry is labor intensive, and since it is unable to cut costs by developing labor-saving machinery, the canning companies strive desperately to hold down the costs of labor. The canneries seek out the cheapest labor pool, usually drawing from the ranks of immigrants, national minorities, and women.

In addition to this economic imperative, the seasonality of cannery work also affects the workforce. The canneries operate only when crops are being harvested, and thus in most areas 80 to 90 percent of the cannery workers are employed for only four to six months of the year. Both the seasonality of cannery work and the drive of the canning companies to hold down wages explains why the cannery workers in California and other parts of the world are among the worst paid and most exploited group of workers employed by any sector of monopoly capital.

In addition to Del Monte's quest for a cheap cannery workforce, the company's investments in farming also gave it a vested interest in keeping wages low. By the 1930s the company owned 21,500 acres of choice California land and employed thousands of field workers at subsistence wages.[10] Thus when the Depression struck and labor unrest spread throughout California's factories and fields, Del Monte more than any other large corporation in the state had a direct economic stake in busting unions and employing all available means to repress labor militancy.

Financing Vigilantes

The impact of the Depression on agricultural workers was devastating. Their ranks had been swelled in the previous decade by immigrants from Mexico and the Philippines, and by U.S. migrants who came to California as the "new land of opportunity," only to wind up as field hands. By the early 1930s there were at least 250,000 agricultural workers in the state, many of whom could not find even seasonal work once the Depression set in. The growers took full advantage of the labor glut, driving wages down to all-time lows.

Due to these desperate conditions, a statewide campaign to organize agricultural workers was launched in 1930 by a new union with close ties to the Communist Party, the Cannery and

Agricultural Workers Industrial Union (CAWIU). As agricultural conditions worsened the union became more militant.[11] By 1933 this labor strife sent shockwaves through the ranks of California's agribusiness interests: thirty-one major strikes occurred, affecting 48,000 workers, four-fifths of whom were led by the CAWIU. As one worker said, "we would have to starve working, so we decided to starve striking."[12]

Del Monte was directly affected by the labor strife. In August 1933, at the height of the peach harvest, 2,000 pickers under the leadership of the CAWIU walked off the job at Del Monte's Fancher Ranch. They demanded that the prevailing wage of 15–17.5¢ per hour be increased to 30¢. Other peach farm workers in the region also went on strike. The growers and police initially offered stiff resistance, with newspapers reporting that deputies and ranch guards were armed with shotguns and rifles. But Del Monte gave in to the strikers because its peach canneries as well as its farms were tied up by the strike. The workers were granted a pay increase to 25¢ per hour. After Del Monte settled, the other peach growers followed suit.[13]

To combat the increased labor militancy, however, Del Monte and the state growers organized the Associated Farmers of California, Inc. Soon, the Associated Farmers had about 40,000 members across the state, all of whom pledged that in case of any "disturbances," they would report to the local sheriff's office for deputization. The organization functioned as a rightwing vigilante group. As *Fortune* magazine noted in 1938, the Associated Farmers of California was "violently anti-union," and "run by the big growers but supported and manned by the little ones who pay dues and wield pick handles and rifles in case of trouble."[14] Stockades for holding striking workers were built with the aid of the Associated Farmers. The organization also had an espionage system and maintained special files in San Francisco on over 1,000 labor organizers. These files were made available to local sheriffs and the state police whenever necessary.[15]

Del Monte was a major force behind this new organization. It served as the chief fundraiser for Associated Farmers, soliciting contributions from corporations such as Standard Oil of California and Pacific Gas and Electric Company (PG & E). According to a U.S. Senate report, Del Monte directly or indirectly raised 41 percent of the money received by the Associated Farmers from 1934 to 1939. In 1935 the president of the Associated Farmers wrote to Alfred Eames, a vice-president of Del Monte, thanking him for recent contributions and proclaiming: "The dreams of my childhood are coming true—there really is a Santa Claus."[16]

In 1934 the growers and their allies confronted the farmworkers and the CAWIU head on, breaking strikes violently. The state government threw its weight behind the anti-union drive, and in July 1934 the police raided the offices of the CAWIU and threw the union's main leaders in prison.[17] Confronted by the naked power of the growers the farmworkers organization was crushed. The great wave of strikes came to an end.

Repression in the Canneries

The struggle in the fields was followed by a long and equally vicious struggle to unionize the canneries. Like the agricultural workers, the cannery employees came largely from the ranks of California's immigrant labor pool. Wages were low and employment seasonal, making the lot of the cannery workers among the worst of any industrial workers in the state. Del Monte, the largest employer of cannery workers, used all available means to repress labor militancy in the canneries just as it had in the fields.

The struggle to organize the cannery workers is interwoven with the conflict that developed among U.S. unions for control over the labor movement. Initially, in the mid-1930s, most of the unions organizing in the canneries, including the International Longshoremen's and Warehousemen's Union (ILWU) and the International Brotherhood of Teamsters, worked under the auspices of the American Federation of Labor (AFL). But the craft union orientation and conservative policies of the AFL drove the more progressive members (including many who had belonged to the now defunct CAWIU) to look to the new Congress of Industrial Organizations (CIO) for support. By 1937 two competing labor camps were active in the California canneries—one led by the state AFL office which worked closely with the Teamsters, and the other led by local labor councils and supported by the CIO and ILWU.[18]*

In response to cannery organizing, Del Monte adopted tactics similar to the ones used against the agricultural workers. Its first move was to found the California Processors and Growers Association, an organization in which all the state canners formed a united front against the cannery workers. The association was instrumental in getting the Teamsters and the AFL to collaborate in undermining the more militant union locals. Like the association, the Teamsters and the AFL wanted to end class conflict in the canneries. They espoused "bread and butter unionism," and advocated quiet negotiations with the employers. For these unions, the militant activities of the locals were viewed as a threat to their control.

When a wave of strikes erupted in the canneries in 1937 the processors were ready. In Stockton, California the cannery owners called upon the Associated Farmers to put together an army of 1500 deputized vigilantes who violently repressed the cannery strikers with tear gas and arms. Of the 300 picketers attacked, 50 were seriously injured and one was "riddled with buckshot from his mouth to his abdomen."[19]

In San Francisco and Oakland the processors relied more heavily on the Teamsters to do their dirty work. Following a meeting of the Teamsters with J. Paul St. Sure, the lawyer for the Processors and Growers Association, the union instructed its members to cross the picket lines. A key battle erupted in Del Monte's Oakland plant where the Teamster local refused to obey the strike-breaking orders. The leaders of the local were sacked, but the members still refused to strike break. Finally, Dave Beck, the fast-rising national Teamster leader, came from Seattle, promised large pay increases to the local's members, and persuaded them to cross the picket lines at the Del Monte plant.[20]

These tactics succeeded in undermining the more militant unions, and the Teamsters, under the auspices of the AFL, became the major union representing the canneries in California. Years

---

*In late 1937, the progressive locals formed the United Cannery, Agricultural, Packing and Allied Workers of America (UCAPAWA), an affiliate of the CIO.

later, the lawyer for the Processors and Growers Association, St. Sure, admitted that the association had collaborated with the Teamsters union to ensure its victory over the more progressive unions. He said, "I think we made it clear to them [the Teamsters] at the very first meeting that if there was to be an organization [in the canneries] we would like to tie in with the Teamsters." He also declared that "we had very definite ideas about the kind and shape of union we would like to deal through," and that the Teamsters fit those needs.[21]

In 1945 the Teamsters solidified their hold when the AFL granted them total jurisdiction over the canneries. The cannery workers voted against this change, but the Teamsters worked with the Processors and Growers Association to reverse this vote by ignoring court orders, by bringing systematic pressure to bear on government labor mediators, and finally, by conducting new, rigged elections.[22] The Teamsters won complete control of the canneries, and in succeeding decades they paid off their debt to the cannery owners by containing labor militancy and keeping wage increases to a minimum.

The Dynamics of Expansion

World War II ended the social and economic unrest of the Depression years and ushered in a new era of prosperity for U.S. business. Del Monte plants that had been running at half their capacity in the 1930s strained at their productive limits as the government purchased up to 70 percent of the company's canned goods for the army, navy, and Allied governments. The company's sales almost doubled—from $62 million in 1941 to $111 million in 1945. To augment production in its plants and fields, Del Monte, in its own words, used "Mexican nationals, Jamaicans, prisoners of war, and thousands of American soldiers and sailors who worked during furloughs or on special passes."[23]

The postwar years brought yet another wave of prosperity, as consumers rushed to purchase canned convenience foods that had been scarce at home during the war. In 1947 Del Monte profits were up more than 300 percent over previous years. The company solidified its productive position throughout the United States, and by 1950 it owned major canning and processing facilities in fourteen states. Del Monte's drive to develop the U.S. market for special delicacies like pineapples and sardines led the company to extend its foreign operations. It expanded its pineapple plantations in the Philippines and then in 1954, due to the dwindling catch of sardines off California's coast, it began fishing for sardines in Walvis Bay off South West Africa.

However, further domestic expansion was limited by the mid-1950s. The per capita consumption of canned goods showed signs of leveling off, with a growth rate of less than half a percent per year. The canning industry was now dominated by a handful of large companies. Market expansion at the expense of competitors was virtually impossible. The other fruit and vegetable canning leaders, like Libby, McNeill, Libby and Stokely-Van Camp, were too firmly established for Del Monte not to have had a difficult time taking over a significant portion of their sales. Furthermore, one of the features of monopoly capitalism is that the major firms in a given industry usually refrain from price wars or other severe forms of economic competition which could lead to the destruction of one or more of the leading corporations and adversely affect the entire industry.

But Del Monte had to expand in spite of these obstacles. The development of new markets is central to the survival of any big corporation. As a vice-president of the company said, "In industry you can't get into a static situation—you've got to grow."[24] Del Monte thus focused on two avenues for further growth—opening up foreign markets and diversifying production.

Agro-Imperialism

Whereas Del Monte had gone abroad only in search of such special commodities for the U.S. market as pineapples and sardines, by the late 1950s the company turned to foreign consumer markets, especially those of the Western industrialized nations. Del Monte had been exporting to these countries for years, as one report put it, "We recognized an overseas market potential far beyond what we could serve simply by exporting U.S. products. . . ."[25] Early in 1956, it purchased majority control of Canadian Canners, Canada's largest canner, with forty-nine plants and annual sales of $40 million. The company was older than Del Monte itself, dating back to a merger of Canadian canning companies in 1903.

The firm moved into the Western European markets somewhat more cautiously. In 1956, it contracted with an Italian firm to pack goods with the Del Monte label. Then, several years later, it set up a large cannery in Italy's Po Valley, thereby gaining a solid base for selling in the European Common Market. It expanded in Great Britain and the Commonwealth countries through the acquisition in 1958 of a canning firm in England, and in 1960, the South African Preserving Company started canning Del Monte goods for both the Union of South Africa and European markets.

In the 1960s Del Monte moved its canneries into third world nations with two objectives—to develop markets within the countries themselves and to use them as bases for exporting to the industrialized nations. With low labor costs, countries like Kenya became havens for canneries whose production was destined almost exclusively for the developed countries. One new Del Monte product took advantage of cheap labor in three different regions of the world: tuna from the Philippines and Ecuador was loaded on Del Monte ships and processed in Puerto Rican canneries for export to the United States.

Within the third world countries themselves, Del Monte's strategy called for tapping the relatively limited markets presented by the middle and upper classes. Plants in Venezuela, Mexico, and Brazil produced mainly for these sectors of the population. Tariff concessions enjoyed by these countries under the terms of the Latin American Free Trade Association enabled Del Monte to cater to the elites of neighboring countries.

Del Monte's growth in foreign markets was impressive. By 1967 it owned facilities in twenty countries and international sales were growing three times as fast as domestc sales. But for a global corporation like Del Monte, the tactics of marketing had changed little since the 1910s and 1920s. A sophisticated advertising campaign, rather than technological or nutritional innovations, remained the cutting edge for breaking into new markets. By 1972, the company advertised in at least twenty-five countries, using television, radio, newspapers, and billboards to alter the eating habits and diets of millions of people.[26] In some countries, the impact has been disastrous: people have been persuaded to buy canned goods even though the same fruits and vegetables are often readily available fresh at a fraction of the cost.

Domestic Diversification

By the mid-sixties Del Monte was firmly established in foreign markets and, still seeking new areas for growth, moved to diversify its domestic operations. The drive began in 1966 with the purchase of Granny Goose, a major producer of potato chips and snack foods in California. The next year Del Monte purchased Service Systems Corp., a supplier of meals to institutions around the country, which also runs a chain of vending machines and provides private security police for multinational firms.

Next Del Monte began selling frozen "culinary delights" by acquiring O'Brien, Spotomo, Mitchell, a firm that caters to airlines, restaurants, and hotels. The fresh fruit markets also drew the company's attention: it began to import bananas in 1968 and increased its imports of fresh pineapples from Hawaii and the Philippines. Del Monte's acquisition of companies involved in trucking, shipping, and international air freight helped cut its transport costs.

By the early 1970s Del Monte boasted that it was not merely a canning company but a diversified corporation engaged in the "worldwide business of feeding people." Statistics bore out this claim: by 1973 slightly more than half of its sales came from domestic canning; snack foods, institutional food services, and fresh produce operations accounted for 25 percent; and foreign investments made up another 25 percent.[27]

The Home Front

While expanding its worldwide operations, Del Monte confronted new challenges on the home front that led to basic changes in its domestic operations. California's farmworkers, who had been brutally repressed in the 1930s, continued to push for unionization in succeeding decades. Finally in the 1960s, they made significant advances under the leadership of Cesar Chavez and the United Farm Workers. Del Monte of course joined with other California agribusiness interests in trying to destroy the new union movement.

On its Union Island asparagus ranch the company used several different tactics against the farmworkers. In 1960 it brought in three hundred Arabs from nearby Stockton to replace the more militant workers who were demanding better wages. In addition it hired undocumented Mexican immigrants and tightened security around the labor camps to keep out union organizers. A former security guard for Del Monte told NACLA investigators that the ranch supervisors were so worried about "outside agitators" that the guards were even instructed to keep prostitutes out of the labor camps.

But Del Monte soon found out that the Arabs were not the docile labor force that the company had hoped for. In 1971 a strike broke out in one of the Arab labor camps and Del Monte fired the 70 to 80 workers involved. But continued agitation eventually forced Del Monte to raise wages and improve working conditions on Union Island.[28]

Confronted with worker militancy and the drive for collective bargaining throughout the state, Del Monte began to move its asparagus operations to Mexico. First the company stopped growing white asparagus, which since it can only be harvested by hand, is more labor intensive than the green variety. Then in 1975, Del Monte sold its Union Island ranches and ended asparagus production completely in California. All of Del Monte's white asparagus production has been shifted to Mexico, where it is packed and shipped abroad for sale.

Next Del Monte moved to sell off the remainder of its agricultural holdings in California. Because of rising labor costs and the highly competitive nature of farming in the United States (in which no one producer controls a significant percentage of the market), many companies found their returns in agriculture were diminishing in relation to other corporate investments. Del Monte, like other large agribusiness corporations, began to abandon the risky business of direct agricultural production, choosing to concentrate on food processing and canning where it had greater control of the market and of the process of production itself. In 1978, it sold the Fancher Ranch, the huge peach farm near La Merced that once formed the cornerstone of its agricultural operations. According to one Del Monte executive, the ranch had become a "less productive asset." To get "adequate tonnage in the future" for its peach canneries, the company decided to rely exclusively on contracts with local growers.[29]

But the abandonment of agriculture did not enable Del Monte to avoid the rising tide of labor discontent in California. The militancy generated by the United Farm Workers spilled over into the canneries. There the workers, long held in check by the collaborationist policies of the Teamsters union, began demanding fundamental changes in the employment practices of the canning industry. A rank-and-file organization called the Cannery Workers Committee fought for higher wages and an end to an antiquated seniority system that discriminated against women and minority workers. Dissident cannery workers also undertook affirmative action suits in the courts that forced the California canneries to end some of their more discriminatory policies.

Del Monte could not escape this militancy by moving its canneries abroad. Fresh produce operations can be shifted to countries like Mexico, but high tariffs on imported canned goods make it economically unfeasible for Del Monte to do the same with canneries. Since it cannot shift production abroad it must fight to hold down wages in California canneries. It is the major power in California Processors, Inc. (the successor of the Processors and Growers Association), the organization that represents the state's largest canners in their contract negotiations with organized labor. Just as in the 1930s, Del Monte's wage and labor policies set the standard for the industry.

But in spite of repressive labor policies, the canning industry has not been able to recover the dynamism that characterized its expansion in earlier decades. It is a "mature industry," and expansion in foreign markets was not sufficient to offset the limited growth at home. Throughout the 1970s profits were low in the canning industry and corporate investors began to look upon Del Monte and other canners as "dogs," i.e., slow-growth companies with stagnating stock market prices and low dividends.

This downturn in the canning industry occurred at a time when a new wave of mergers was gripping the corporate world. In the mid- and late 1970s, corporations with excess cash in their tills began expanding by buying up firms with sagging stock market prices. Often the mergers were between companies in entirely unrelated areas. For example, IC Industries, a metal fabricating company, acquired the Pet Milk Company, while Mobil Oil bought Montgomery Ward, a huge merchandising firm. The acquired companies usually benefit from the mergers since surplus cash from the new parent often goes to expand the operations of the newly acquired company.

The merger phenomenon hit the canning industry in the latter part of the 1970s. In 1975, Libby, McNeill, Libby, an historic rival of Del Monte, was acquired by Nestlé, the second largest agribusiness firm in the world. Then in 1977, Green Giant merged with Pillsbury, another agribusiness corporation that was busy gobbling up an array of food- and agriculture-related enterprises.[30] Del Monte was next: it went even further afield to find a corporate white knight to rescue it from the doldrums of the canning industry. In 1978, after two years of merger discussions, Del Monte decided to join R. J. Reynolds Industries, one of the giants of the tobacco and cigarette industry.

But R. J. Reynolds was more than a tobacco company. Ever since the late 1960s, Reynolds had been acquiring companies in order to diversify out of the cigarette industry where market growth was limited due to the publicized dangers of smoking. In 1969, R. J. Reynolds acquired Sea Land, the world's largest container shipping company, and then in the early 1970s it moved into the petroleum industry by purchasing Aminoil and the Burmah Oil company.[31]

For Del Monte, a merger with Reynolds made economic sense.

The executives and directors of Del Monte were guaranteed a leading role in plotting the expansion of R. J. Reynolds' push into the food industry. Although Reynolds' headquarters are located in Winston-Salem, North Carolina, the Del Monte executives continue to run the food processing operations from San Francisco. Reynolds' two small food companies, Hawaiian Punch and Chun King, which were acquired earlier, were both incorporated into the Del Monte division in San Francisco.

The Del Monte executives also looked forward to tapping R. J. Reynolds' huge advertising budget. In the year before the merger, Reynolds spent 5.6 percent of its consumer product sales on advertising while the comparable figure for Del Monte was 1.2 percent.[32] For cash-poor Del Monte, the sudden access to the revenues of R. J. Reynolds meant that the Del Monte brand could be pushed more aggressively than ever in consumer markets.

Del Monte's six decades of expansion illustrate many of the forces of monopoly capital that have shaped U.S. agribusiness. Del Monte led the way in transforming the canning industry from a highly competitive sector with many small firms into an industry dominated by a handful of corporations. The labor intensiveness of canning plus the seasonal nature of agricultural production made Del Monte a leading force in repressing and manipulating labor organizations. Another major dynamic of the corporation— the quest for international markets—began in the 1950s when the domestic market for canned foods began to stagnate.

But this imperialist solution, while enabling Del Monte to surmount the limits of the domestic market, has created new contradictions for the corporation. As the succeeding articles will show, Del Monte's operations in the third world have internationalized its conflict with labor, posed new problems for the company in dealing with governments increasingly sensitive to foreign exploitation of their natural resources, and demonstrated the basic inability of agribusiness corporations like Del Monte to deal effectively with the problems of hunger and malnutrition.

9. Canned Imperialism: Del Monte in Mexico

Around the world, agribusiness corporations like Del Monte are moving into regions that are struggling with the problems of malnutrition, poverty, and land distribution. The corporations usually pose as saviors, claiming that their fertilizers, tractors, hybrid seeds, and food processing plants will help solve the world's problems by expanding food production and providing employment opportunities. However, these corporations exert enormous control over the economic life of countries where they operate, and often control their most important sources of foreign exchange. They dominate vast tracts of land which are used to produce export crops, instead of being used to produce staple foods or to provide a source of income for the local population. Further, because their profits depend on control of vast land-holdings and the exploitation of cheap labor, plantation operators like Del Monte must oppose progressive changes in the third world, and consistently align themselves with the most conservative forces. A case study of the Bajio Valley in Mexico shows how Del Monte's operations merely accentuate the extremes of wealth and poverty, turn out highly processed foods that are priced beyond the reach of most of the country's population, and force peasants off their lands.

The Bajio Valley is one of Mexico's richest agricultural regions. Located 200 miles north of Mexico City in the state of Guanajuato, the valley is endowed with fertile soils and a mild climate suitable for a wide variety of crops. The valley itself is sizeable—about 100 miles in length and from 20 to 50 miles wide. Bustling cities and towns dot the Bajio, linking the region to greater Mexico and the rest of the world.

The cradle of Mexican independence, the Bajio today finds itself invaded by foreign agribusiness interests. For over a decade and half, U.S. corporations have been at work altering the region's agriculture and integrating the valley into the network of international capitalism. Three multinational food processing corporations—Del Monte, Campbell's, and General Foods—operate canning and packing plants in the valley. Ford and John Deere tractors till the land, insecticides from Bayer are used to control plant diseases, and cattle are fed special formula feeds milled by Ralston Purina and Anderson Clayton. As one Del Monte vice-president noted, "When you go to the Bajio today, it's almost like being in one of California's valleys."[1]

Del Monte has had a more profound impact upon the people and agriculture in the valley than any other corporation. Its factory in Irapuato at the west end of the valley employs more people than any other food processing company in the region, and the plant turns out the largest variety of fruits and vegetables of any Del Monte facility in the world. The tillers of the land as well as the factory workers have felt Del Monte's presence: agricultural techniques have been altered and crops that were never seen before in the valley are now cultivated on large tracts of land for Del Monte.

Contract Farming

When Del Monte first sent its technicians to look at the Bajio in 1959, they found a region ill-suited to the needs of the world's largest canner of fruits and vegetables. Grain production predominated, with corn and beans serving as the mainstays of the local diet. In Del Monte's own words, "vegetable production was small and limited to a few crops grown exclusively for the local fresh market."[2]

The Bajio's land tenure system was also incompatible with Del Monte's needs. Due to the valley's population density and the breakup of the large landed estates under Mexico's agrarian reform laws, the average landholding was small, ranging from ten to twenty acres. Some of the land was held in ejidos, large, communally owned farms that are subdivided into many small plots and worked by peasants, or ejidatarios. Mexican law prohibited the sale of these lands, and it also placed restrictions on land ownership by foreign corporations. For a company used to owning plantations and working with U.S. growers who own hundreds or even thousands of acres, the conditions in the Bajio did not appear auspicious.

But Del Monte found the perfect tool for changing the valley's agriculture—contract farming. Under the contract system, the farmer or grower agrees to plant a set number of acres of a particular crop, and the company in return provides financial assistance which usually includes seeds and special machinery, as well as cash outlays for purchasing fertilizers and hiring farm labor. All these costs are discounted from the farmer's or grower's income when the crop is delivered to the cannery.

In Mexico, where agricultural credit is limited or nonexistent, contract farming was an attractive offer. As such, it was influential in changing the structure of agriculture in the Bajio. Del Monte revealed just how influential its crop financing was when it noted that "in the early 1960s, Productos Del Monte was practically the only source that many of its growers could turn to for short term crop loans."[3] By skillfully using its financial leverage, Del Monte affected the valley in several ways: it introduced crops that had never been grown there, favored the development of the larger growers at the expense of the smaller, more marginal producers, and gained operating control over large tracts of land.

From the start of each growing season, Del Monte exerts tight control over its contract growers. It specifies seed varieties and fertilizers and often supplies special planting equipment. After the land is sown, frequent visits are made by Del Monte technicians who insist that the company's irrigation and cultivation specifications be strictly followed. If these specifications are not carried out, the contract gives Del Monte the right to take over direct control of the crop. Harvest time also finds Del Monte in the field: the company maintains the largest pool of machinery in the valley, much of which is sent to harvest its crops.[4]

Viewed from a productivity perspective, this paternalistic system of agricultural production has some positive effects. As Del Monte boasts, "from 1962 to 1972 yields per acre among Productos Del Monte contract growers rose steadily," while gross income per acre sometimes rose by 50 percent.[5] But these results must be placed in the larger context of agricultural changes in the valley. Although the Bajio's landowners are small by U.S. standards, those with more land tend to be favored by the changes in agricultural production, while the smaller producers or ejidatarios are increasingly marginalized.

From the start, Del Monte worked with the larger growers in the valley. In 1964 the company had contracts with 21 growers for 413 acres, or an average of 20 acres per grower. Since most of the growers contracted only a portion of their land to Del Monte, their landholdings were actually much larger than the average 10- to 20-acre farms that predominated in the valley. Since then, Del Monte has tended to work with even larger tracts of land. In 1974 the company had 110 growers with a total of 5,000 acres, or an average holding of 45 acres.[6] In 1977 NACLA investigators were told that the company has contracts with approximately 150 growers who work 7,500 acres, or an average of 50 acres.[7]

Many of the reasons for working with larger growers are implicit in capitalist agriculture. For Del Monte it is easier to supervise a contract with one grower who owns 50 acres than with five growers who each own 10 acres. Ownership of capital assets also influences the company's choices. Although Del Monte provides much of the credit for each vegetable crop, anywhere from 10 to 60 percent of the actual cash needs must come out of the grower's pocket. Del Monte also insists that the grower put up some agricultural equipment or machinery as collateral. For the small producers who rent most of their machinery, this stipulation automatically prevents them from becoming Del Monte's contract growers.[8] As one agricultural technician in the valley noted, "the small landowner doesn't have the economic resources to plant vegetables."[9]

Thus Del Monte's contract farming leads to an increasing concentration of wealth among the valley's larger growers. As the American Chamber of Commerce in Mexico noted in a recent study: "In the Bajio, as elsewhere in the Republic, there is a sharp split between relatively prosperous commercial farming and the fragmented plots of ejidal land starved for investment and technology."[10] The growers who already have capital or land can enter into new areas of production which will further augment their wealth, while the ejidatarios or small producers are increasingly marginalized and often forced out of production. Agricultural experts at several government agencies in the valley noted that a large number of small landowners are already renting or selling their lands to the larger growers. The dispossessed either serve as paid farmworkers for the new owner, or search for other ways to eke out a living in a valley that is already noted for its high rate of unemployment.

Although the growers who work with Del Monte are relatively prosperous, their relationship to the company is a difficult one. Crops delivered to the factory have to be of prime quality or be subjected to price discounts. Sometimes the poor condition of the produce is Del Monte's fault: one grower lost his entire pea crop because the company failed to send out its pea harvester on time. As one grower commented, "The company does what it wants with the contract."[11] Throughout the valley Del Monte has a reputation as a tightfisted and manipulative company that drives a hard bargain and takes advantage of the growers whenever it can.

The growers who survive the pressures of capitalist agriculture are driven to produce for the national and international markets instead of raising staples for local consumption. The three largest crops that Del Monte contracts for are sweet corn (1,000 acres), peas (1,500 acres), and asparagus (2,250 acres). The first two were introduced to the valley by Del Monte, while the last one was brought in by Campbell's, although Del Monte is now the largest contractor for the crop.[12] None of these crops figures prominently in the diet of the Mexican people. Canned peas and sweet corn are marketed as delicacies and purchased exclusively by the middle and upper classes, while over 90 percent of asparagus is shipped abroad to markets in the industrialized countries. In 1974 alone, over $4 million worth of canned goods from the Irapuato plant were shipped to twenty different countries.[13]

Del Monte's Workforce

Del Monte's employment policies at the Irapuato plant contribute to the economic and social instability of the Bajío. During the course of a year the company employs approximately 1,750 workers. But only 120 are permanent workers. The remainder are seasonal employees, 90 percent of whom work no more than four to six months of the year. Wages for these workers are the minimum required by Mexican law—61 pesos per day in 1977, or approximately $4.90. Even people who have worked at the cannery for six years receive no more than the minimum wage.[14]

To keep its wages low, Del Monte draws on the valley's large pool of unemployed laborers, using those who most desperately need work. The majority, around 75 percent, are women. Some are young women, still in their mid teens, who come to Del Monte looking for their first job, while others are older women who need any kind of work to sustain their families. As one woman told NACLA: "I don't work at Del Monte because I like it—I have to feed my children."[15] Many of the men and women who work at the plant are the sons and daughters of ejidatarios or small landowners who migrated to the valley's cities and towns looking for jobs that did not exist.

Because the workforce needed at the plant varies from day to day, Del Monte has a hiring hall where workers report to find out whether or not they are needed on a given day. There they often sit and wait for hours before being told if there is work. Some spend hours traveling from their homes in the countryside, only to find no work available at Del Monte. For some at the hiring hall the situation is desperate. As one woman said: "If I don't get work today, how will I manage to eat?"[16]

In theory the workers at Del Monte are represented by a union affiliated with the Confederacion de Trabajadores Mexicanos, or the CTM. But the CTM is an official government union that is known more for its efforts to quell labor militancy than for its defense of worker interests. The union representatives at the plant are all men, and none of the workers with whom NACLA talked could remember when an election had ever been held. During Del Monte's fourteen-year history in Irapuato, there has been only one strike, in 1969, which only lasted several hours. One woman said that a couple of years ago "we wanted to strike for better wages, but the union leaders said no, that people would be brought in from the countryside to take our jobs."[17] The strike never occurred.

Although the local head of the CTM told NACLA that the union had made efforts to improve workplace conditions, the workers said they saw no improvements. The moving cans and the assembly lines produce a loud, deafening noise that often impairs hearing for hours after one leaves the plant. Lax safety standards have resulted in many chemical burns from acids used in the canning process. Plant supervisors harass the workers to move faster, thereby causing industrial accidents as the workers try to speed up the process.

In addition to the 1,750 cannery workers, Del Monte says it provides employment for another 3,500 people in the Bajio. These are mainly the field hands who work for the company's contract growers. Some of these agricultural workers have been dispossessed of their lands, others maintain small plots that they and their families work to help sustain themselves, and still others form part of the migratory workforce that moves around the valley looking for employment. The field workers do not have even an official government union to represent them, and minimum wage levels are ignored. On one Del Monte asparagus field visited by NACLA, the workers received $3 a day for backbreaking, menial work. These workers, like the factory employees, can expect only seasonal employment since the asparagus harvest season lasts only a hundred days.

Law and Order: Del Monte Style

Conditions in Mexico are thus ideal for Del Monte. A cheap labor force and collaborative government unions, along with export subsidies, are several of the factors that the company looks for wherever it operates. A Del Monte vice-president, William Druehl, said in an interview that the company will move out of any country if these conditions change. He insisted "the countries have to remain competitive if Del Monte is to stay," and that "labor is one of the main factors that has to be kept under control."[18]

But Del Monte, while demanding low wages and a stable political environment in the countries where it operates, often violates the local laws that do not suit its interests. For example, according to Mexican law, 51 percent of the stock of local subsidiaries of foreign food processing companies must be held by Mexican nationals. On paper, Del Monte has fulfilled this requirement: José Ignacio Mendoza, a Mexican with interests in a large strawberry freezing plant in the valley, heads up a small group of Mexicans who legally hold 51 percent of the stock in Productos Del Monte. But according to a plant administrator who worked for Del Monte for a number of years, neither Ignacio Mendoza nor his associates actually own a single share of stock in the company.[19] They are merely "hombres de paja" or straw men who lend their names to Del Monte to give its Mexican operations a legal facade. One office manager at Productos Del Monte stated bluntly: "The Mexican shareholders don't have anything to do with the plant." Del Monte, like other multinationals in Mexico, has complete control over its subsidiary.[20]

As elsewhere, advertising has been the key to Del Monte's marketing expansion in Mexico. McCann Erickson, Del Monte's U.S. advertising agency for half a century, works closely with company executives out of its offices in Mexico City. When Del Monte entered Mexico in the early 1960s, it found that the Mexicans had little need or use for its products. The company itself admitted it confronted a difficult situation:

> Del Monte was an expensive brand in the minds of the consumers in the large population centers where our products could be found, and in the countryside Del Monte Brand awareness was virtually nonexistent.[21]

But Del Monte and McCann Erickson moved aggressively to change this situation, using radio, television, billboards, magazines, and other media to create a public awareness of Del Monte products. McCann Erickson even developed a new symbol for the campaign—a talking parrot with the Del Monte emblem emblazoned across its chest. By 1968, Del Monte propaganda had made an imprint on the public mind: a survey found that 70 percent of the Mexican people were aware of the Del Monte brand name.[22]

Del Monte makes no secret of the fact that its primary market is not the working masses who make up the majority of Mexico's population, but the new urban middle class and the upper class. The company boasts:

> Canned foods are becoming more and more accepted, and are no longer found only in the homes of the wealthy. The middle class, developing as a result of the jobs created by companies like our own, is a fast growing consumer of our products.[23]

Del Monte did not point out that of the more than 5,000 people who work for the company in the Bajio, only a small fraction receive wages adequate to fulfill their minimal dietary needs, let alone purchase Del Monte canned foods.

Del Monte is only one of the many multinationals that dominate the Mexican food industry. During the past two decades, foreign food processing companies such as Kraft, General Foods, Carnation, Anderson Clayton, and Nestlé have established new plants and acquired locally owned companies. Del Monte itself has two snack food factories in Mexico, besides its plant at Irapuato. The far-reaching impact of these companies in Mexico was summed up by Fernando Camora, a former director of the Economic Research Institute at the National Autonomous University of Mexico:

> The multinational food processing firms . . . act as monopolies, increasing the cost of food, . . . determining the zones of production and the types of crops, and deciding what is to be exported. They also determine what seeds, fertilizers, insecticides, and machinery should be used, and they fix the salaries of the field and factory workers. . . . In the broadest sense Mexican agriculture is victimized and controlled by the foreign firms in the food industry.[24]

10. Modern Plantation Systems: Del Monte in the Pacific

The early history of Del Monte's plantation operations is also the story of U.S. expansion in the Pacific Basin. By the early 1900s the United States had secured its position in the Pacific with the annexation of the Hawaiian Islands and the acquisition of the Philippines as a U.S. territory. The main impetus behind this expansion was the desire on the part of expanding business interests to gain access to the markets in the Far East. But capitalists were also drawn by the rich natural resources of the Pacific Basin to make direct investments in production. In both Hawaii and the Philippines, Del Monte was in the forefront of the move to exploit the fertile lands and develop an export-oriented plantation economy.

Hawaii: Planting the First Pineapples

The economy of the Hawaiian Islands, where Del Monte acquired its first plantation, was by 1900 already dominated by vast sugar plantations, most of them owned by the descendants of U.S. missionaries and traders. In fact, formal annexation of the islands in 1898 was due largely to the lobbying efforts of the sugar planters, who wanted duty-free access to mainland markets. Annexation also opened the way for other agricultural investors to exploit the land for export production. Thus the stage was set for the emergence of the pineapple industry, which together with the sugar industry was to shape the islands' political, economic, and social structure.

Like the sugar industry, the pineapple industry was started by a handful of entrepreneurs who went to the islands to make their fortunes. Among these were the young James Dole (whose Dole and Company was years later acquired by the agribusiness multinational Castle & Cooke) and Alfred Eames (whose son and grandson were both to become president of Del Monte).

James Dole left his home in New England to settle in the islands, where his relatives were prominent political figures. His cousin, Sanford Dole, had been one of the leaders of the 1893 "revolution," when white planters and merchants overthrew the Hawaiian monarchy with the help of U.S. marines. Sanford then became the first president of the short-lived republic. These family connections undoubtedly proved useful to the young Dole, who in 1901 planted the first pineapples on the islands (the plant being native to South America). A short time later he set up a canning factory and began to export pineapples to the United States mainland.[1]

Alfred Eames, a farmer who had left California to homestead in the new colony, soon began his own pineapple plantations, and by 1906 had set up the Hawaiian Islands Packing Company. The pineapple business flourished and before long the Eames family business linked up with the emerging forces of monopoly capitalism on the mainland. In 1917, when Del Monte had consolidated its position in the California canning industry, it took over the Hawaiian Islands Packing Company. With this business as a nucleus, Del Monte soon became one of the three largest pineapple producers in the islands.[2]

As the sugar and pineapple industries expanded, Hawaii was turned into a virtual agricultural outpost. But the rapid colonization took its toll on the population. Some natives were pushed off their lands; more were killed by new diseases. A 1930 *Fortune* article on the pineapple industry summed it up from the industry perspective:

> Hawaii has become so thoroughly Americanized that it is the few remaining natives who seem forlorn and foreign. . . . It is regrettable that pineapples do not grow in Boston or Maine. But Mr. Dole has, in effect, brought Boston and Maine out to Hawaii with him.[3]

Organizing the Plantation

The plantation companies needed a sizeable labor force to work in the fields and canneries. But not only were the native

Hawaiians reduced in numbers, the planters also complained about their "indolence." To solve their labor supply problem, the planters turned mainly to the Asian mainland for a limitless source of cheap but "reliable" agricultural workers. Tens of thousands of Chinese, Japanese, Filipinos, and a smaller number of Puerto Ricans were lured to the islands.[4] They and their descendants became the workforce that made sugar and pineapple the islands' most important industries and made Hawaii one of Del Monte's most lucrative profit centers.

Ironically, however, these workers have built a strong and effective union movement. For years, Del Monte resisted unionization, along with the major sugar companies. As in California, divide and conquer was a main technique, and the companies constantly tried to exacerbate conflicts between the different ethnic groups. Before World War II organizing was done along ethnic lines. Thus, when an all-Japanese or all-Filipino union went out on strike, the companies simply hired workers of another nationality.[5]

During the war, the CIO-affiliated International Longshoremen's and Warehousemen's Union (ILWU) began a massive organizing drive among Hawaiian workers, including those in the sugar and pineapple industry. But this time the strategy was to organize workers of all races into one union. Recognizing their common interest in resisting unionization, the Big Five and Del Monte set up the Hawaii Employers' Council in 1943 to coordinate their antiunion strategies. They were unable to stop the union drive, however, and in 1946 the ILWU succeeded in organizing both the sugar and pineapple industries.

Almost immediately, the Employers' Council and the Pineapple Growers Association mounted a counterattack on the ILWU, focused mainly on the pineapple industry. They maneuvered the union into a five-day lockout in 1947, and when thousands of unorganized seasonal workers crossed the picket line the strike was broken. After this blow, Del Monte and the other companies kept the union in a weak position for the next eighteen years, and held salary increases to a minimum. Finally, in 1965 and again in 1967, the pineapple workers were able to mount successful strikes that won them the first significant wage and benefit increases. By 1972 Hawaii's agricultural workers had become the highest paid in the world (though they also had one of the highest living costs in the world), earning an average of about $30 a day.

The pineapple companies reacted predictably. Claiming the wage increase would make their operations unprofitable, both Dole and Del Monte announced plans in early 1973 to close a significant part of their plantation and cannery operations—a move that would mean the loss of thousands of jobs.

However, there is little evidence to support the companies' claim that their Hawaiian canning operations are not profitable. One small pineapple company in Hawaii, with none of the advantages of the multinational corporations, reported a sixfold gain in earnings in 1972–1973,[6] at a time when the multinationals were claiming losses. The truth is more likely that Hawaiian plantations are less profitable than the companies' operations in low-wage third world countries where there are no unions to protect the workers.

Sugar workers, faced with similar cutbacks, joined the pineapple workers for a strike in 1974 to protest the runaway plantations. The strike, however, had no effect on the companies' decisions, since without some coordination with workers in other countries, Hawaiian workers had little leverage on the multinationals. Dole proceeded to follow through with its cutback plans, closing down one plantation and putting 175 workers out of a job.

Del Monte, however, continued to delay the cutback, and has recently announced it may continue Hawaiian operations in full force until 1985.[7] But the reason for the turnaround has nothing to do with Del Monte's concern for its workers' welfare or the possible adverse effect on the islands' economy. Rather, it flows out of the corporation's long-term growth strategy. In response to booming world demand and high prices for fresh fruit, Del Monte has decided to focus its Hawaii operations on fresh fruit production. But because only the highest quality fruit can be exported to the fresh market, the cannery will be maintained to provide a profitable outlet for lower quality fruit. In order to implement its new marketing strategy, Del Monte recently purchased the Hawaii-based Aloha Papaya Company, a large distributor of fresh tropical fruit on the mainland.[8]

The company's decision to remain in Hawaii also reflects Del Monte's generally cautious strategy of keeping all its options open. Commenting on the decision to stay in Hawaii, one company vice-president said in an interview, "No company can afford to put all its eggs in one basket."

Even though the company has production facilities in every corner of the globe, Del Monte's corporate strategists realize that its position in many of these countries may not always be secure. Historically, the main alternative source of pineapple supply has been the Philippines. There, in spite of a cheap and highly exploitable labor force that brings the company huge profits, explosive political conditions undoubtedly make Del Monte worry about the future.

The Philippines: Expansion in the Pacific

The Philippine Islands were the site of one of Del Monte's first foreign investments. When an insect infestation threatened to wipe out its pineapple fields in Hawaii in the early 1920s the company was forced to seek an alternative source of supply for the growing U.S. market. In addition to starting plantations in Haiti (an unsuccessful venture which it sold several years later), the company turned its attention to the Philippines, which had been brought under U.S. political and economic domination at the end of the Spanish-American War in 1898.

On the island of Mindanao Del Monte found the ideal conditions for a lucrative venture: rich agricultural land, the largest and southernmost island in the Philippines, Filipino workers already familiar to the company from its California and Hawaii operations, and the political and economic stability guaranteed by the islands' status as a U.S. territory. Although Mindanao was inhabited by Moslem tribespeople, company executives viewed the area simply as "untamed tropical wilderness."

In 1926 Del Monte created the Philippine Packing Corporation (Philpack) and planted pineapples on large tracts of land in the Bukidnon province. By 1930 Del Monte's cannery on the coast in Cagayan de Oro was packing and shipping canned pineapples to the United States.[9]

For the next three decades, Del Monte had a monopoly on the

Philippine pineapple industry. Although the Depression caused sales of pineapples to plunge and Del Monte to temporarily convert the plant to tuna production, by 1934 pineapple sales were booming. In 1937, Philpack was exporting $1.7 million worth of canned pineapples and the company was a major supplier for Del Monte's world markets.[10] However, when the Japanese occupied Mindanao in 1942 Del Monte was forced to abandon its plantations and cannery. Not to be deterred by wartime hostilities, Del Monte stepped up production in Hawaii to make up for the loss of the Philippines. Wartime labor short-ages were solved when, under the islands' military government, authorities arranged for school children to work in Del Monte's fields and canneries.[11]

With the defeat of Japan, U.S. hegemony in the Far East was firmly established and Del Monte was able to move back into its old base in the Philippines. As the company reported in 1949, it was able to reconstruct its cannery and plantations rapidly "thanks to the cooperation of General MacArthur and the assistance of our friends in the Philippine government." The cooperation of the American military extended to providing army engineers to construct a temporary dock to replace the company pier destroyed during the war.[12]

The postwar period saw a tremendous expansion in Del Monte's Philippine operations, along with the increasing penetration of U.S. capital. Today U.S.-based multinationals dominate the Philippine economy, with U.S. capital accounting for one-third of the invested capital in the country's 900 largest corporations. Del Monte is the largest food processing company in the Philippines and ranks among the top twenty corporations in terms of sales. It is also the leading exporter of two of the country's top ten foreign exchange earners—bananas and pineapples.[13] The company has branched out into other areas as well: it conducts a broad range of tropical fruit and vegetable canning; produces livestock feed from pineapple waste and operates one of the country's largest cattle feedlots; has a large rice-growing operation; manufactures its own cans; operates a trucking fleet; and purchases tuna from local fishermen for shipment to the company's cannery in Puerto Rico.

Politics and Profits

Today, Del Monte's privileged position in the Philippines is protected by the dictatorship of President Ferdinand Marcos. But even before the advent of his martial law regime, Del Monte had long relied on ties to the Philippine government and bourgeoisie which allowed the country's resources to be exploited by U.S. interests.

From the beginning, Del Monte's ownership of the Mindanao plantation was in conflict with a long-standing Philippine law limiting corporate ownership of public agricultural lands (i.e., those considered to be previously unexploited) to 2,253 acres. When this limitation was written into the 1935 constitution, the colonial government obligingly intervened on Del Monte's behalf to get around the restriction. In 1937 the government created a special body, the National Development Corporation (NDC), which was empowered to *hold* public agricultural lands in excess of the established limit. Soon after, the corporation sub-leased 17,429 acres of prime "public" lands in Mindanao to Del Monte on highly favorable terms, even though the NDC was not empowered to sublease lands, much less those in excess of the constitutional limit. Thus, while other American interests were prevented by law from directly controlling large planta-tions, Del Monte's exploitation of the land was protected for decades to come.

Formal independence in 1946 did little to alter the Philippines' status as an appendage to the U.S. economy. That same year the U.S. Congress passed the Philippine Trade Act, which reaffirmed the "free trade" policies that had made the country a supplier of agricultural commodities.[14] This allowed Philippine agricultural exports into the United States duty free, while U.S. manufactured goods could enter the Philippines on the same terms. Even more important to Del Monte, U.S. interests were exempted from a Philippine restriction on foreign exploitation of natural resources. The law gave U.S. companies the right to "parity," that is, the same right as Filipinos to exploit the islands' natural resources.

During the 1950s, in the midst of rising anti-U.S. nationalism, the Philippines adopted a number of protectionist measures aimed at fostering national development. But Del Monte once again proved to have privileged status. In 1956, seven years before its land leasing contract with the National Development Corporation was to expire, the government renewed it for another twenty-five years (until 1988).[15]

When President Macapagal took office in 1962, he scrapped the protectionist policies of the previous decade and adopted a free trade, foreign investment-oriented stance. Del Monte had a special friend in Macapagal, whose association with the company dated back thirty years. When Del Monte first arrived in the Philippines, it shared offices in Manila with its law firm, Ross, Selph and Carrascoco, one of whose attorneys was the young Macapagal. Even after he left the firm to enter politics, Macapagal continued to maintain close relations with the head of Philpack.[16]

In the early 1970s Del Monte's position was increasingly threatened by the growing strength of nationalist elements in the Philippine bourgeoisie. In this situation, Del Monte found its most important ally in President Marcos. As head of the Philippine senate in the early 1960s, Marcos made a reputation as a staunch defender of U.S. agribusiness when he blocked nationalist moves to prevent the expansion of pineapple plantations in Mindanao. As president, Marcos has had close personal ties with Del Monte. He has been hosted several times by the company at its Mindanao plantation, where he stays at the house reserved for the corporation's president.[17] And on the occasion of a special meeting of the Del Monte board of directors in Manila, Marcos had a personal consultation with them.

The challenge of pronationalist anti-foreign capital sentiments came to a head in 1972. At a national convention to draft a new constitution, several strong provisions limiting foreign investment were introduced, and these were supported by large popular demonstrations in Manila. Then, in the summer of 1972, nationalist forces won an important victory when the Philippine supreme court made several rulings that effectively voided U.S. parity rights. The court ruled that U.S. corporations would be allowed no more than 40 percent ownership in their Philippine subsidiaries, that they could not have direct representation on their subsidiaries' boards of directors, and, in a direct blow to Del

Monte, that U.S. companies could not hold agricultural lands.[18]

In a move that saved the day for Del Monte, Marcos acted swiftly to block the nationalist movement. In September, he declared martial law, adjourned congress, and undertook a massive round-up of his political opponents. Del Monte's corporate executives undoubtedly heaved a sigh of relief when Marcos issued decrees reversing the court decision that would have prohibited U.S. landownership, and ensuring the safety of U.S. property and profits (including complete freedom from any restrictions on capital and profit repatriation).

With anti-U.S. nationalism held in check by the martial law regime, U.S. investors have been assured of the "stable" investment climate they need. But even more significant for Del Monte, the Marcos "development" strategy has been tailored to correspond to the interests of U.S. agribusiness investors. First, the cornerstone of Marcos' Five Year Development Plan is increasing exports in two sectors where U.S. multinationals dominate—agriculture and labor-intensive light industry. And second, Marcos' land reform program, supposedly designed to improve the plight of hundreds of thousands of impoverished peasants, applies only to lands devoted to the cultivation of rice and corn, thus exempting the two-thirds of Philippine agricultural lands used by multinationals like Del Monte to grow export crops.[19] Although the National Development Corporation was dissolved after martial law was declared, today Del Monte leases its lands from a newly constituted body, the National Economic Development Authority, headed by Marcos himself.

Plantation Plunder

Despite the nationalist challenge, the 1970s were a time of prosperity and expansion for Del Monte in the Philippines. The company added about 7,000 acres to its pineapple lands, and along with its two major competitors in the Philippines, Castle & Cooke and United Brands, branched out into banana production. Del Monte is now the leading supplier to the rapidly growing

Japanese market, which imports about 90 percent of Philippine bananas.[20] The Philippines have also replaced Hawaii as the company's main source of canned pineapples.

The availability of a cheap and docile labor force has made the Philippines an ideal haven for "runaway plantations." Del Monte, like other pineapple companies, is expanding production in the Philippines not just to be near the Japanese market, but also to escape steadily rising labor costs in Hawaii. Along with completely curtailing civil liberties, martial law has meant a harsh crackdown on the labor movement, creating a situation where labor-intensive businesses like Del Monte's can thrive. All strikes in "strategic" industries which are major foreign exchange earners—like agribusiness—are outlawed. And with unions directly under the control of the government's labor department, Del Monte has no worry of being challenged by an independent union. For most of the 10,000 workers who pick and process pineapples for Del Monte, the average daily wage of $1.70 is one-third less than the average cost of living for a family of six. By one estimate, over half of the company's field workers are kept on permanent "temporary" status as a way of avoiding wage increases and benefits.[21] The thousands of field workers who pick the bananas exported by Del Monte are even worse off, earning from $1.00 to $1.50 a day.[22]

Del Monte's expansion has also taken place at the expense of thousands of small peasant farmers who now find themselves landless. The company's attempts to incorporate new acreage under its control have not always gone smoothly, however. In the pineapple growing province of Bukidnon, observers report that Del Monte has been involved in a classic case of landgrabbing. One pressure tactic has been to threaten small farmers with encirclement and loss of access to their own lands if they do not lease to the company. In other instances, local officials have facilitated the company's landgrabbing by refusing to process disputed land title claims unless the farmers first agree to lease to the company. Those who agree to the lease arrangement are presented with a legal document that is made to look like an attractive subcontracting agreement. The company agrees to provide technical assistance and financing if they will sell their pineapples to Del Monte. But as the farmers (who are often illiterate) discover, they have actually signed away all rights to cultivate the land. A letter appended to the contract reads: "Due to the technical ability needed to grow these crops and the sizeable amount of finances and equipment needed, I cannot comply and meet this particular condition. In view of this, I am giving the company or your representative the absolute authority to take over the entire area as agreed."[23] Unable to survive on the lump-sum payment they receive from the company, these contractees often wind up as hired laborers on their own lands.

When intimidation and deceit have failed, Del Monte has resorted to strong-arm tactics. Some of those farmers who steadfastly refused to abandon their fields have seen their lands fenced and cattle driven onto their cultivated fields by Del Monte employees protected by armed guards.[24] An American priest, arrested for helping peasants resist, described the landgrabbing by U.S. companies: "They bulldozed people right off the land. Now they're using aerial sprays, harming farm animals and giving people terrible rashes."[25]

Del Monte's expansion into the banana business in the Davao region of southern Mindanao has taken a different form, but one with no less severe social consequences. Instead of operating banana plantations directly, Del Monte and the other banana multinationals have production contracts with large-scale local plantation owners (in a system similar to the associate producer program pioneered in Guatemala). Many of these plantations are owned by wealthy and powerful Filipino entrepreneurs drawn into the banana business by the lucrative contracts being offered by the multinationals. (Marcos himself is part owner of the plantation that is United Brands' major supplier.) Once again, the expansion of these large landowners has taken place at the expense of small farmers in the area.

The social unrest sparked by this process of land concentration has contributed to the strength of two important insurgent movements operating in Mindanao. One is led by the (Moslem) Moro National Liberation Front (MNLF). The MNLF says it is fighting to regain the lands of Mindanao's native Moslem inhabitants— lands lost partially because of the "imperialist" expansion of foreign corporations like Del Monte.[26] Del Monte's plantations have thus far been spared from direct attack, since the heaviest fighting has taken place in adjacent provinces. However, since 1974 another guerrilla force, the New People's Army (NPA), has begun operating in precisely those areas where Del Monte's facilities are located—Davao and Bukidnon. The NPA, which is the military arm of the newly constituted Philippine Communist Party, has developed a strong base among the peasantry of the northern islands, and Marcos has characterized the NPA as a serious threat to his regime's stability. The NPA also presents a threat to Mindanao agribusiness interests like Del Monte, since its estimated 10,000 peasant members there are the same small and landless peasants who are being pushed off the land by agribusiness expansion.[27]

The government's massive counterinsurgency campaign on Mindanao is indicative of the high priority the regime places on protecting the status quo in the region. Since the declaration of martial law, about two-thirds of the Philippine army has been deployed in Mindanao, along with a sizeable force of the Philippine Constabulary, the national police. For Del Monte, its future in the Philippines rests on the continuing protection under the shield of martial law and the U.S.-backed Marcos regime.

Profits Are a One-Way Street

After decades of exploiting the country's labor and natural resources, Del Monte has left behind little of the wealth created by its operations, contrary to its claim. The terms of its land leasing and tax arrangements are an example of how the company minimizes its contribution to the Philippine economy in order to maximize profits. For the years covered by its first contract with the National Development Corporation (1937–1956), the company paid the ridiculously low annual rental of about $40,000 for over 17,000 acres of prime land. Del Monte also escaped from its obligation to pay the government a share of its profits. The contract was written to apply only to profits made on raw pineapple, rather than the canned product, where most of the profits are made. Under Del Monte's contract with the NDC the land rental was still a fraction of its market value, and since it is set in pesos rather than dollars, the government's real income decreased each time the peso devalued. Moreover, the contract set the value of raw pineapple (the tax basis) at the 1938 level, which is about 95 percent less than the value of pineapples Del Monte produces in Hawaii.[28]

Although it can claim that its pineapples and banana exports bring sizeable foreign exchange earnings to the Philippines, Del Monte is in fact the main beneficiary, since the revenue is either repatriated as profits or plowed back into the company to finance expansion. In its position as a major exporter, the company naturally acts to maximize its profits on a global scale, regardless of the detrimental impact this may have on the country's foreign trade position. In 1973, for example, Del Monte and other pineapple producers, responding to world market conditions, cut back on exports from the Philippines by 20 percent. While this did not hurt the company's profit picture, it was a significant setback for the country's foreign trade balance.[29]

The Philippines is today one of Del Monte's most profitable operations. Philpack's profit rate in the early 1970s was a spectacular 33.4 percent, or four times that on consolidated equity in the United States.[30] The Philippines has become a key offshore production center, allowing Del Monte to serve more affluent markets in the industrialized countries: only an estimated 10 percent of its production is sold locally (including those canned goods that do not meet foreign health specifications) and 90 percent is exported.[31]

Del Monte's continuing expansion in the Philippines is a reflection of capital's tendency to roam the globe constantly in search of a more exploitable labor force and higher profits. As long as Marcos can keep the lid on the explosive social situation there, the Philippines will undoubtedly remain a key profit-making center. But Del Monte is not taking any chances. The company currently is experimenting with pineapple production in Guatemala—a country closer to home and still securely protected by the shield of U.S. imperialism. As we will see in the next chapter, Guatemala has rapidly become a kingpin in Del Monte's plantation empire.

11. A New "Banana Republic": Del Monte in Guatemala

Talking to a reporter from *Forbes* magazine recently, Del Monte's chairman Alfred Eames mused, banana trees "are like money trees. I wish we had more of them."[1] Unlikely as it may seem, eight short years ago Del Monte did not own a single banana tree. But today, the corporation owns or controls an estimated 38,000 acres of banana plantations in Costa Rica, Guatemala, and the Philippines.[2] It is one of the three U.S.-based multinationals that dominate the world banana economy: Del Monte, Castle & Cooke, and United Brands together account for 70 percent of the world's $2.5 billion banana trade. Because of this dominance, the companies also exercise considerable influence on the economic life of the banana producing countries, many of which depend on banana exports as a principal source of foreign exchange.

Guatemala: Going Bananas

The kingpin of Del Monte's banana empire is its plantation in Guatemala, which was purchased from the old and infamous United Fruit Company in 1972. When Del Monte took over from United Fruit, it stepped into the shoes of a company that had long been the symbol of U.S. imperialism in Central America, particularly in Guatemala. As Guatemala's largest landowner and major foreign investor, United Fruit had dominated the country's economy, exploiting its natural resources and workers and consistently opposing organized labor, and it was the leading force in pushing for the CIA-engineered overthrow of the progressive government of Jacobo Arbenz in 1954.[3]

By the time Del Monte entered the picture, United Fruit had lowered its political and economic profile in Guatemala and the rest of Central America as part of a sophisticated strategy to rationalize its operations and undercut nationalistic resentments. But beneath this facade, Del Monte continues the old tradition of the United Fruit Company in Guatamala. It still operates as though it were above the law; it is allied with the most reactionary elements within the Guatemalan bourgeoisie; it manipulates its workers to avoid labor unrest; and along with the other banana companies, it has tried to torpedo efforts by Central American governments to gain greater control over their natural resources. Like the United Fruit Company, Del Monte reinforces economic underdevelopment and political reaction in Guatemala, and acts as a formidable obstacle to change.

The Guatemala plantations that Del Monte took over from United Fruit in 1972 are the most productive in Central America, assuring Del Monte's position as a major force in the world banana trade. For United Fruit the acquisition meant the further erosion of its dominance, unchallenged before the 1960s when it controlled 75 percent of the world trade.

Ironically, the original impetus for Del Monte's entry into the banana business in 1968 came from the United Fruit Company itself. In an apparent bid to take over the food processing company, United Fruit purchased a large chunk of Del Monte's stock. To thwart the takeover attempt Del Monte went out and bought a banana company—the one line of business United Fruit was legally blocked from acquiring. A 1958 antitrust ruling had found United Fruit guilty of monopolizing the banana trade, and in fact the company was under court orders to sell off about 10 percent of its banana operations. With the purchase of the Miami-based West Indies Fruit Company and its Costa Rican subsidiary, the Banana Development Corporation (known as BANDECO), Del Monte was able to make its first inroads into the U.S. banana market.

The banana business proved highly profitable and Del Monte began looking for ways to expand its Central American holdings. Again, United Fruit provided the opportunity. The final deadline for United Fruit's required divestiture was approaching, and the company still had no buyers when Del Monte approached United Brands (which had purchased United Fruit in 1970) with a purchase offer for its Guatemala plantations. By the end of 1970 the two companies agreed that Del Monte would purchase United Fruit's holdings in Guatemala for about $10 million, provided the Guatemalan government agreed.

For Del Monte, Guatemala was the ideal place for expansion. Not only would the plantations there double the company's banana production, but just as important, fifteen years of U.S.-sponsored counterrevolution since 1954 had made the country safe for U.S. investors, providing the kind of "stable" political climate Del Monte demands wherever it operates. However, Del Monte had one formidable obstacle to overcome—a provision of the Guatemalan constitution that prohibits the sale of border lands (as United Fruit's lands were defined) to foreign interests. To complicate matters further, several purchase offers were put forward by Guatemalan nationals, including two entrepreneurs who had even lined up bank loans.[4] But in the best tradition of U.S. multinationals overseas, Del Monte did not let ethics or legal technicalities stand in its way.

Despite personal lobbying visits by Del Monte executives to then president Carlos Arana and several cabinet officers, in late 1971 the government denied permission for the purchase.[5] Not to be deterred, company officials simply dipped deep enough into corporate coffers to change the Guatemalan government's decision. Following the advice of then ambassador to Guatemala, Nathaniel Davis, to retain a local "consultant," in the summer of 1972 Del Monte hired Domingo Moreira, a Cuban-born Guatemalan entrepreneur. Moreira agreed to help swing the deal in return for a $.5 million "consultant's fee." He soon proved his political clout. Even before the Guatemalan government officially reversed its position, Del Monte received the go-ahead from the government to conclude the deal with United Brands. One month later, in September 1972, Arana formally issued a decree approving the sale.[6]

Del Monte, of course, claimed that there was no bribe involved, since the corporation did not make any direct payment to a government official. But the truth of the matter is that Del Monte was carefully covering its tracks. The $.5 million fee was paid through several of the company's Panamanian shipping subsidiaries and charged to general and administrative expenses.

Thus, Del Monte managed to stay within the formal limits of the law by satisfying Securities and Exchange requirements that accurate records be kept, and no secret slush funds be used to channel funds abroad. Del Monte also went to great lengths to conceal the transaction with Moreira. No company record was ever made of his name, and Del Monte has promised never to reveal his identity.

In spite of Moreira's disclaimers that no bribery was involved, in Guatemala the universally accepted assumption is that Moreira handed over a good-sized chunk of his "fee" to then President Arana. Some sources in the Guatemalan bourgeoisie even claim to have personal knowledge of the transaction.[7]

But more important than the question of the impropriety of the payment is what the Moreira connection reveals about Del Monte's ties with the most reactionary and corrupt elements of the Guatemalan bourgeoisie. Moreira is a fast-dealing entrepreneur whose holdings have expanded greatly since he came to Guatemala from Cuba. He is a well-known backer of conservative political forces in Guatemala and has close ties with a group of rightwing business executives who promote their political and personal gain through Mafia-like tactics. In Nicaragua he had business links with former dictator Anastasio Somoza.[8]

Plantation Enclave

The United Fruit plantations Del Monte took over lie in the hot tropical lowlands of northeastern Guatemala, not far from the Atlantic coast ports which face the markets of Europe and the United States. The most notable change at the plantation since Del Monte's takeover are the new signs on company buildings. They now read BANDEGUA, for Banana Development Corporation of Guatemala, the subsidiary that runs Del Monte's operations there. Recognizing that the plantation system developed over the years by United Fruit serves its interests well, Del Monte has made few basic changes. In fact, several of the workers interviewed by NACLA wondered whether the company had really changed ownership.

For the $20.5 million Del Monte finally paid to United Brands in 1972, the company acquired 55,000 acres of prime agricultural land, plus an agro-industrial complex that stretches from plantation to port. It also inherited a position of privilege and influence that had long characterized United Fruit's operations.

Though no longer the major representative of monopoly capital in Guatemala, where U.S. multinationals now have sizeable industrial investments, Del Monte is still a formidable economic and political power. It is the country's largest single private employer and totally monopolizes the export of bananas, one of the top five sources of foreign exchange for Guatemala. Del Monte continues to run the plantations like an independent enclave within the Guatemalan state, where government officials are barely tolerated. It is Del Monte, not Guatemalan officials, that supplies official export statistics on bananas. Del Monte pays no tax on its lands, and has only 9,000 acres under cultivation. The remaining 48,000 acres are grazed by 7,000 head of company cattle—not to produce meat, but, as a company official explained, as a tactic designed both to keep squatters off the property and to prevent the goverment from expropriating it as idle land.[9]

While Del Monte does not dominate the country's key transportation networks as United Fruit once did, it still benefits from special privileges. When its port facilities at Puerto Barrios on the Atlantic were destroyed by the earthquake in 1975, the company was immediately able to relocate to choice facilities at the nearby government port of Santo Tomás. The corporation also enjoys a special relationship with the government-run national railway, Ferrocarril de Guatemala (FEGUA). Del Monte is one of FEGUA's creditors and also repairs the company's rail cars at its plantation machine shop.[10]

The first thing that strikes a visitor to the town of Bananera, where the plantation headquarters are located, is the highly stratified social system typical of plantations everywhere. On one side of the railroad tracks, behind fences and guard posts, is the company compound. Amidst country club surroundings, a few North American executives and their Guatemalan aides oversee Del Monte's vast lands and its 4,500 person workforce. The compound's manicured lawns, spacious tropical mansions, its pool and tennis courts, stand in sharp contrast to the dusty com-

pany town on the other side of the rail tracks. The evident poverty
of the town, which exists mainly as an adjunct to the plantation,
belies Del Monte's claim that its presence has a beneficial effect on
the surrounding economy.

Most of Del Monte's workers and their families live on the
plantation itself, isolated even from the small town of Bananera.
The company-owned housing camps are conveniently clustered
around the banana farms where the men work, along the edges of
the railway line. The workers' housing is spartan and barely
adequate, a far cry from the luxurious company compound.
Since there are no roads going into the plantation, the only access
to the outside world is the company operated rail wagon, which
runs only twice daily—at the beginning and end of each work day.
No one, neither workers, their families, nor company executives,
is allowed to board the train without a special pass given out daily
by a company office. To further assure "law and order" there is a
Guatemalan army post in the middle of the plantation, staffed by
armed Guatemalan soldiers. A company executive explained to
NACLA interviewers that the soldiers take care of any disturbances which occur on the plantation. He also recalled the original
reason for the post: in the late 1960s, guerrillas were active in the
area, and a United Fruit pilot was killed. Given the social unrest in
the Guatemalan countryside, Del Monte is clearly not taking any
chances.

Plantation Workforce

Many of the workers at the BANDEGUA plantation were once
peasant farmers from the neighboring provinces who were either
forced off the land, or were unable to survive by farming. Now,
with their sole source of sustenance the salary they receive, the
plantation workers have become part of the Guatemalan proletariat. However, with salaries averaging about $870 a year, and
with benefits such as free housing, water, electricity, and medical
facilities, Del Monte's employees are better off than the bulk of
the Guatemalan working class.[11]

Although the policy of maintaining a *relatively* well-off work-force was originally pioneered by United Fruit, today it has become an integral part of the strategy of all the multinational banana companies. Like other monopolistic corporations, they recognize their own self-interest in ensuring labor peace by paying high salaries—something their hefty profit rates allow them to do. For the banana industry, however, a docile and cooperative labor force is a special imperative. Bananas are a highly perishable commodity, and time is critical in the marketing process. A plantation or port work stoppage of even a day can mean the loss of hundreds of thousands of dollars in overripe bananas. Thus, harvesting at BANDEGUA's plantation is carefully timed to coincide with the arrival of Del Monte's ships at Puerto Barrios. Within one day, the bananas are cut, washed, packed, and sent by train to the nearby port. There they are immediately loaded onto specially refrigerated ships which will transport them to the U.S. and European markets. The whole process must be regulated like clockwork, and delays avoided at any cost. In this context, it is possible to understand why Del Monte is willing to pay its dock-workers, who hold the key to the whole marketing process, up to $600 a month on a piecerate basis.

The plantation workers, most of whom earn between $2.80 and $4.00 a day, are not nearly so well off. And in fact, their relative privilege is more than anything a commentary on the miserable living conditions of the rest of the Guatemalan people. In spite of the free benefits provided by the company, the salary of a banana worker is still not sufficient to sustain a family. To supplement their income, wives and children of the banana workers are usually forced to find jobs, often in the banana packing sheds, where salaries are the lowest on the plantation. According to a recent study in Guatemala, the workers and their families spend an average of 64 percent of their income on food, clothing, and fuel; and 17 percent of the plantation families do not have an income adequate to obtain a minimum satisfactory diet.[12]

Work conditions on the plantation are also extremely difficult. Banana production is highly labor intensive, and requires continual painstaking work of weeding, trimming, marking plants, and spraying with insecticides. Under the hot tropical sun, crews of workers roam among the banana trees under the constant supervision of the BANDEGUA foremen. When one of Del Monte's ships is in port, workers often do the grueling job of harvesting for twelve or thirteen hours at a time—one man cutting down the banana stem with his machete, and another carrying the stem (which can weigh up to 150 pounds) in a sack slung across his back. As one of the U.S. executives on the plantation told NACLA, "It's backbreaking work, and you couldn't get a single person in California to do it, especially for $2.80 a day. . . . I wouldn't do it for any money." But, as he explained, cheap labor is key to the company's profits. "If you can pay a worker 35¢ an hour, why buy an $8000 tractor?"

The main device the company uses to extract the maximum value from the workers' labor is payment on a piecerate basis. While this gives the banana workers the possibility of earning more, it also means a higher level of exploitation. Workers drive themselves to the limit, often with disastrous long-range consequences for their health. This system also makes the workers extremely productive. For the company, this productivity translates into a higher rate of profits, far out of proportion to the meager wage increases.

As Del Monte realizes, in spite of its "enlightened" labor policies designed to coopt the workers, there is always an underlying danger of labor unrest. Historically, the banana workers in Guatemala have a strong tradition of struggle. During the years when Jacobo Arbenz was president (1950–1954) the United Fruit-workers' union was one of the most militant and progressive unions in Guatemala. It was only as a result of the massive repression unleashed against the labor movement after the 1954 coup— when banana union leaders were especially targeted to be jailed, killed, or exiled—that the militancy of banana workers was quelled in Guatemala.[13]

Recently, in other Central American countries, there have been renewed signs of militancy among banana workers. In Honduras, 18,000 workers at United Brands' subsidiary voted in 1975 to oust the conservative, pro-U.S. union leadership, installed twenty years ago in a U.S.-engineered effort to undercut the then progressive leadership. In May 1976, Del Monte was itself the target of a strike at its Costa Rican subsidiary, where workers were demanding higher wages, recognition of their union, and reinstatement of fifty-four fired workers.[14] Like other corporations, Del Monte attempts to prevent worker discontent from bursting into open conflict by identifying and weeding out the most outspoken and militant workers—a tactic one of the company's plantation supervisors admitted using.

To further control its labor force, Del Monte relies on the union itself—Sindicato de Trabajadores de BANDEGUA or SITRABI— which is known in Guatemala as a "sindicato blanco," or a sell-out union. In a pattern familiar in the United States, the union performs the function of the loyal opposition—it may oppose the company on bread-and-butter issues, but promotes an ideology of cooperation and common interest with the company, rather than one of anticorporate class interest.

The BANDEGUA union has cooperative relations with the American Institute for Free Labor Development (AIFLD), an organization funded by AID, supported by the AFL-CIO and U.S. corporations, and often used by the CIA to undercut genuine progressive unionism in Latin America. Every year a handful of chosen BANDEGUA workers spend months at AIFLD-sponsored courses in Guatemala City learning U.S.-style unionism, and some are sent to AIFLD schools in Honduras and Colombia. Many of these AIFLD graduates become union officials or are given supervisory jobs on the plantation.[15]

The Banana War

The most serious challenge Del Monte has faced in Guatemala has come not from labor, however, but from rising third world nationalism. Barely a year after the company took over the plantations in Guatemala, Latin America's major banana exporting countries—Guatemala, Costa Rica, Panama, Honduras, Colombia, Nicaragua, and Ecuador—proposed forming a producers' organization, the Union of Banana Exporting Countries, or UBEC. Like the oil producers who formed OPEC, those who controlled the governments of banana producing countries were rebelling against the disadvantages raw material producers face in world trade. For most of these countries, bananas constitute a major source of foreign exchange. Yet the world market price of bananas remained unchanged for twenty years while the cost of their manufactured imports skyrocketed. Whereas in 1960 a tractor cost three tons of bananas, in 1970 the same tractor cost eleven tons of bananas.[16] Instead of the mere 11.5¢ of every $1 of banana sales staying in producing countries,[17] UBEC governments set out to capture a larger share of the banana dollar. Their chief target was the multinationals like Del Monte who reap the lion's share of profit from the banana dollar.

When in 1974 UBEC proposed a $1 tax on each box of bananas exported, the banana companies moved quickly to confront the challenge. Documents submitted to the U.S. Senate Committee on Multinationals allege that the three companies met in Costa Rica in early 1974 to coordinate a strategy for confronting the UBEC challenge.[18] The Costa Rican foreign minister also charged that the companies had set up a secret fund to "destabilize" the UBEC member governments in order to prevent them from levying the banana tax.[19] The companies of course denied the charges, but they all proceeded to move against the UBEC countries.

Castle & Cooke took the lead by cutting back on exports and destroying 145,000 boxes of bananas rather than pay any tax. United Brands, it was later revealed, bribed Honduran government officials $1.25 million to reduce their tax, a scandal that eventually led to the suicide of the company's president, Eli Black, and the removal of the president of Honduras.

By comparison, Del Monte was careful to keep a relatively low profile in its campaign against UBEC. In Costa Rica, the company agreed under protest to pay the tax but began judicial proceedings to challenge the government.[20] By 1975 the Guatemalan government had not yet levied the tax, arguing in effect that the company was above the law. Its case rested on the grounds that it assumed all the rights and privileges granted United Fruit in its contract with the government, namely, that the export tax could not be raised above 2¢ per stem until the contract expired in 1981. Del Monte found its strongest allies in extreme rightwing members of the Guatemalan congress, who blocked attempts to impose the tax.[21]

When the new government of General Kjell Laugerud responded to public pressure and announced it would support the tax, Del Monte countered with a new public campaign aimed at intimidating the government. In a full-page advertisement in the Guatemala City papers, the company brazenly threatened that it would reconsider expansion or even cut back operations if the tax passed, leaving Guatemala with even less foreign exchange earnings than previously.[22] When another attempt to pass the tax was defeated, there were once again rumors that Del Monte had resorted to bribery.[23]

When the tax was finally pushed through the Guatemalan congress in late 1975, the company showed that it was indeed above the law. That year Del Monte managed to pay no tax at all on its banana exports by declaring a volume of over three million boxes lower than the year before. The company's export figures were suspiciously low given that the area of land under production remained the same and there were no adverse weather conditions to affect productivity.[24] However, without an independent count of the number of boxes exported, the Guatemalan government had no way of knowing whether the company had manipulated export figures. So hefty were Del Monte's profits in 1975 that the Guatemalan minister of the economy predicted the company would recoup its entire investment in Guatemala in three years.[25]

The outcome of the so-called banana war highlighted the limits of the brand of nationalism that led to UBEC. First, whatever monetary gains the ruling elite who control the Guatemalan government reaped had no effect on the well-being of the majority of Guatemalans. Moreover, producers of nonstrategic raw materials like bananas have very little leverage vis-à-vis global corporations like Del Monte who wield decisive power because of their control over marketing and distribution channels. A clear sign of the success of the banana companies' intimidation campaign was the failure of a single member government of UBEC to impose the full $1 tax. Even when a smaller tax was levied, it was the multinationals who came out on top by jacking up prices. Just after the tax was first imposed, the box price of bananas in the United States shot up from $2.50 to $5.20, an increase way out of proportion to the tax. This gave the companies a profit of 9¢ a box, more than four times the profit rate company spokespeople usually call reasonable.[26]

Hedging Bets

This is not to say that Del Monte and the other banana companies are immune to pressures from reformists and nationalists. In fact, the threat of land expropriations has forced the banana companies to modify their investment strategies significantly—a necessary adaptation which they have turned to their own advantage.

Instead of relying solely on their own lands, the companies now purchase a significant amount of bananas from "associate producers"—local growers who contract to sell their production to the companies. This associate producer program, first pioneered by United Fruit in Guatemala in the 1960s in response to the land reform attempts of the previous decade, has allowed the companies to lower their profiles without cutting into their profits.[27] The companies also use the associates to buffer themselves against fluctuations in the world market. When demand for bananas is strong, the companies turn to associates for increased supplies. On the other hand, when there is oversupply and the danger of falling prices, the companies simply purchase less fruit from associates by raising their quality specifications.[28]

The companies also use the associate producer system as a public relations ploy to demonstrate their beneficial impact in helping local farmers. But in reality, those who are helped are usually large and wealthy landowners—those who have the capital and technological sophistication required to produce the uniformly high quality fruit demanded by the multinationals.

Del Monte's associates are a prime example. In Costa Rica, about two-thirds of Del Monte's bananas come from the company's thirteen associate producers, each of whom has an average plantation of 612 acres.[29] In Guatemala, where United Fruit never set up an extensive associate program, Del Monte obtains nearly all of its contract production from one business group, headed by Spanish-born Julian Presa. Presa and his family contract about 3,000 acres to Del Monte, partly through a joint venture with a Florida-based U.S. company, Taylor Enterprise of Guatemala. Such associates provide the multinationals with important political allies within the local bourgeoisie. Del Monte's associates, for example, were prominent in arguing the company's case against imposition of the UBEC tax.

Although the associate producer scheme has given the companies some security that their profits could survive a new wave of land expropriations, the multinationals still have a strong vested interest in maintaining the status quo. Del Monte's plantation lands are the most productive in Central America, and for all of the banana multinationals profit margins are significantly higher on their own plantations, which are able to produce quality fruit more cheaply and efficiently than are the associates.

Given this, Del Monte and the banana multinationals will remain a highly conservative force in the third world, in spite of their image of flexibility. They are likely to oppose progressive changes like land reforms, and will certainly be a major obstacle to the basic social changes necessary to meet people's needs.

12. The Grain Trade: A Seedy Business

Worldwide grain shortages, skyrocketing grain prices, and multibillion-dollar grain deals with the Soviet Union—all these developments during the past decade have pushed into the limelight the small group of companies that dominate the grain trade. Five large companies—Cargill, Continental Grain, Bunge, Dreyfus, and the Andre-Garnac complex—control about 85 percent of U.S. grain exports and are the major grain traders in the world market.

The "Big Five"

The five companies are controlled by just eight families.* Eschewing publicity, the families have cloaked the operations of their companies in secrecy: since they are not public corporations the companies do not regularly report their profits, annual sales, or new investment plans. No other major business sector in the world is as secretive and as tightly controlled by such a small group of families.

These eight families have a stranglehold over the world's grain supply system and literally hold the power of life and death over millions of people. Each year their companies move tens of billions of dollars of grains from the surplus producing countries to the food deficit areas of the world. The companies run integrated merchandising structures extending from the farmer's fields to foreign markets. Domestically they control local grain elevators, storage bins, railroad cars, shipping barges, and port elevators;

---

*The eight families are the Cargills and MacMillans (Cargill), the Borns and the Hirschs (Bunge), the Fribourgs (Continental Grain), the Andres and the Hedigers (Andre-Garnac), and the Dreyfuses (Dreyfus).

they operate charter companies that control shipping to every part of the world; and in scores of countries they own port facilities and processing plants.

In the age of monopoly capitalism, these companies hold a unique position. Founded in the nineteenth century, they are actually similar to the British merchant firms or commercial houses, which bought and traded agricultural products as well as manufactured goods and raw materials. These merchant houses relied heavily on banks to finance their trading operations, and they made direct investments in port facilities and shipping.

Most of these merchant firms were eclipsed by the rise of the multinational corporations. Whereas the commercial houses had focused their international activities on the buying and selling of commodities, the multinationals gained direct control of mining and manufacturing facilities. Control of the means of production then enabled the multinationals to bypass the merchant houses and set up their own marketing networks.

This did not happen in the grain trade however. While the production of plantation commodities such as sugar and bananas passed into the hands of the multinational corporations, grain farming did not lend itself to large-scale, plantation-like methods of production, and accordingly, multinational corporations never tried to gain direct control of grain production. To this day, family farms and medium-sized commercial units supply most of the world's grain.

Throughout their history the grain companies have profited from this arrangement. With no ties to the land, the companies are free from the risks of falling prices, bad weather, and land mortgages. Buying and selling on the open market, the companies act as intermediaries and profit regardless of the calamities the farmer may be facing.

Playing the Free Market

However, as many grain company executives are fond of pointing out, the trade is highly competitive. Bids are made in fractions of a penny per bushel as a company strives to beat out a competitor for a potential sale. The intense competitiveness of the grain trade was demonstrated in 1977 when one of the giants of the grain trade, Cook Industries, was forced into bankruptcy. The company had negotiated contracts for the delivery of soybeans based on the supposition that soybean prices would hold steady or even fall. When market prices in fact rose, Cook lost $80 million, and was compelled by its financial backers, the banks, to sell its grain facilities.[1]

The decline of Cook Industries illustrates the closed nature of the grain trade and the tremendous power of the companies that remain. Cook had always been regarded as an upstart in the grain trade: it entered the trade only in the 1960s, while the other companies had commercial roots dating back to the nineteenth century. To keep up with the more established grain companies, Cook Industries gambled more heavily on the fluctuations of the market. And in 1977 it gambled one too many times and lost. The lesson will not be lost on any potential rivals who think of challenging the Big Five.

Although competitive, the grain companies use their enormous size to manipulate the marketplace and to maximize profits at the expense of farmer and consumer alike. As one government officer investigating the grain trade observed, "In the U.S. there's a free market, but freedom exists only for the few and not for the many."[2]

To manipulate the market the companies have developed a sophisticated intelligence network. They run offices in every corner of the globe, and their system of gathering information is so extensive that even the CIA turns to them.[3] Profits turn on their ability to project the movement of market forces with a high degree of accuracy and to adjust their strategies accordingly.

This explains the companies' interest in the more speculative mechanisms of capitalism such as the grain futures market. Before each year's crop is harvested, billions of dollars of grain are already sold to buyers. The prices on these preharvest sales, or futures contracts, are determined by what the buyer and seller predict will be the value of the grain when it is delivered. Marketing information is crucial in the transaction. Thus a large grain company with advance knowledge, or the ability to project the movement of the market, will profit from the futures contract, while the farmer is least likely to come out ahead. As one company representative noted, "the grain companies can adjust much quicker than a farming community" to changing market conditions.[4]

The companies also speculate heavily in international shipping. Each company buys and sells contracts for shipping space, never intending to use all of the space, but rather to keep its options open and to maximize profits. The grain itself is often transferred on paper from country to country. Depending on the rise and fall of grain prices, a shipment originally destined for Europe may be assigned to Panama, only to ultimately wind up in Japan. Since most of the companies' international transactions are in foreign currencies, they also maintain divisions that deal solely in foreign exchange. The companies manipulate every possible market mechanism—the more the better. Besides dealing in grain, the companies have diversified into everything from food processing to real estate and steel.

The grain inspection scandals, which broke in 1975 and resulted in the indictments of many grain inspectors and company officials, must also be seen in the light of the companies' market manipulation. By bribing inspection officials to raise the grade or alter the classification of grain, the companies in effect increased their earnings by millions of dollars. As one Senate aide who investigated the trade noted in an interview, "by controlling the inspectors, the companies control the price mechanism."[5]

With their ability to thrive on market fluctuations, the grain companies are among the most vociferous defenders of the so-called free market. Government intervention to iron out the rises and falls in agricultural prices is abhorred by the companies, since this would limit their ability to profit from the cyclical nature of agricultural trade. The companies oppose all forms of export controls and some of them have lobbied against international grain reserves. Rather than establish mechanisms that would stabilize food prices and help provide an adequate diet for people around the world, the companies prefer free-swinging markets that maximize profits. "The free market serves the oligopolies," as one government official observed.[6]

The companies also use their global trading networks to escape government regulations. Due to the companies' profiteering from the grain shortages of the early seventies, many public interest and consumer groups called for tight government controls over the grain trade. Congress responded feebly to this demand; it passed one piece of legislation requiring the grain companies to report all large export sales. The companies, however, quickly made a mockery of even this law by having their foreign subsidiaries contract for some of the export sales. These subsidiaries were not required to report the sales.[7] To this date, there is still no effective monitoring system of the companies' trading activities.

While evading government regulations, the companies strive incessantly to influence and control the government. Key business associations, such as the National Grain Trade Council and the National Grain and Feed Association, lobby in Washington on behalf of the grain trade. One former under secretary of agriculture declared: "The political and bureaucratic influence of the grain companies is very pervasive."[8] Be it detente with the socialist world, tariff negotiations with the European Common Market, or the cutoff of grain exports to the Soviet Union, the companies work closely with the U.S. government to formulate foreign policies. The power of the trade rests not only in its manipulation of the market, but also in its ability to use the government for its own interests.

Many critics of the grain trade view the companies as nineteenth-century robber barons and propose government regulation to force them to respond to public needs. This approach, however, ignores the fact that the companies are modern enterprises that vividly illustrate the basic tendencies of capitalism. The maximization of profits, the manipulation of the government, the insatiable thirst for foreign markets, and the exploitation of people's fundamental needs—these are all characteristics of capitalism which the grain companies embody.

To better understand the dynamics that drive the grain companies, each of the five major ones is studied in profile. The profiles focus on the origins of the companies, their role in the U.S. grain market, and the activities of the companies outside of the grain trade. The following chapter then looks at the largest of these, Cargill Inc., in greater depth.

Cargill, Inc.

Founded in 1865, Cargill is the only major grain company founded in nineteenth-century America. The Cargills ran the enterprise alone until 1909, when the MacMillans were brought in to rescue it from the brink of bankruptcy. Today, the two families own 85 percent of Cargill's stock, and Whitney MacMillan serves as chairman. Based in Minneapolis, the company projects an all-American image.

In May 1979 the company's worldwide sales stood at about $12.6 billion, making it the largest private corporation in the United States.[9] About half of this income derives from the grain trade; the remainder is generated by activities ranging from feed milling to metals trading. The biggest of the grain companies, it contols about one-quarter of U.S. grain exports, and is the largest single contributor to the U.S. balance of payments. High profits in recent years have enabled the company to acquire a number of agribusiness and other firms.

Continental Grain Company

Run by the Fribourg family, which owns 90 percent of the stock, Continental Grain originated in Belgium in 1813. The company operated mainly in the European market until the rise of Hitler forced the family to flee to the United States with its business. Michael Fribourg assumed control of the company in 1944 at the age of thirty, and quickly turned the firm into one of the world's largest grain merchandisers.

Today, Continental Grain and Cargill control almost half of all U.S. grain exports. The bonanza of profits from grain trading in the early 1970s enabled Continental, like Cargill, to make a number of acquisitions. Continental now owns two important processing companies, Oroweat Bakeries and Allied Mills (a manufacturer of livestock feeds), and operates large flour mills in Venezuela, Ecuador, Puerto Rico, Guadeloupe, and Zaire.[10] But Continental is not as diversified as Cargill, with less than a quarter of its annual sales coming from nonmerchandising activities. Based in New York, Continental Grain, more than any other grain company, projects a cool, corporate, Wall Street image. Fribourg is a leading proponent of detente with the Soviet Union and has entertained Soviet officials on yacht cruises since 1961.[11]

Bunge Corporation

The Bunge Corporation, based in New York, forms part of the worldwide financial empire of Bunge & Born. The enterprise began operations in Argentina in 1884 when Ernesto Bunge, a descendant of an old Belgian trading family, joined with Jorge Born to set up a grain exporting firm. In 1897 the Hirsch family linked its fortunes to the company, and eventually displaced the Bunges as one of the two dominant families in the company. Bunge & Born became so powerful in Argentine agriculture that the following expression became common: "Bunge gives the farmer his credit, sells him his seed and buys his grain. And when the crops are in, Bunge sells the farmer the rope to hang himself."[12]

Bunge & Born began operating in the United States in 1919, but its real growth in this country occurred after World War II. Cutting corners to compete with the two giants of the U.S. market (Cargill and Continental Grain), Bunge, more than the other grain companies, turned to bribery to get grain inspectors to misclassify and overweight grain shipments destined for foreign markets. Finally caught in the 1970s, Bunge officers were sent to jail. But this hasn't halted the company's growth in the U.S. market: today, it has export sales of well over $2 billion.

The parent firm, which owns flour mills, chemical and textile plants, and an array of other industrial operations throughout Latin America, also encountered problems in the mid-1970s. Two Born brothers were kidnapped by Argentine guerrillas in 1974 and released in exchange for a $60 million ransom.[13] To prevent such future occurrences, Bunge & Born's headquarters were moved to Brazil and the company expanded its operations there. Today, Bunge & Born is one of the leading industrial conglomerates in Brazil. And after the military coup in Argentina in 1976, Bunge & Born began reinvesting in Argentina once again.

Louis Dreyfus Corporation

Like the Fribourgs of Continental Grain, the Louis Dreyfus family (which owns the company of the same name) was forced to abandon France when Hitler's armies invaded. The family had been active in the French grain trade since 1842. But unlike the Fribourgs, who maintained their corporate headquarters in the United States after the war, the Louis Dreyfus family returned to their French offices. However, they did leave behind a U.S. firm which is one of Louis Dreyfus' main subsidiaries and controls some 10 percent of the U.S. grain trade today.[14]

Back in France, the company expanded rapidly. Louis Dreyfus had especially close relations with the regime of General Charles DeGaulle, and the company's banking and shipping interests flourished, often with state assistance. Today, it owns France's fifth largest commercial bank, the Banque Louis Dreyfus et Cie., and controls the Banque Hypothecaire Européen, one of the largest mortgage banks in Europe.

Internationally, Louis Dreyfus also has diversified holdings. The company manufactures glass, shipboard, and particleboard in Argentina and Brazil. Louis Dreyfus owns two merchant shipping firms, one based in London and the other in Paris, and is a part owner of DWS, Inc., a New York firm that owns and manages real estate in the United States and Canada. Dreyfus moved into the international meat trade in the early seventies and today is a major meat trader in Argentina, Canada, and France.[15]

Andre-Garnac

Andre-Garnac is actually two legally separate grain companies—Andre based in Switzerland and Garnac located in the United

States. However, the two companies work so closely together that they can be regarded as a single business complex. Garnac was established in the United States in 1937 by Frederic Hediger, a Swiss immigrant who worked for Andre. According to Hediger, "Andre helped us. Without their finances, we couldn't have made it—and without us they had no connection here in the United States."[16]

Andre, which was founded in 1877 by a family of the same name, relies totally on Garnac for grain from the U.S. market. And Garnac in its own right is one of the big grain traders in the United States. In 1977 Garnac had U.S. export sales of $1.5 billion. It owns the Midwestern Grain Company, which is a major trader in the American heartland, and runs a large terminal in San Diego which handles West Coast grain exports.

In addition to Garnac, Andre also has grain trading affiliates in Africa, Western Europe, and Latin America. Through these affiliates and its own operations, Andre controls at least 7 percent of the world's grain trade. The Argentina affiliate, the La Plata Cereal Company S.A., is particularly important; in addition to grain trading, it is also involved in flour milling, oil seed crushing, textile manufacturing, and machine tool manufacturing.[17]

13. Harvest of Profits:
The World Empire of Cargill, Inc.

Cargill, Inc. is the largest privately owned U.S. corporation.* Two Minneapolis-based families—the Cargills and the MacMillans—own 85 percent of the company's stock and run one of the world's most secretive and far-flung commercial empires. Over a century old, Cargill buys and sells commodities in every corner of the globe while also operating manufacturing plants that process everything from feed grains in the Midwest to salt in Louisiana and soybeans in Brazil. As Cargill itself boasts, "Few facets of modern life are unaffected or unreached by Cargill today."[1]

If Cargill were placed on the list of the 500 leading public industrial corporations, it would rank fourteenth, ahead of such well-known giants as RCA, General Foods, and Dow Chemical. Since Cargill, however, is more involved in the buying and selling of commodities than in industrial production, it is more accurate to compare it to the leading merchandising firms where it would rank fourth, just behind K-Mart but ahead of J. C. Penney and Kroger. As of May 31, 1979, Cargill's worldwide annual sales stood at about $12.6 billion, making it the largest grain trader in the world.[2]

In spite of Cargill's sprawling business empire, its name is not a household word. The executives who run the enterprise keep a tight lid on its activities, permitting only an occasional article to be written by a trusted business journal or newspaper. The company headquarters reinforce the air of secrecy. Located in a French-style chateau outside of Minneapolis, the company's officials deal in billions of dollars worth of commodities in pastoral surroundings seemingly far removed from the modern corporate world.

---

*Unlike most large U.S. corporations, Cargill does not sell its shares to the public. Examples of other large private corporations are the Hearst Corporation and the Bechtel Corporation.

Cargill's Corporate Origins

Cargill's history reflects many of the forces that have shaped U.S. capitalism for the past century and a half. In the 1830s William D. Cargill, a Scottish Presbyterian, migrated to the northeastern United States, where he worked as a captain in the merchant marine. Several sources suggest that Captain Cargill's quest for profits led him into the slave trade. He sold his shipping interests just before the bottom dropped out of the maritime industry in the panic of 1857 and moved to Wisconsin to become a gentleman farmer.[3]

His sons soon adapted their father's trading talents to the agrarian economy of the Midwest. In 1865, the oldest son, Will, went to Iowa where he bought an interest in country grain elevators along the new railway lines. With the close of the Civil War, railroads began to crisscross the Midwest, thereby providing wheat farmers with ready access to national markets, while at the same time opening up new lucrative opportunities for the merchants and grain traders. Within several years, Will was joined in the grain trading business by two of his brothers, and they built elevators and grain storage houses in Iowa, Minnesota, and Wisconsin.

In the early years of Cargill, just as today, financial backing played a crucial role in the company's growth. Aside from obtaining loans from many of the smaller midwestern banks, Will Cargill befriended a prominent Milwaukee banker, Robert Elliott, who "backed his friend not once, but again and again to their mutual benefit."[4] The Cargills also extended their commercial influence by forming partnerships with a number of other grain merchants to erect or control elevators; then, when the opportunity arose, the partners would be bought out, since the Cargills preferred complete ownership.

Because Cargill in many cases controlled the only elevator at major railroad stops, the local farmers were often forced to accept the price offered by the company for their grain. The railway owners and the grain elevator operators, such as Cargill, sometimes conspired to fix grain prices. By the 1880s, Cargill operated along major railway arteries in five states—North and South

Dakota, Iowa, Minnesota, and Wisconsin. Even Cargill's official historian admits that by the late 1870s and 1880s the company held monopolistic trading positions "in southern Minnesota and South Dakota."[5]

The growing domination of the farmer's economic life by the railroads, the grain traders, and the eastern banking interests led to the formation of an independent political party called the Populists, whose impassioned protests against this destruction of the land rose in strength throughout the Midwest, West, and South in the 1880s and 1890s. However, Cargill, like the other ascendant business interests, emerged largely unscathed from the revolt. The rise of agricultural exports after the depression of the 1890s along with the continued growth of the national economy eventually provided the farmers with new markets, thereby alleviating their financial plight and defusing the Populist movement. The emergent corporate interests in the United States never forgot the lessons of this period: farmer discontent against big business could be contained only by constantly expanding market outlets.

Cargill was in the forefront of the push by business to develop new markets for farm production. It erected large grain terminals on the Great Lake ports, and even built short railway lines to link major commercial and transportation routes in the Midwest.

By the turn of the century, Cargill's profits enabled the family to expand into new areas totally unrelated to the grain trade. However, many of these endeavors were speculative, and the new family scion, William S. Cargill, proved incapable of managing the company's overextended businesses in the face of the economic downturn that began in 1906. Three years later, most of Cargill's properties were placed in receivership, and the Cargill grain merchandising empire appeared to be on the brink of dissolution.

But the Cargill fortune was saved by the infusion of new blood into the company administration. John H. MacMillan, a member of the prominent business family from LaCrosse, Wisconsin, married into the Cargill family in 1895 and soon assumed important administrative positions. When the Cargill properties were placed in receivership, John MacMillan persuaded the Creditors Company to allow him to assume management of the ailing company. From that time onward, the MacMillans joined with the Cargills to forge the destiny of the midwestern grain company.

Expansion at Home and Abroad

By the early 1920s Cargill had fully recovered from its brush with bankruptcy and embarked on a new expansive phase. When eastern grain trading interests began moving into the Midwest markets to bypass the regional grain dealers, Cargill responded by establishing direct sales offices in the East. The company now had a completely integrated trading network which handled grain from the small country elevators to its final sale in the eastern markets. And at the end of the decade, Cargill joined the growing list of U.S. companies with foreign operations when it established sales offices in the principal European grain centers and in Argentina, one of the world's major grain exporters.

The Great Depression did little to deter the company's expansion. In 1932 Cargill assumed control of the new grain export elevator at Albany, New York, at the time the largest facility of its kind in the world. Then in the mid-1930s, Cargill moved abruptly into the Chicago market. There it forced out the old trading giant of the city, the Rosenbaum Grain Company, and soon became the largest grain merchant in the Chicago area.[6]

Cargill's use of cut-throat business practices and its rapid pace of expansion upset many of the established grain trading interests. They rallied around the Chicago Board of Trade to curtail Cargill's expansion. Nominally set up to control speculation and profiteering in the grain trade, the board in reality is dominated by the grain trading interests which it is supposedly regulating. In 1938 the board, still controlled by well-established local traders, filed suit against the upstart company, charging Cargill with manipulating prices on the corn market. Cargill issued a countersuit and demanded that the federal government "clean-up" the Chicago Board of Trade. Although Cargill lost the legal battle when its Illinois subsidiary was excluded from trading on the Chicago market, it won the economic war. The subsidiary was already in the process of dissolution and the Chicago Board of Trade abandoned its efforts to keep the parent company out of the Chicago grain market, where it continued to expand.[7]

World War II brought with it a new commercial framework for the operations of the grain companies. Maritime hostilities ended direct private grain exports, and the government stepped in to regulate the domestic grain market as well as other sectors of the economy. Though Cargill complained about the "frequent and serious incursions by various government agencies," it diversified its operations and profited from the war.[8] The company established feed milling and vegetable processing divisions that moved into domestic manufacturing, and it also built tankers for the navy and army. Thanks to the stimulation of production caused by the war, Cargill and many other U.S. corporations extended their reach into new areas of the economy.

The postwar period proved to be an even greater boom for Cargill. With most of the economies of the world in disarray, the United States became the world's principal food supplier. Realizing that prosperous export markets could develop only if the major economies of the world were rebuilt, the United States used first the United Nations Relief and Rehabilitation Administration (UNRRA) and then the Marshall Plan to send unprecedented quantities of grain to the European and Asian nations. The main U.S. agricultural exports, wheat and flour, jumped from 48 million bushels in 1944 to 503 million in 1948.[9]

Government Support: Public Law 480

Although the U.S. strategy led to an immediate increase in exports, the resurgence of agricultural production in Western Europe at the end of the 1940s lessened the demand for U.S. grain. The outbreak of the Korean War caused only a brief spurt in grain exports. But just as it appeared that Cargill and the other grain companies would have to reconcile themselves to a smaller role in the world export markets, the U.S. government in 1954 forged the perfect instrument for their continued expansion—Public Law 480.

This piece of legislation served as a two-pronged instrument in Cargill's market expansion. First, it enabled the company to directly increase its export sales. For example, between 1964 and 1965 Cargill exported $200 million under PL 480 while its total exports stood at $700 million.[10] As Table 13.1 shows, Cargill was a principal beneficiary of PL 480 Title I financing.

Secondly, Cargill (and other grain companies) used PL 480 to "whet the appetites" of many countries.[11] Once they had opened up the market in a given country with PL 480 concessional sales, it was much easier for them to follow up with direct commercial sales. As one former grain company official who went to work in the export division of the Agriculture Department noted, with PL 480 "we taught people to eat wheat who didn't eat it before, particularly in the Far East."[12] One grain company representative summed it up even more bluntly: "PL 480 enabled the companies to gain entrance into a market at the smallest expense possible."[13]

Table 13.1
Exports of Grains and Vegetable Oils Under Title I, PL 480
(figures in thousands of dollars)

Company	1969–78	1954–67[1]
Continental Grain	925,795	1,626,472
Cargill	629,462	1,572,968
Louis Dreyfus, Inc.	439,999	678,651
Bunge Corporation	258,834	641,022
Andre-Garnac	209,374	N.A.

Source: U.S. Department of Agriculture, internal reports, 1976, 1979.
1. Figures not available for 1968.

Aside from PL 480, other government programs also stimulated company exports. The Commodity Credit Corporation (CCC) granted one- to three-year loans to foreign governments to purchase its surplus grain reserves, while the Barter program, which exchanged grain for strategic and war materials, provided an effective subsidy for U.S. exports. Among the grain companies, Cargill was the major firm to take advantage of the latter program.

In some years 70 percent of total U.S. grain exports involved government concessional financing of one type or another.

Cargill's Domestic Structure

"The Reign It's Plain is Mainly in the Grain"
(from a Cargill pamphlet)

By the 1950s, Cargill had expanded and consolidated its control over a huge network of merchandising, storage, and transportation facilities. Domestically, the company operates at the three main points of grain collection and distribution: the local elevators where the farmer sells the grain, the subterminals and terminals at the major transportation crossroads, and the large export elevators located in major U.S. ports. In recent years, the subterminals have assumed a special role in the company's expansion. Since they are able to handle large volumes of grain in relatively short periods of time, Cargill uses these subterminal elevators to bypass the smaller country elevators that are often under the control of local cooperatives and usually located in smaller communities. Like other large corporations under monopoly capitalism, Cargill seeks to limit the commercial options available to the small producer.

Due to the accumulation of grain surpluses in the 1950s and 1960s, the operation of storage facilities by the large grain companies figured prominently in their market strategies. The federal government, through the CCC, nominally controlled these surpluses, since it purchased the excess agricultural production each year to keep farm prices from falling. Companies such as Cargill stored the CCC grain in their facilities in return for government storage payments. From 1958 to 1968, for example, Cargill received over $76 million for storing grain.[14]

Purchases were made from the CCC reserves whenever the companies wanted grain to cover their own marketing needs. Their manipulation of the CCC reserves was dramatized in 1966 when the large grain interests bought most of the government corn reserves in anticipation of shortages and rising prices.

Both small country elevator owners and the farmer cooperatives complained bitterly that the companies were able to take advantage of subsequent price rises at their expense.[15] And, of course, the CCC also lost a sizable amount of potential revenue since it could have waited for corn prices to rise before selling the surpluses.

Transportation has figured prominently in Cargill's manipulation of the domestic market. Since World War II the development of new transportation techniques has enabled the company to stay one jump ahead of its competitors and to extract the maximum profit from every bushel of grain it handles. First, in the late 1940s Cargill opened a new access route to the Mississippi River by widening the Minnesota River channel, thereby making it possible to bypass Minneapolis where labor costs and municipal regulations made grain handling more expensive. Then in the late 1950s the company began to use the inland waterways for transporting grain through its shipping subsidiary, Cargo Carriers. Its barges and tow boats plied the Missouri, Ohio, Tennessee, Illinois, and Mississippi rivers, making Cargill one of the largest shippers in the United States.

However, Cargill still depended heavily on land transportation for moving much of its grain. Worried about the growing power of the teamsters union and the trucking industry in the 1960s, the company took the lead in pressuring the Interstate Commerce Commission to restructure railway rates and regulations so that rail transportation became more economical for the grain companies.[16] Regulations were first altered so that the companies could take control of entire train units at special rates. Then in 1968 Cargill carried the process one step further when it initiated the concept of Rent-A-Train (RAT): under this system Cargill rented the engine, the train crews, and the railroad right-of-way for extended periods of time.*

Through these changes Cargill and the other major grain companies gained control of much of the country's grain carrying capacity, a position they used to their utmost advantage in 1972. When the increased foreign demand for wheat placed an enor-

---

*Cargill also has interlocking directorates with some of the railroads.

mous strain on the U.S. transportation system as grain was moved from internal markets to the ports, the companies used their control of the railways to hold down the price they paid for wheat. In many instances the companies discounted 10 to 25¢ per bushel from the market price they paid the farm coops and the locally controlled elevators for their grain.[17] The lack of shipping alternatives meant that the local merchants and farmers had no choice but to sell at the price the grain company dictated.

In the late 1970s Cargill gained an even tighter hold over the transportation system. It invested heavily in transportation facilities, and by 1980 owned over 500 barges, 5,000 rail cars, and 14 ocean-going vessels.[18] The Interstate Commerce Commission did nothing to curtail Cargill's growing power. In fact, under the Carter administration, the commission has been even more lax in its regulation of the grain companies than it has been in earlier years. The stranglehold the big grain companies exercise over the grain transportation system makes it virtually impossible for the cooperatives or the smaller grain traders to stay in the grain market and offer the farmers competitive prices. And for the farmers, the growing concentration in grain handling in turn means that they have fewer and fewer options in choosing to whom to sell their grain.

Financing the Cargill Empire

Banks and financial institutions play an especially important role in Cargill's sprawling commercial empire. From the moment the grain is purchased until the time it is finally sold abroad, Cargill and other exporting companies must have sufficient funds to cover the costs of carrying these large quantities of grain. Not even Cargill, the "Cadillac of the grain trade," possesses anywhere near the amount of capital needed to finance these seasonal grain inventories.

To satisfy these capital needs, Cargill maintains credit lines with over forty banks, including eight of the ten largest U.S. commercial banks. Cargill draws on these credit lines to pay for its grain purchases. In one recent year, Cargill borrowed more short-term cash than any other corporate entity in the United States.[19] For Cargill and the other grain companies, three Chicago-based banks—the Continental Bank of Illinois, the First National Bank of Chicago, and the Harris Savings & Trust—play an important role in financing grain inventories.

Cargill enjoys a particularly close relationship with the Chase Manhattan Bank: for Cargill, as well as for the grain industry as a whole, Chase is the "lead bank."[20] The relationship between the two goes back decades, at least to 1933, when John Peterson left Chase to join Cargill as its chief financial officer. In 1945 Cargill noted that among its many creditors, "the most important of these to Cargill is the world's largest bank, the Chase [Manhattan] Bank."[21] No major financial moves are made by Cargill without first consulting with Chase. One company official noted that hardly a month goes by without Cargill and Chase officials holding consultative meetings. Nevertheless, company executives denied that Chase "calls the shots" or has the ultimate say in Cargill's business decisions.

Aside from Cargill's special ties with Chase, company executives also sit on the boards of banks in the Minneapolis area. Cargill's closest link is with the First National Bank of Minneapolis, which served on the Creditors Committee in 1909 when Cargill entered into receivership. The current president of the First National Bank, George H. Dixon, also serves as a director of the Cargill Foundation. Although the First National Bank provides Cargill with only a small part of its capital needs, it heads up the First Bank System which controls eighty-three banks in five midwestern states.

Not all of Cargill's capital needs are satisfied by lines of credit with commercial banks. When Cargill erects grain elevators, storage bins, or any other type of fixed asset, it often turns to insurance companies for long-term loans. Such giants as Prudential, Metropolitan Life, and John Hancock are among the insurance companies that collect the savings of U.S. workers to relend to large corporate interests, including the grain companies.[22]

Over the years Cargill and the other grain companies have become especially adept at tapping public financing. Port facilities are frequently financed and constructed by urban port authorities which then lease them to the grain companies. In 1973, for example, the Duluth, Minnesota Port Authority and Cargill announced a $15 million project for constructing new port facilities. Cargill did not put up any of the money: $13.5 million came from revenue bonds backed by the Port Authority, while the remainder flowed from special federal and state programs. When the new facilities were completed in 1977, Cargill leased them for thirty years.

Overall, Cargill is astute at using public and private funds to sustain its commercial empire. In 1973 the company possessed net assets worth only $352 million, but with this relatively small capital base it conducted a volume of trade worth $5.3 billion.[23]* When one recalls that Cargill controls much of the flow of grain on the railway system without owning a single locomotive, that it received millions of dollars in storage payments for holding CCC grain surpluses which it could buy and sell at a moment's notice, and that much of its international trade is financed by PL 480 and other government lending programs, then one has some understanding of how its commercial system is run. The company is a stunning example of modern corporate capitalism, where small amounts of capital are used to control vast financial and commercial empires.

Foreign Marketing Activities: "The Sun Never Sets on Cargill's Corn"

Since its first trading offices were established in Europe in 1929, Cargill's international operations have penetrated into every corner of the globe. Today, the company operates in thirty-six different countries and has 140 affiliates and subsidiaries. Its international trading operations are directed by Tradax, a subsidiary with headquarters in Geneva. As one company official noted, "Tradax and Cargill are mirror images." Tradax performs the same merchandising functions abroad that Cargill carries out

---

*Since that date, Cargill has not declared its net assets.

in the United States: it owns grain elevators and storage facilities, arranges regional financing with foreign banks, employs a large number of sales agents, operates its own shipping network, and deals heavily in buying and selling foreign currencies. Among other places, it has offices in Manila, Tokyo, Panama, Buenos Aires, Amsterdam, and London.[24]

Not only is Cargill involved in exporting U.S. grain, it also buys and exports grain in the other major agricultural producing nations. Cargill is Argentina's leading exporter of wheat, barley, maize, and other grains[25] and through Tradax is the leading exporter of grain in France.

Although grain exports in Canada have been controlled by the Canadian Wheat Board ever since 1935, Cargill is maneuvering with Canadian agribusiness interests to open up the trade to private companies. A "free market" now exists for feed grains, and Cargill already markets some grains internationally. The company became a major force in the Canadian grain trade in 1974 by acquiring the National Grain Company, a firm that owned a number of grain elevators, five feed manufacturing plants, and port facilities at Vancouver and Thunder Bay.[26]

As part of its expansionist strategy in Canada, Cargill is building large-scale regional grain terminals that bypass the smaller country elevators located in most of the farm communities and owned by cooperatives. Cargill's regional terminals favor the large-scale farmers who can buy or contract for trailer trucks to haul their grain long distances to the terminals where they receive premium prices that compensate for the shipping costs. Thus Cargill's operations are undermining not only the cooperatives, but also the smaller farmers who receive less for their grain because they cannot ship it to the terminals.[27]

Cargill's interests in the Philippines have flourished under the dictatorship of Ferdinand Marcos, and today Cargill is a heavy trader in two of the islands' key agricultural exports—copra and sugar. Cargill opened up the Philippines international trade in copra, the dried coconut which is processed and used to make vegetable oil products such as margarine. Initially the copra was processed in San Francisco, California, but as the trade expanded, Cargill set up a plant on the Philippine island of Mindanao where it could take advantage of the cheap labor force. In addition to copra, Cargill is heavily involved in the Philippine sugar and molasses trade, and its Shaver Poultry division is a major factor in the Philippine poultry industry.[28]

Cargill and the four other major grain companies dominate the grain markets of Western Europe. These companies control export-import facilities in Europe, operate large shipping and transportation networks, have close relations with European bankers, and even own manufacturing subsidiaries in Europe that process imported grain. For four of the five firms—Continental Grain, Bunge, Andre, and Dreyfus—these extensive European operations are attributable to their family and commercial roots in nineteenth-century Europe.

Cargill of course possessed none of these ties. However, its complex U.S. marketing and transportation system gave it far more control over the basic export commodity, grain, and enabled it to move strongly into European markets after World War II. While the companies of European origin built elevators, terminals, and other marketing facilities in the United States similar to Cargill's, the native grain giant cornered a large share of the European market. As a newcomer, Cargill's market initiatives met with resistance. When the company began selling grain directly to feed millers in West Germany, that country's merchants initiated a boycott which lasted for almost eight years before it finally collapsed.[29]

Japan is one of the world's leading grain importers. Although the U.S. grain companies export to Japan, the huge Japanese trading companies control much of the internal movement of grain, and two Japanese firms, Mitsui and Mitsubishi, are even active in the U.S. grain trade. (Mitsui bought up most of the grain handling facilities of the bankrupt Cook Industries.) Cargill did enter into a joint venture with Toyo Futo Company in 1966 to construct new grain handling facilities in Japan. Cargill is also active in the Japanese poultry and meat industries.

Although they import less grain than Western Europe and Japan, the third world countries represent lucrative markets for the grain traders. Some of the countries import large quantities of grain under U.S. concessional programs, while others have "graduated" from PL 480 and now use their meager foreign exchange to satisfy the new demand for U.S. grains. The quality of the grain that these countries receive under PL 480 sometimes leaves much to be desired. As one U.S. Senate aide noted: "PL 480 recipients have not been in a position to complain about the grain and food they receive. The stuff they get is probably shit."[30]

Some of the companies bribe local government officials to gain marketing concessions in the third world countries. One small grain company executive caught bribing a Salvadorean official proclaimed that such payoffs are "not at all unusual. They're a way of life." He went on to add, "I understand many of the grain companies do it. You're either going to pay or not do business."[31] One retired Cargill official, after first stating that his company was not involved, proceeded to name some of the Latin American countries most susceptible to bribery in arranging grain deals. The companies would probably prefer to operate abroad without providing funds for kickbacks, but if such payments become necessary for closing an important grain deal, then the dictates of business require that the bribe be paid.

A Multinational Industrial Corporation

Cargill's expansion into foreign manufacturing in the 1960s was built on its U.S. industrial base and its foreign marketing network. By 1962, through its wholly owned Nutrena subsidiary,* it operated twenty-seven domestic feed mills, and in addition owned fourteen vegetable oil processing plants. Cargill's first manufacturing investment abroad was in Peru: by 1960 it had become a major international distributor of Peruvian fishmeal—a high-protein meal used for animal feed—and in 1963 it purchased a large fishmeal plant in Peru, as well as a fishing fleet to supply it.

At about the same time, Cargill began constructing a soybean processing plant in Spain. Then in 1964 it acquired the Hens companies, a major feed manufacturing chain with subsidiaries

---

*Nutrena is the largest U.S. feed manufacturer.

in Belgium, West Germany, and France. In 1966 Cargill built another soybean processing plant in the Netherlands, and in 1970 opened a third such plant in France.[32] Almost overnight, Cargill had become a major factor in the vegetable oil and animal feeds industries of Western Europe.

The company also expanded into related areas of international agribusiness. In 1965, it purchased Shaver Poultry Breeding Farms, a Canadian firm that ships breeding stock abroad. Today, Cargill uses Shaver to form an integrated package of feed mills and poultry breeding stock when it moves to establish operations in other countries. Although a relative newcomer as a multi-national industrial corporation, Cargill has rapidly expanded its feed and food processing operations into many third world markets, establishing subsidiaries in El Salvador, Guatemala, the Philippines, Argentina, Pakistan, Brazil, Taiwan, and South Korea during the sixties and early seventies.

Cargill's operations abroad have been assisted by the imperialist policies of the U.S. government, as can be seen in the case of South Korea. In 1968 the company announced it would build an integrated poultry operation that included a poultry breeding farm, a large feed processing plant, and a poultry processing unit. Cargill received 95 percent of its financing from the U.S. government to establish this subsidiary. One loan for $500,000 came from PL 480 under the special provisions of the Cooley amendment. This amendment allowed multinational corporations to use local currency from the proceeds of PL 480 sales to finance the establishment of local subsidiaries. The other loan, for more than $1 million, came from the private trade entity provisions of PL 480, which extends credits to foreign subsidiaries of U.S. corporations to import U.S. agricultural commodities to be processed in their plants. The companies can either sell the commodities and use the proceeds to finance their operations, or use the commodities to supply their processing plants.

Cargill's subsidiary (called Korea Cargill) also provided lucrative opportunities for Koreans who had served the U.S. empire abroad. Seung Man Park, Cargill's local partner and the president of Korea Cargill, "was a supplier to U.S. military forces during and after the Korean War."[33] The chief construction and engineering manager, Myung Cho Chang, worked for the U.S. AID mission in South Vietnam from 1966 to 1968. Many employees of the feed plant are veterans of the Korean War, and almost all of them have had military training. E. C. Fuller, the assistant vice-president of Cargill in charge of its Korean operations, believes the employees' training in the martial arts makes them ideal workers. He noted: "They have an awareness of danger, a familiarity with hardship and an eagerness to face the future that is enviable."[34]

Despite large loans from the U.S. government, Korea Cargill began experiencing financial difficulties in 1972. Due to the exhaustion of Cargill's PL 480 credits for importing grain, and the Korean government's restrictions on the use of its limited foreign exchange, it became difficult for Korea Cargill to import the feed grains and poultry breeding stock necessary to sustain its operations. At the same time, the South Korean government became less responsive to the demands of multinational corporations. In 1974 Cargill representative S. D. Ward, Jr., in a letter to the Department of Agriculture, summarized the problems the company and other multinationals faced in South Korea:

> I do not like what is going on and I am not alone. Many other investors feel as I, that inwardly Korea appears not to want foreigners. I know that is a strong statement but in view of continued harassment, new decrees and restrictions, I cannot help but draw that conclusion. The decline in new investments over the past year certainly leads one to suspect that many prospective investors have a similar view.[35]

Dissatisfied with profits from its Korean operations, Cargill again fell back on the resources of the U.S. government. First it asked U.S. officials to intervene on its behalf with the Korean government to try to obtain a relaxation of the import restrictions and the domestic price controls. The State Department instructed its representatives in Korea to see that the "poultry and livestock industries" receive special consideration from the government.[36] Cargill itself went to the highest levels of the Korean government to seek concessions. When this failed to reverse Korea Cargill's financial fortunes, it called upon the U.S. government for another favor: it asked for and received permission to defer payments on its two PL 480 loans.

Although less is known about the operations of many of Cargill's other subsidiaries, the corporation is heavily involved in two South American countries—Brazil and Argentina. Its subsidiaries in these two countries are in effect "mini-Cargills." In Argentina, aside from exporting wheat and other grains, Cargill owns and operates export facilities, produces hybrid seed corn for the domestic market, and owns two large feed mills that manufacture livestock and poultry feeds. In late 1979, Cargill announced a new $18 million investment in a linseed oil and sunflower seed oil processing plant. This is one of the largest foreign investments made under the military government that replaced Isabel Perón in 1976.

Although involved in Argentina since 1929, Cargill's Brazilian operations are of much more recent origin. Cargill failed on two earlier occasions to gain a foothold in Brazil—once in 1947 and again in the 1950s. Determined to gain access to the large Brazilian market, Cargill sent a new representative to Brazil in 1959 who succeeded in breaking into the export-import trade. Its operations grew rapidly, especially after the installation of the military regime. Cargill Agrícola was established in 1965 and by the early 1970s it was engaged in hybrid seed production, feed manufacturing, and poultry farming, as well as grain merchandising.[37]

Cargill figures prominently in Brazil's emergence in the early 1970s as one of the world's largest soybean producers. Aside from engaging in the soybean export trade, Cargill built one of the world's most modern soybean processing facilities in Ponta Grossa, Brazil. Once again, timely backing from the U.S. government aided Cargill's expansion. The Overseas Private Investment Corporation (OPIC) lent Cargill Agrícola $2.5 million for the soybean processing plant, while the Eximbank has helped out on three separate occasions with loans totaling over $1 million.[38]

Recent acquisitions have carried Cargill into other areas of the Brazilian economy. When it acquired C. Tennant & Sons, an international metals trading firm, Cargill gained a foothold in the Brazilian metals trade and picked up a chemical plant. As one Cargill official noted in an interview: "Cargill has a stupendous growth rate in Brazil."

Cargill and the State

Thus although the company loudly proclaims the need for free trade and abhors government regulation, it would be virtually impossible for the world's largest grain trader to operate without the continued support of many governmental institutions and organizations. PL 480 enables the corporation to sell grain to the third world, Eximbank and loans from the Overseas Private Investment Corporation help it to set up foreign subsidiaries, and American military and economic assistance to repressive regimes in Taiwan, South Korea, El Salvador, and Guatemala help maintain the environment necessary for Cargill operations. Domestically, federal and state governments finance port facilities, grant the company tax concessions for new capital investments, and generally maintain a legal and financial system that is essential for the survival of Cargill and other monopolistic corporations.

The most politically active of the grain companies, Cargill in the early 1960s set up a Public Policy Committee within the company which formulates positions on key issues and works out guidelines for the company representatives who speak out publicly. Cargill's influence pervades both of the major political parties. Politically, the twenty-odd people who run Cargill are rock-ribbed Republicans almost exclusively, and within the party they support the more conservative positions. But ideological considerations do not stand in the way of the company's business interests. Minnesota state politics for most of the 1970s was dominated by the Democratic Party (or the Democratic Farmer Labor party, as it is called locally), and Cargill worked closely with many of its party leaders. As one former employee of Cargill observed in an interview: "If a person has the power, Cargill finds the way to influence the person."

Minnesota's most well-known politician, Senator Hubert Humphrey, had ties with Cargill. According to one informed source, the company or its officers "have given money to Humphrey for every campaign since he ran for mayor of Minneapolis."[39] Humphrey knew many of the Cargill officials on a first-name basis and he made occasional visits to the company chateau outside Minneapolis. Although he did not openly defend the grain companies, Humphrey moved to control and dilute congressional efforts to regulate the grain trade. A former president of General Mills summed up the attitude of Minnesota agribusiness interests toward Hubert Humphrey: "It's a lot cheaper to give Humphrey a few thousand dollars than to fund the Republican Party."[40]

Although less directly tied to the grain companies, Vice-President Walter Mondale "toes the line with Cargill." As a senator from Minnesota, Mondale read public statements by Cargill into the *Congressional Record* as recently as 1972. In January 1980 he played a key role in the U.S. government's decision to buy up the grain company's contracts with the Soviet Union when the grain embargo was announced. Among the grain companies, Cargill was the biggest beneficiary of this decision.

Cargill had especially close ties to Richard Nixon. A former Cargill employee noted that "Cargill was closer to Richard Nixon than it has been to any president." The ties go back at least as far as Nixon's vice-presidential days when he was entertained several times by the company in Minnesota. After his defeat in the California gubernatorial race in 1962, Nixon went to work for the Wall Street law firm of Mudge, Stern, Baldwin & Todd, which counted Cargill among its corporate clients. When Nixon traveled to Minneapolis in early 1964 to review his firm's accounts with Cargill, the company helped him arrange a conference at the Minneapolis Press Club. As Nixon's first formal press conference since the California debacle, it proved to be a success and encouraged many people to take a second look at him. Cargill, of course, rallied behind Nixon in 1968 and in 1972.

Cargill officials also serve in government positions. William Pearce, a vice-president of the company, was a leading architect of the Williams Commission report (which drew up the blueprint of U.S. agriculture in the 1970s). He served as deputy special trade representative with the rank of ambassador and headed up an interagency team that guided the 1973 Trade Reform Act through Congress. In all of these instances legislation or policies were adopted that reflected the general interests of the grain trade.

Finally, sections of the Department of Agriculture are virtually run as the private bailiwicks of Cargill and the grain trade. As one former under secretary of agriculture noted, "The grain companies are always at the elbow of people in the USDA."[41] Some times personnel go from the grain companies to work for the Department of Agriculture, while in other instances people who leave the department are hired by the grain trade. These links led one government investigator to label the situation as one of "structural corruption."[42]

The grain trade companies have been very active in pushing detente with the Soviet Union. Although the company executives are generally doctrinaire defenders of the free enterprise system, the quest for new agricultural markets in the Soviet Union and China led many of them to favor a relaxation of East-West tensions at an early date. Cargill is a member of the U.S.-U.S.S.R. Trade and Economic Council, while its retiring president, Fred M. Seed, serves as a director of the National Council for U.S.-China trade. According to a Continental Grain officer, the president of the company, Michael Fribourg, "has felt since the late 1950s that it is better to trade with the Communist countries than to fight them."[43]

Profiteering and the Future of the Grain Trade

The shift in U.S. agricultural policies in the 1970s led to a boom for the grain trade. Profits soared as the price of grain on the international market reached unprecedented levels. The leading grain trader, Cargill, also proved to be one of the leading beneficiaries. A former employee noted in 1975 that "for the past five years Cargill has consistently earned profits in excess of 20 to 25 percent."

The Soviet wheat deal played an especially important role in Cargill's profiteering. Although the company was not the leading exporter to the Soviet Union in 1972, the unloading of the large U.S. grain surpluses set off a price spiral as other nations rushed to secure the remaining grain supplies. In fact, while Continental Grain, Dreyfus, and Cook Industries tied up most of their elevator and shipping capacity in moving grain to the Soviet Union, Cargill later picked up the more lucrative grain sales to other overseas customers—after the world price of grain had soared to unprecedented levels. At the same time Cargill used its control over railroads and elevator facilities to exploit the farmers. With no alternative means of moving grain, farmers were sometimes forced to accept price discounts of 10 to 25 and, in some cases, as much as 50¢ on each bushel of grain sold to Cargill.

Cargill's financial statement for 1973 reveals that the company's net assets increased from $246 million to $352 million, an increase of over 40 percent. Profits were $107.8 million, or over 43 percent return on assets.[44] No other large corporation in recent history has reported such astounding profit margins.*

In the late 1970s, Cargill used these profits to expand its grain handling facilities throughout the capitalist world. Today it is the largest private grain exporter in four of the world's five leading grain exporting nations—the United States, Canada, France, and Argentina. And in the fifth country, Australia, it is unclear which company is dominant, although we do know that Cargill is a major force in that country's grain trade. In the United States, Cargill is hoping to increase its market share from 25 percent to 35 percent in the early 1980s by investing $150 million per year in building up its grain handling facilities.

Cargill is also using the high profits of the early 1970s to rapidly diversify its holdings outside of the grain trade. The company realizes that the agricultural policies of the United States government mean widely swinging markets with boom and bust periods in agriculture. This is precisely what Cargill and the other grain companies want in order to maximize their profits. But at the same time Cargill is diversifying so that it is well protected during the lean years. One company official said in an interview, "Cargill wants to spread the risk base and the profit base."

In the late 1970s, Cargill's biggest acquisitions were Leslie Salt and MBPXL Corporation, the nation's second largest meat packer with sales of over $1 billion. Earlier in the same decade, Cargill had purchased Summit National Holding Company, an insurance firm, AENCO Inc., a solid waste processing center, C. Tennant

---

*The figure of 43 percent *return on net assets* should not be confused with *annual percentage increase in profits*. Return on net assets means the return on invested capital, not the annual increase in profits from year to year.

& Sons, a large international metals trading firm, and the North Star Steel Company, a manufacturer of steel sheet rolls. In addition Cargill has set up new subsidiaries such as Cargill Leasing, and bought up scores of small businesses around the world. Cargill in effect is now a mini-conglomerate involved in an array of operations that have no direct relations to the grain trade or to food. Approximately one-half of Cargill's sales now come from activities other than grain trading.

Despite Cargill's expansion and prosperity, the officials who run the company are uneasy about the future. Under increasing scrutiny because of the food crisis, the company fears that public discontent may lead to government intervention. As one grain company executive noted in an interview, "I see no way to keep the government out of the market if we go through another bout of exploding prices."[45] For decades, Cargill has shrouded itself in a veil of secrecy precisely to ward off this possibility: it realizes that publicity about the company's operations can only lead to increased public hostility.

Exploiting people's most fundamental needs and making enormous profits in the process, firms like Cargill vividly illustrate the basic injustices of capitalism. Although capitalism requires these types of enterprises to keep the system functioning smoothly, they are located in the system's most exposed flank. To protect itself, Cargill will strive to maintain the veil of secrecy and attempt to use friendly politicians and bureaucrats as a protective shield. But in the long run its insatiable quest for profits and markets can only increase the discontent felt by working people in the U.S. and abroad.

Appendix

The following chart lists the investments of the sixty largest U.S. agribusiness corporations in Latin America. Most of the corporations are active in food processing, fertilizer production, or farm implement manufacturing, a few own large tracts of land or plantations, and some have diversified into nonagribusiness areas of production.

Due to the difficulty in obtaining recent data and the increased reluctance of the corporations to reveal their foreign assets, the list of investments from 1973 to the present does not reflect the full intensity of foreign investments in recent years. In spite of these limitations, however, the chart reflects roughly 80 percent of all U.S. agribusiness investment activity that has occurred in Latin America during the twentieth century.

This chart is based on information gathered by Marc Herold for an ongoing project entitled "Multinational Enterprise Data Base," Economics Department, University of New Hampshire, Dover, NH. Hank Frundt, who worked with Harris Gleckman at the United Nations Center on Transnational Corporations, provided some additional information, and Sarah Stewart helped in the early stages of work on the chart.

The data is organized for each corporation as follows: country, year of entry (most refer to year established, other information as noted: acq=acquired; jv=joint venture), year of exit, if any (nat=nationalized), principal product(s), name of subsidiary, where known, % owned by parent company, where known (maj=majority; min=minority).

Multinational Investments in Latin America

Aguirre Corp.

Dom. Rep. 1966 acq / agric. dev. project / CODDEA / maj
P. Rico 1899 / 1970 / sugarmill, molasses / 100
1931 acq / 1970 / sugarmills / Santa Isabel Sugar / 100
1974 acq / constr. materials, ag. equip. / Rodriguez Portela y Cia / 100

Anderson, Clayton & Co.

Argentina 1935 / cotton compress, cottonseed oil mill
1962 acq / cake, pudding, pizza mixes / Instantix SA
Brazil 1934 / cotton compress, cottonseed oil mill, fertilizers
1936 / vegetable oil ref.
194– / vegetable oil ref., soap, can plant

253

1946 / cottonseed oil mills
1948 / vegetable oil ref.
1950 / insecticides
1952 acq / insecticides / 100
1960 / solvent process, soybean mill
1960 acq / cottonseed oil mill
1961 acq / softdrinks / Cia Refrigerantes Guanabara / maj
1962 / soaps
1967 / formula feeds
1972 / animal & poultry feed mills
1975 acq / cheese / Norremose SA / 100
1976 / soybean proc. / 100
1978 / foods
1961 / soft drinks / Grapette SA
1975 acq / cheese / Lacticinios Luna SA / 100

Colombia 1966 acq / 1971: sold / coffee processing / A. Aristizabal y Cia / 100
1966 acq / 1971: sold / coffee processing / Villegas Hermanos / 100

Mexico 1921 / cotton lint, purchasing / 100
1946 / cotton compress
1947 / vegetable oil ref. / 100
1950 / cottonseed oil mill
1951 / cottonseed oil mill
1952 / cottonseed oil ref., shortening
1954 / cottonseed mill
195– / insecticides mixing
1957 / feed mill
1961 acq / cake, pre-cake mixes / Pronto SA
1963 acq / candy / Luxus SA / 100
1966 acq / mixed formula feeds / Productos Api Aba SA / 100
1966 / cheese, oils, cocoa, sauces / Anderson Clayton y Cia SA / 68
1967 / pet foods
1968 / hatcheries
1969 acq / foods / Empacadora Rico SA / 100
1969 acq / institutional foods / Empresas Maier / 100
1976 acq / hatchery / Reproductora Shaver SA / 100
1976 acq / poultry, eggs, prepared feeds / Granjas Progenitoras SA / 100
——— / poultry / Productora de Aves
——— / poultry / Granjas del Norte
——— / foods / Nacional Pecuaria SA

Paraguay 1935 / vegetable oil ref.

Peru 1933 / 1971: sold / cottonseed oil ref. / Fabrica de Aceite Shapaja SA / 100
1955 acq / 1971: sold / cotton gins, soap, oil / Fabricas Unidas SA / 100
——— / 1971: sold / coffee processing
——— / 1971: sold / veg. oil products / Fabrica Monserate SA

Archer-Daniels-Midland Co.

Brazil	1974 acq / soybean proc, edible oil ref. / Tecnologia em Vegetais e Proteinas SA / 50
	1974 acq / soybean proc, edible oil / ADM do Brasil Productos Agricolas
Cayman	1974 / soybean meal / Agriproduct / 100
	1975 / offshore insurance / Agrinational / 100
Mexico	1956 acq / 1966: sold / grain mill products / Productos Api Aba SA / 50
	1964 acq / 1967: sold / plastics, synth. resins / Admex SA / 40
	1966 / plastic resins / Quimica Organica SA
Peru	1956 / whaling station / Balanerna del Norte SA / 50

Bangor Punta Corp.

Argentina	1971 jv / light plane assembly / Chuincul SA
Brazil	1970 acq / large & small arms mfg. / maj
	——— / Piper assembly kits / Piper Aviacao do Brazil
Cuba	1883 / sugar plantation, mill / Atkins / 100
	1916 acq / —: sold / sugarmill / Trinidad Sugar / 100
	1916 acq / 1961: nat / sugarmill / Florida Sugar / 100
	1917 / 1951: sold / sugarmill / Punta Alegre Sugar / 100
	1923 acq / —: sold / sugarmill / Antilla Sugar / 100
	1924 acq / —: sold / sugarmill / Tacajo Sugar / 100
	1925 acq / —: sold / sugarmill / Cia Azucarera Fidelidad / 100
	1925 acq / —: sold / sugarmill / 100
	1932 acq / 1961: nat / sugarmill / Baragua Sugar / 100
	1951 acq / 1961: nat / sugarmill / Caribbean Sugar / 100

Beatrice Foods Co.

Brazil	1975 / luggage / Sampsonite / 100
Colombia	1963 acq / candy, gum / Fabrica de Dulces Gran Colombia / 75
	1966 acq / milk, snack foods / Jack's Snacks de Colombia SA / 100
	——— / confectionery, gum, drugs / Industrias Beatriz SA
	1971 acq / Hacienda la Rosita, SA / 100
Dom. Rep.	1972 acq / snack foods / La Estrella C. por A. / maj
	1968 acq / ice cream & dairy plant / Frig. C. por A. / 70
	——— / Industrias Unidas SA
Guatemala	1970 acq / snack food, meat, confectionery, plastics / René SA / maj
	——— / confectionery / Prod. Alimenticos Peter Pan SA / 60
	——— / textile mill prod. / Asunto Carimba
	——— / cookies, crackers / Asunta

Honduras ——— / cookies, crackers / Chitos de Honduras
Jamaica   1966 acq / dairy & ice cream, frozen foods, fruit juices / Cremo Ltd / 75
1968 acq / dairy & ice cream / Northshore Dairies / 100
Mexico   1962 acq / ice cream & bakery / Lactoproductos La Loma SA / 75
1968 acq / chemical finishes / Stoffel y Cia / 100
1968 acq / ice cream / Helados Holanda SA / 60
1970 acq / brushes, toiletries / Perfect Brush / 100
1973 acq U.S. parent / luggage / Samsonite SA / 100
1973 acq U.S. parent / luggage, plastic prods / Altro SA / 50
——— / chemicals / Stoffel SA / 96
Nicaragua 1969 / leather, chemicals, plastics / Quimic Stahl Centroamer. SA / 90
——— / cookies, crackers / Adams Korn Kurl
Peru   1966 acq / cookies, crackers / Productos Chipy SA / 75
P. Rico   1962 acq / ice cream, frozen biscuits / Mantecados Payco / maj
1966 acq / snack foods / Eric's Swiss Products / 100
——— / draperies
——— / ice cream
Venezuela ——— / confectionery / Caremelos Royal
——— / Granos de Oriente
1977 / confectionery / Industrias Anita
1977 / confectionery / Industrial Savoy
——— / chemical finishes / Quimicas Stahl / Polyvinyl SA
——— / Marlon

Beker Industries Corp.

Brazil   1974 jv / phosphatic fertilizers / Fertilizantes Beker / 100
1977 acq / fertilizers / Ricassolo SA Ind. e Com. de Adubas / 98
——— / fertilizers / Beker Com. e Ind. de Fertilizantes / 100

Borden, Inc.

Argentina 1947 / plastics, resins, indust. chem. / Casco Cia
Bermuda 1960 acq / dairy products / Devon Creamery / 40
Brazil   1967 / shrimp fishing & proc. / 100
1973 acq / pasta products / Productos Alimenticias Adria / 100
——— / Pastificio Romanini SA
——— / sausages, meatpacking / Frig. Borden
1947 / paints, adhesives, sealants, plastics / Alba SA / 97.5
Colombia 1944 acq / dairy products / Lecheria Higienca SA / 50
1975 / dairy products / Pasteruizadora de Valle SA
1953 / dairy / Colomb. de Alimentos Lacteos SA
1960 / chemicals / Quimica Borden SA
C. Rica   1965 acq U.S. parent / shrimp trawling & proc. / Henderson y Cia / 100

1971 / shrimp proc. / Peseuy Mariscos SA / 100
Fr. Guiana 1965 acq U.S. parent / fresh, frozen & canned seafoods / Pecheries Int. / 80
Mexico 1957 / formaldehyde / Industrias Quimicas Formex SA / 100
1959 acq / 1968: sold / ice cream / Holanda SA / 100
1959 acq / ice cream, cond. milk / Mixturas SA / 100
1972 acq / Prolesa SA / 50
1973 jv / fruit juices, cheese
Nicaragua 1966 jv / medicinals, plastics / Quimica Borden Centro-ameri. SA / 85
Panama 1953 acq / dairy products / Chiricana de leche SA / 25
————— / fresh, frozen & proc. fish / Hendersons / 100
P. Rico 1959 acq / fluid milk / Puerto Rico Dairy / 100
1961 acq / fluid milk / United Dairies / 100
1961 acq / fluid milk / Caribbean Dairy / 100
1965 acq U.S. parent / CO Mason / 100
1969 / proc. meats / Borden Pan America / 100
Trini. Tob. ————— / cane sugar refining / Trinidad Processing
Uruguay ————— / plastics, medicinals / Halcolar SA / 60
Venezuela 1941 jv / powdered milk, dairy / Industria Lactea Venezolana / 51
1956 / dairy products / Industrias Lacteas de Occidente / 51
1960 acq / ice cream, dairy / Helados Club / 51

Campbell Soup Co.

Brazil ————— jv / condensed soups / C. do Brasil Ind. e Com.
Mexico 1961 / canned soups / Campbell de Mexico / 100

Cargill, Inc.

Argentina 1964 / animal feeds / Cargill SA / 100
1964 acq / animal feeds / INSA / 50
Barbados ————— / hatcheries, bread / Shaver Poultry
Brazil 1948 jv / grain & oilseeds processor
1965 / hybrid corn
1965 / animal feeds / 100
1972 / soybean proc., poultry, cereals / Cargill Agricola SA / 100
Guatemala 1964 acq / fats & oils, animal feeds / Cargill Americas
El Salv. 196– / animal feeds / Adria
————— / poultry products, feeds / Cargill
Honduras 1969 / animal feed, egg & broiler prod. / Centrocom SA / 100
————— / animal feeds / Alimentos Concentrados SA
Peru 1963 jv / 1973: nat. / fishmeal / Pesquera Delfin SA / 50
1963 jv / fishing trawlers / Bolicheros Unidos / 50
————— / alkalies, detergents

———— / canned, cured seafoods / Cargill Peruana SA
P. Rico   1948 / flour mill / 100

Carnation

Brazil   1957 jv / 1971: sold / powdered milk, cans / Leite Gloria / 60
Cuba   1937 / 1960: nat. / dairy products / 24
———— / 1960: nat. / metal cans / 100
Dom. Rep. 1971 jv / evaporated, condensed milk / Dominicana de Alimentos Lacteos SA / 50
Jamaica   1931 / powdered & fluid milk / Jamaica Milk Products / 30
Mexico   1946 / milk products / Carnation de Mexico SA / 100
———— / evap & fluid milk / General Milk Cannery
Panama   1935 / powdered milk / Cia Panameña de Alimentos Lacteos / 30
1961 acq / metal cans / 100
———— / General Dairy / 100
Peru   1941 / dairy products / Leche Gloria SA / 97

Castle & Cooke, Inc.

Brazil   1975 acq / mushroom processor / Kinoko SA / 75
———— / general crop services / Brasdole / 100
———— / horticultural products / Monte Belo SA / under 50
Br. Hond. 1975 jv / brewery / Belize Brewing / 51
Colombia ———— / crop prep services, bananas / Castle & Cooke
C. Rica   1961 / paperboard boxes / Envases Industriales SA / 34
———— / Cia Financiera
Cuba   1943 acq / wharf facilities / 100
Ecuador   1950 / crop prep services / Standard Fruit
1977 / canned, cured seafood / Castle & Cooke
Haiti   1935 / bananas / Standard Fruit & Steamship / 100
Honduras 1948 acq / brewery / Cerveceria Tegucigalpa SA / 60
1948 acq / beer, soft drinks / Cerveceria Hondureña / 64
1948 acq / soap, oils, paperboard / Fabrica de Manteca y Jabón / 51
1961 / paperboard boxes / Manufacturera de Carton / 70
1965 acq / cement / Cementos de Honduras SA / 25
1965 acq / cottonsed oils / Industria Aceitera
1968 / extruded polyethylene bags / 100
———— / wood containers / Envases Industriales / 95
———— / plastic materials, synthetics / Plasticos SA / 100
Jamaica ———— / bananas / Banana Co. of Jamaica
Mexico ———— / bananas / Southern Banana
Neth. Ant. ———— / commercial fishing / Marine Resources / 100

Nicaragua 1971 / bananas, other fruits / Standard Fruit
Panama ——— / bananas / Bananera Antillana SA / 100
P. Rico 1975 acq / tuna fishing / 100
1977 acq / tuna cannery / 100
Surinam 1969 / canned seafoods, wire, paperboard / Surinam American Indus.
1969 / commercial fishing / Surinam Industrial Marine Corp.

Caterpillar Tractor Co.

Brazil 1954 / repair parts / Caterpillar do Brasil SA
1974 / diesel engines, bulldozers / Caterpillar do Brasil SA
Mexico 1962 / mfgs replacement parts / Caterpillar Mexicana SA / 100

Central Soya Co., Inc.

Brazil 1970 / feed mill / Central Soya-Racoes Granjeiro / 100
1972 acq Dutch parent / cattle feed
1974 / prepared feeds / Central Soya Alimentos
1974 / prepared feeds / Granjas Reunidas SA / 100
1974 / prepared feeds / Provimi do Brasil SA / 100
1974 / prepared feeds / Riberiarao Bonita SA / 93
Guatemala 1968 acq / feed mill / Alimentos Mariscol SA / 80
1968 acq / poultry proc. / Industria Nacional de Concentrados
Integrales / 100
Jamaica 1971 jv / feed mill / Central Soya of Jamaica / 55
P. Rico 1963 / feed mill / Central Soya of Puerto Rico / 100
1977 / feed mill / Central Soya of Puerto Rico / 100
Trinidad 1968 jv / feed mill / Master Mix Feeds of Trinidad / 85

Clark Equipment Co.

Argentina 1960 acq / constr. equip. / Eximia Indust. Clark Argent. SA /100
Brazil 1958 / axles & trans, farm mach. / Equipamentos Clark SA / 96
1961 acq / trucks / Empilhaderais Clark SA / 98
1970 / refrig. equip. / Industrias Campos Salles / 95
1971 / truck trailers
1974 / constr. equip. / Equipamentos Clark SA / 100
Mexico 1965 jv / trans., constr. equip. / Trans. e Equipos Mexicanos SA / 26
1966 / trucks, constr. mach. / Prod. Indust. Metalicos SA / 40
1969 acq / refrig. equip. / Refrigeracion Ojeda SA / 45
P. Rico 196– / truck trailers
Venezuela 1966 acq / refrig. equip. / 13

Coca-Cola Co.

Argentina	1941 / bottling & concentrates / Coca-Cola SA Argentina de Bebidas / 100
Brazil	——— / instant coffee
Colombia	1955 / bottling & concentrates / Coca-Cola de Colombia SA / 100
	——— / bottling & concentrates / Coca-Cola Indust. e Comer. SA / 100
	——— / Embotelladora de Barranquilla SA
	——— / Embotelladora Tropical SA
C. Rica	——— / concentrates / Coca-Cola Inter-american Corp.
Cuba	1935 / 1960: nat. / bottling & concentrates / Cia Embotteladora Coca-Cola SA / 100
El Salv.	1960 acq US parent / instant coffee
Ecuador	——— / bottling / Guayaquil Bottling
Guatemala	1961 acq / confectionery, canned foods / Productos Alimenticias Sharp SA / 51
	1967 acq / coffee, confectionery, syrups / Industria de Cafe SA / 51
	——— / Industrias del Pacifico SA
Mexico	1977 jv / shrimp farm
	——— / frozen orange juice / Cléaver-Brooks de Mexico SA
	——— / concentrates / Cia Coca-Cola de Mexico SA
Panama	bottling / Coca-Cola Export Co.
Peru	bottling & concentrates / Coca-Cola Inter-american Corp.
P. Rico	1974 acq / Coca-Cola Bottling Co. / 100
	——— / concentrates
Uruguay	——— / concentrates / Coca-Cola SA Fabrica de Bebidos Carbonates
Venezuela	1960 / bottling & concentrates / The Coca-Cola Export Corp.
Vir. Is.	——— / bottling / Coca-Cola Bottling Co.

Colgate Palmolive (Riviana Foods)

C. Rica	1970 acq
Mexico	1972 / Riviana de Mexico SA
Guatemala	1970 acq / fruits, ketchup, babyfoods / Alimentos Kern SA
	1970 acq / 1971 / canned foods / Ducal SA / 100

ConAgra Inc.

P. Rico	1958 / flour milling / Molinos de Puerto Rico / 100
	1958 / mixed feeds mill / Molinos de P. Rico de las Piedras / 100
	1960 / corn mill / Molinos de P. Rico de Hatillo / 100
	1961 / bagasse dehydr. plant / Molinos de Guanica / 100
	1965 / livestock dev. farms / 100

1965 / poultry proc., poultry hatcheries / 100
1966 acq / 1966: sold / poultry proc., baby chicks
1970 / mixed feeds mill / Molinos de P. Rico de las Piedras / 100
Venezuela 1978 acq / grain storage, animal feed, proc. seed / 49

Consolidated Foods Corp.

C. Rica 1979 acq US parent / women's hosiery
Cuba 1920 acq / sugar mills, lands / Cardenas American Sugar / 100
Dom. Rep. 1979 / bras, swimwear
Jamaica 1969 acq US parent / cleaning products, brushes
Mexico 1964 acq US parent / shrimp proc. / Booth Fisheries / 100
1979 acq US parent / women's hosiery / Bal-Mex SA
1979 acq US parent / women's hosiery / Canon Mills SA
Nicaragua 1964 acq US parent / shrimp proc. / Booth Nicaragua SA / 54
1968 jv / shrimps, lobsters / Nicarmar SA / 50
P. Rico 1979 acq US parent / women's hosiery
1979 acq US parent / knitwear
1979 acq US parent / bras, swimwear / Bali Puerto Rico
Venezuela 1959 acq / 1961: sold / vinegars, sauces / Alimentos Mundiales / 51

Continental Grain Co.

Brazil 1976 / soybean proc.
Ecuador 1966 jv / flour mill / Harinas del Ecuador
Guadaloup ——— / flour mill
Nicaragua ——— / crop prep services / Continental Milling
P. Rico ——— / large flour mill
Venezuela ——— / flour mill

C.P.C. International

Argentina 1928 / oils, adhesives, feeds / Refinerias de Maiz SA / 100
1966 / synth. adhesives / 100
1968 acq / cheese / Quelac SAIC / 100
Brazil 1930 / corn milling / Refinacoes de Maiz / 100
1963 / dextrine, chemicals / CPC Brazil / 100
1969 acq / biscuits / Aymore Industrias Alimenticias / 100
1972 / soup cubes, mayonnaise / 100
1973 / feeds, soups, oils, textiles / Refinacoes de Milho / 100
——— / dehydrated foods, soups / Knorr Brazil / 100
——— / wet corn milling / Refinacoes de Milho Monde Ste
——— / Aymore Productos Alimenticos e Domesticos / 100

Chile   1961 jv / hybrid seeds / Industrias Agro-pecuarias / 57
        1963 / starches, glucose, dextrines / Industrias de Maiz / 75
        ———— / canned fruits, vegetables / Alimentos Knorr
Colombia 1933 / wet corn milling, pancake bread, baby foods, soups / Maizena
        SA / 100
        1961 / fruits, vegetables / Frutera Colombiana SA / 100
        ———— / Empresa Agrícola Occidente SA
Dom. Rep. 1930 acq / 1951: sold / tapioca, tapioca starch / 100
Guatemala 1965 acq / corn processing / E. Castellanos Crocker Sucs. / 100
        ———— / wet corn milling, oils, feeds, adhesives / Productos de Maiz y
        Alimentos SA
Honduras 1973 acq / corn starch, veg. oil / Almidones del Istmo SA / 100
Mexico   1930 / starches, glucose, dextrine / Productos de Maiz SA / 100
        1970 acq / aerosol cosmetics / Aerobol SA / 100
        ———— / wet corn milling, confectionery / Productos de Maiz SA
Nicaragua ———— / fertilizers, chemicals / Cia Fertilizantes Superior / 59
Peru   1961 jv / corn starch, glucose, cereals / Alimentos y Productos de Maiz
        SA / 75
        ———— / wet corn milling / Alimentos y Productos de Maiz SA / 75
P. Rico   1973 / corn & soya oil ref. / 100
Uruguay   1959 / corn processor / Industrializadora de Maiz SA / 100
        1964 acq / corn oil & starch / Maizola SA / 100
Venezuela 1960 / bouillon cubes, soups / Primaven SA / 100
        1968 acq / farming land for peanuts, sorghum, beans / 100
        ———— / wet corn milling, oils, flour / Alfonzo Rivas
        ———— / dehydrated fruits, vegetables / Aliven SA
        ———— / dehydrated fruits, vegetables / Productos Knorr SA

John Deere & Co.

Argentina 1957 / tractors / John Deere Argentina / 100
        1962 acq / iron & steel foundries / Cindelmet SA / 36
Mexico   1956 / farm implements, tractors / John Deere SA / 70
Venezuela 1978 jv / tractors / 20

Del Monte Corp.

Brazil   ———— / canned fruits, veg. / Conservas Del Monte
        ———— / fruits & veg. / Legumes Frescos do Brasil
C. Rica   1966 acq / fruit & vegetable / Del Campo / maj
        1968 acq US parent / banana plantation / Bandeco / 100
        ———— / canned fruits, veg / Del Campo / under 50
        ———— / bananas, farm management / Banana Dev. Corp
        ———— / food prep / Monte Libano SA

———— / bananas / Productores Unidos de Banano SA
Cuba 1960 / 1961: nat. / canned foods / 100
Ecuador 1966 / tuna freezing, storage / Del Monte SA / 100
Guatemala 1972 acq / banana plantations / Cia de Desarrollo Bananero
———— / food prep / Del Monte Int'l
Haiti 1929 / 1933 / pineapple plantation / Haitian Pineapple / 100
Mexico 1960 / canned tomatos, chilis, fruits / Productos Del Monte SA / 60
1965 acq / snack foods / Papas y Fritos de Monterrey SA / 50
P. Rico 1962 / 1977 / canned tuna / Del Monte de Puerto Rico / 100
———— / canned vegetables, juices / Conservas Del Monte de Puerto Rico / 100
Venezuela 1965 / canned fruits, vegetables, meats / Cia Venezolanos de Conservas / 60

Diamond Shamrock Corp.

Brazil 1961 jv / chlorine & caustic soda / Carbocloro SA / 50
1978 / chlorine & caustic soda / Carbocloro SA / 50
Chile 1978 / chlorine & caustic soda / Petroquimica Nacional SA / 100
Mexico 1956 / D.D.T. / Insecticidas Diamond del Pacifico / 51
1956 / 1974: sold / D.D.T. / Insect. y Fert. Diamond del Norte / 69
1959 / insecticides
1965 jv / 1971: sold / metal & paint finishes / Diacromex SA / 52
1965 jv / agric. defoliants, synth. detergents
1967 acq US parent / Nopco Industrial SA / 50
1968 / tanning plant / Quimica Retzloff Interamericana SA / 100

Esmark (-Swift)

Argentina 1909 / meatpacking / Cia Swift de la Plata SA / 100
1943 / veg. oil ref., dairy & poultry, grain mill / 100
1958 acq / dairy & poultry / 100
1958 acq / poultry / 100
1960 acq / cattle ranches
———— jv / cattle ranch
Barbados ———— / playtex products / IPC Barbados / 100
Brazil 1916 / meatpacking / Cia Swift do Brasil / 100
1954 jv / cattle breeding / Cia Swift do Brasil
———— / cottonseed oil mill
———— / packing plant
———— / cottonseed oil mill & refinery
———— / bras, toiletries / Playtex Industrial / 100
Cuba 19— / 1960: nat. / meat products, cottonseed oil refinery / 100
Mexico 1954 acq / chicken hatchery / Swift y Cia SA / 100

1968 acq US parent / petroleum white oils / min
1969 acq / phtalic anhydrides / SOSA / 100
1969 acq / ethylene glycol, propylene glycol / IDESA / 100
1970 acq / maleic anhydride / 18
———— / bras, toiletries, rubber prod. / Playtex de Mexico SA / 100

Panama 1962 / meatsmoking / Swift & Co. / 100
———— / Nutriproducts / 100
Paraguay 1917 / 1921 / meatpacking / Frigorifico de Carnes
P. Rico 1975 acq US parent / women's lingerie, bras / Playtex Manati
Uraguay 1912 / meatpacking / Cia Swift de Montevideo / 100
Venezuela ———— / fertilizers / Swift Chemical SA / 100

Ford Motor Co.

Brazil 1962 / 1967 / tractor assembly / Ford Motor do Brasil SA / 100
1975 / farm tractor assembly / 100

Foremost-Mckesson, Inc.

Argentina 1961 acq / dairy products / 41
———— / cheese, milk / La Vascongada / 100
Colombia 1960 acq / drugs / Organizacion Farmaceutica Americana / 50
1960 acq / drugs / Quimica Schering Colombiana SA / 50
1960 acq / cosmetics / Productos de Belleza SA / 100
1960 acq / cosmetics / Industrial de Cosmeticos SA / 100
———— / 1978: sold / mfg., mkt. drugs / 20
———— / drug prep. / Calox Colombiana SA / 100
———— / drug prep. / Organizacion Farmaceutica Americana SA / 100
El Salv. 1960 acq / 1979: sold / dairy products, cheese / Empresas Lacteas
Foremost SA / 70
1964 acq / drugs / Corp. Bonima de El Salvador / 98
Equador ———— / drugs, toiletries / Calox Ecuatoriana SA / 100
Guatemala 1960 acq / dairy products / Foremost Dairies de Guatemala SA / 70
Honduras 1970 / ice cream, condensed milk / Famosa SA / 75
Mexico 1961 acq / drugs, cosmetics / Laboratorios McKnal SA / 50
1965 acq / drugs / Celco SA / 100
———— / scientific instruments / Curtin de Mexico SA
———— / chemicals / Drogas y Productos Quimicos SA / 60
Panama 1966 / grain mill products
———— acq / drugs / 100
Venezuela 1949 / dairy products / 10
1960 / dairy products / Industrias Lacteas de Carabobo / 26
1963 acq / drugs / Laboratorios Biogen de Caracas / 20

1964 acq / dairy products / 100
——— / 1978: sold / mfg, mkt drugs / 20
——— / drugs / Laboratorios Calox / 90

General Mills, Inc.

Brazil 1965 jv / 1977: sold / methyl, cellulose, epoxy resins / Indusquima SA / 50
Cayman ——— / shellfish, finfish / Aquaculture Farms / 100
Chile 1967 / flour, cereals / General Mills de Chile Alimentos / 50
Guatemala 1959 jv / flour milling / Industria Harinera SA / 47
1962 / flour, cereals / Industria del Maiz SA / 50
Mexico 1956 acq / plastics / 100
1957 / epoxy resins / General Mills de Mexico SA / 100
1967 acq / cookies, pasta & flour prod. / Productos de Trigo SA / 50
1970 acq / toys / Novedades Plasticos / 75
——— / Jamarex SA / 92
——— / Lili-Ledy SA / 100
Nicaragua 1962 jv / flour / General Mills de Panama SA / 50
——— / grain mill prods / Panalimentos SA / 100
Peru 1968 acq US parent / 1973: nat. / marine oils, fish proc. / Glouster Peruvian SA / 100
Venezuela 1958 acq / flour / 20
1965 / grain mill prod. / General Mills de Venezuela / 67
——— / grain mill prods. / Poliamidas de Venezuela / 49

General Foods Corp.

Bahamas 1942 / canned foods / General Seafoods / 100
Brazil 1957 / beverages / Industrias Alimenticias Gerais SA / 60
1960 acq / ice cream, confectionery / Kibron Industrias Alimenticias SA / 100
1978 / chewing gum / Kibon SA
Mexico 1946 / 1960 / licensing co. / General Foods SA / 100
1950 / 1952: sold / shrimp proc. / General Seafoods de Mexico
1960 acq / confectionery / Industrial Fenix SA / 100
1961 acq / dehydrated soups / Rosa Blanca SA / 100
1962 acq / instant coffee / Cafes de Mexico SA / 85
1967 / vegetables / Birdseye de Mexico SA / 100
1970 acq US parent / burpee farm
Peru 1956 / confectionery / General Foods Peruana / 100
P. Rico 1964 jv / instant coffee / Cafe Instante de Puerto Rico / 50
Venezuela 1956 / proc. chocolate products / La India / 67

Gerber Products Co.

C. Rica 1968 / babyfood / Productos Gerber de Centro-america SA / 100
Mexico 1959 / babyfood / Gerber Products / 80
P. Rico 1966 / babyfoods / Gerber Products of Puerto Rico / 100
Venezuela 1967 acq / babyfoods, preserves / Venezolana Alimentos / 75
1971 / foods

W. R. Grace & Co.

Argentina 1942 / sealing compounds / Dewey and Almy / 100
1954 acq / plastics / 100
Brazil 1952 acq / 1970: sold / electrical magnetic prod. / Eriez / 51
1952 jv / D.D.T., agric. chem.
1954 / sealing compounds / Productos Quimicos Darex / 100
1960 acq / phtalic anhydrides / Industria Quimica Productos Ftalicas
1962 acq / 1970: sold / plastic converting / Vulcan Material Plastico SA
/ 50
1962 acq / 1970: sold / Vulquimica Industrias Quimicas SA / 50
1964 / ammonia plant
1969 jv / shrimp trawling & proc.
1969 jv / 1973: sold / tin dredging / Mineracao Brasilense SA / 50
Bolivia 1918 / 1973: sold / tin mining / Int'l Mining / maj
1925 / cement / 64
1966 jv / tin placer mine / Empresa Minera / 75
1939 acq / 1968: sold / flour milling / 53
Chile 1914 acq / 1963: sold / cotton, rayon / Tejidos Caupolican SA / 79
1916 acq / nitrate lands / Tarapaca and Tocopilla Nitrate
1920 acq / 1969: sold / edible oils, paints, sugar / Cia de Industrias
Azucar / 78
1932 acq / 1963: sold / worsteds, woolen mill / Panos Bellavista SA /
34
1945 acq / 196–: sold / electric light bulbs / Electromat SA / 25
1962 acq / ——: sold / foods / Hucke SA / 58
1968 jv / phtalic anhydrides / Petrocoia
—— / 1969: sold / fishmeal / Eperva SA / 51
—— / Fabrica de Panos las Tres Pascuales
Colombia 1940 acq / 1958: sold / textile mill / Tejidos El Condor
1950 / confectionery / La Rosa SA / 100
1955 acq / paints / Ico Pinturas SA / 55
1956 acq / canned fruits / Conservas California SA / 100
1958 acq / 1969: sold / naphtalene, phtalic anhydrides / Carboquimica
SA / 58
1958 acq / resins, formaldehyde / Quimica Proco SA / 100

1960 jv / pulp & paper mill / Productora de Papeles SA / 50
1965 acq / 1970: sold / coated plastic products / Sinteticos SA / 100
1972 jv / paper mill / 50
1972 jv / paper mill / Productora de Papeles SA / 50

C. Rica 1964 acq / biscuit & candy / Felipe Pozuelo e Hijos / 80

Cuba 1950 / 1960: nat. / bagasse paper mill / 100
1953 acq US parent / 1960: nat. / pyrite sulphur bearing ores / Davison Sulpher

Dom. Rep. 1969 acq / fertilizer mixing / Antilles Chemical

Ecuador 1956 / paints / 67
1961 jv / corrugated boxes / 33
1967 / corrugated boxes / 1

Guatemala 1965 / 1970: sold / canned fruits, ketchup, babyfoods / Ducal SA / 100
1967 acq / 1970: sold / fruits, ketchup, babyfoods / Alimentos Kern

Jamaica 1969 acq / fertilizer mixing / Antilles Chemical

Mexico 1959 / sealing compounds / Productos Darex / 100
———— / 1961: sold / corrugated cartons & containers

Neth. Ant. 1969 acq / 1977: closed / ammonia / Antilles Chemical
1969 acq / fertilizer mixing / Aruba Chemical Industries

Peru 1884 / sugar estate, sugar alcohols / Cartavio / 100
1903 acq / cotton mills / Inca Cotton Mill / 100
1905 acq / cotton mill / Vitarte / 100
1917 acq / cotton mills / Victoria / maj
1926 acq / sugar estate, paper mill / Soc. Paramonga / 100
1946 / bakery, confectionery / Arturo Fields / 70
1959 / 1973: nat. / caustic soda & chlorine / Alcalis Peruanos / 100
1961 / 1973: nat. / extensible paper, multiwall bags / Soc. Agricola Paramonga / 100
1962 acq / canned foods / 61
1964 acq / ————: sold / fishmeal / Cia Pesquera La Gariota / 100
1966 / 1977: sold / copper and tin mine / Minsur
1967 / 1973: nat. / corrugated boxes / 100
1967 / 1973: nat. / paper & pulp mill / 100
1967 / 1973: nat. / paper mill / Papalera Trujillo / 100
1967 acq / base-metal mining / Cia Minera Alianza / min.
———— / 1970: sold / polyvinylchloride / Interquimica SA
———— / 1970: sold / paints / Fabrica de Pinturas Venecedor SA
———— / 1973: sold / paints
———— / 1973: nat. / agric. chemicals / 20
———— / packaging firm / Envases San Martí
———— / copper, lead, zinc mining / Minera Atacucha

P. Rico 1957 / pulp & paper mill / Porto Rican Container
1959 acq / blended fertilizers / San Miguel Fertilizer
1959 jv / 1970 / ammonium sulfates / Caribe Nitrogen / 49
1969 jv / oxo-alcohols / Oxochem Enterprise / 50

St. Lucia 1969 acq / fertilizer mixing / Antilles Chemical

Trinidad   1958 jv / anhydrous ammonia, urea / Federation Chemicals / 100
1975 jv / anhydrous ammonia / Trinidad Nitrogen / 49
Venezuela 1960 / can sealing / Productos Darex SA / 68

Greyhound (Armour Co.)

Argentina 1909 acq / meatpacking / Soc. Anonima La Blanca SA / 33
1917 / 1958: sold / meatpacking / Armour de la Plata SA / 100
1951 / insulin, trypsin / 100
Brazil   1917 / 1958: sold / meatpacking / Armour do Brasil / 100
1923 / 1958: sold / meatpacking / 100
1963 acq / hydroxides, oxychlorides / Quimica Reheis do Brazil / 100
Colombia 1964 / pharmac., surgical sutures / Armour Farmaceutica SA / 100
Cuba   1916 / 1960: nat / fertilizer mixing / Armour Co. SA / 100
Mexico   1964 acq / drugs / Armour Farmaceutica SA / 100
———— / Immobiliaria Dual SA / 50
———— / Industrias Herdial SA / 50
Panama   ———— / foods / Armour Panama SA / 100
———— / meatpacking
Paraguay 1923 acq U.S. parent / meatpacking and lands / Frig. San Salvador /
100
P. Rico   193– / fertilizer mixing / Armour Fertilizer Works
Uruguay 1963 acq U.S. parent / ind. chemicals / Quimica Tec SA / 100
1911 / 1958: sold / meatpacking / Frigorifico Artigas / 100

Gulf & Western Industries, Inc.

Dom. Rep. 1917 / sugar cane lands, mill / Central Romano Corp. / 100
1926 acq / sugarmill & lands / Ingenio Santa Fe / 100
1953 / chemicals / Romano By-Products / 100
1975 jv / cement plant / min
———— / beef cattle
———— / resorts & tourism
Mexico   1969 acq / auto parts / Produciones Auto-motorices SA / 100
Paraguay ———— / farming & cattle lands
P. Rico   1903 / 1970: sold / sugarmill & lands / Guanica Centrale / 100
1926 acq / cigars / GHP Cigar / 100
1940 acq / cigars, cigarettes, boxes / Porto Rican American Tobacco /
100
1951 acq / cigars / Consol Cigar / 100
Venezuela 1973 jv / power & trans. components distr. / Plavica / 100

H. J. Heinz Co.

Argentina	———— / proc. fruits & veg / Alimentos Heinz
Brazil	1972 acq / 1975: sold / convenience foods / Pommy's Alimentos / 100
Mexico	1963 acq / 1973: sold / canned fruits / Empacadora La Cumbre SA / 80
	1964 acq / holding co., canned foods / Social Mex de Credito Indust / 80
	1964 acq / metal cans / Social Mex de Credito Indust / 80
Peru	1963 acq US parent / 1973: nat. / fishmeal / 97
	1963 acq US parent / fishmeal / 100
P. Rico	1963 acq US parent / canned fish / Star-kist Caribe / 100
	1968 / metal cans / 100
	———— / restaurant chain / Caribbean Restaurants / 70
Venezuela	1959 / canned fruits & veg, mayonnaise / Alimentos Heinz / 80

Hershey Foods Corp.

Cuba	1918 / 1946: sold / sugarmill / 100
	1919 acq / 192–: sold / sugarmills / 100
	1926 / 1946: sold / sugar ref
Brazil	1979 jv / pasta, biscuit, margarine / 40
Mexico	1969 acq / candy / Nacional del Dulces SA

International Harvester Co.

Argentina	1963 / farm implements / International Harvester SA / 100
Brazil	1949 / 1967: sold / truck assem. / I. H. Maquinas SA / 100
	1978 acq / combines / Maquinas Agricolas Ideal / 35
Cuba	192– / 1960: sold / sisal fiber, henequen lands / I. H. of Cuba
El Salv.	1965 / truck, tractor assembly / I. H. de Centro-america SA / min
Mexico	190– / hemp ranch / 100
	1947 / farm implements / I. H. Mexico SA / 100
	1964 / truck assem / I. H. Mexico SA / 100

International Minerals & Chemicals

Argentina	———— / pharmac. & veterinary products
Brazil	1917 acq / mines / E. J. Lavino
	———— / pharmac. & veterinary products
Colombia	chemicals, fertilizers, sulfuric acid / Cia. de Productos Quimicos Nacionales
Mexico	1957 acq / barite mine / Minquim Internacional SA / 100

1960 acq / 1963: sold / veg dehydrating / maj
1967 jv / sulphur explor. / Azufrera Intercontinental SA / 16
1968 acq US parent / fluorspar mining / Fluorita de Mexico SA / 100
1971 jv / hydroflouric acid / min
———— / amino products
———— / pharmac. & veterinary products

International Multifoods

Brazil 1977 acq / speciality fruit & vegetables / Pommerening Conservas / 45
1979 acq / pasta, manioc flour, cornmeal / Productos Alimenticios SA / 85
Ecuador 1962 acq / 1976: sold / animal formula feeds / Molinos Champion SA / 100
Mexico 1965 acq / animal formula feeds / La Hacienda SA / 50
1973 acq / fast-food chain / Doni Satellite SA / 66
———— / hybrid seeds / min
———— / hybrid seeds / Procesadora de Semilla SA / 100
———— / prepared feeds / Las Martinez SA / 100
———— / prepared feeds / Molinas Champion SA / 10
Panama ———— / prepared feeds / Fabrico / 100
———— / prepared feeds, hatcheries / Super-Ave Intl SA / 100
Trinidad 1960 / flour mill / 100
Venezuela 1958 acq / flour mill / Molinos Nacionales / 98
1963 / formula feed / Molinos Nacionales / 100
1965 / rolled oats / Molinos Nacionales / 100
1966 / Super-Ave
1970 acq / corn flour mill / Derivados y Alimentos del Maiz / 100
1971 acq / precooked corn flour / 100
1979 / flour mill expansion
———— / Super-S
———— / Harinas Juana Damca
———— / prepared feeds / Agencia Nacionales / 100
———— / prepared feeds / Descarga de Granos / 100
———— / flour / Harinas Juana Damca / 100
———— / prepared feeds, hatcheries / Industrias de Maiz Cumana SA / 100
———— / flour, feeds, bakery prods, poultry / Molinos Nacionales / 98
———— / prepared feeds / Servicios de Computacion y Contabilidad / 100
———— / prepared foods / Super-S / 100

International Proteins Corp.

Ecuador 1971 acq / shrimp proc / Empacadora Nacional SA / 100
El Salv. 1978 jv / langostino proc / Empresa Pesquera Salvadoreña SA

Panama	1969 / fishmeal / Pesquera Taboguilla SA / 100
	1969 acq / fishmeal / Industrias Marinas SA / 100
	1971 acq / fish proc / Excellent Products SA / 100
	1971 acq / Pescadora SA
	1971 acq / Abbattoir SA
Peru	1968 acq / 1973: nat. / fishing & fishmeal / 100
	1969 acq / 1973: nat. / fishmeal / Pesquera Meilan SA / 100

Kellogg Co.

Argentina	1968 / cereals, proc veg / Kellogg Argentina / 100
Belize	1968 acq / Brit. Hond. Fruit Co. / 75
	———— / prepared feeds / Belize Feed Co. / 78
	———— / food prep / Belize Food / 75
	———— / food prep / Caribbean Foods / 75
	———— / food prep / Salada Belize
Brazil	1962 / cereals, cake / Kellogg's Prod Alimenticios / 100
	1970 acq / breads / Dietrigo Indust de Prod Alimenticios / 100
Colombia	1960 / cereals, bakery / Kellogg de Colombia SA / 100
Guatemala	1971 / cereals, proc veg / Kellogg de Centro-america SA / 100
Jamaica	1968 / rolled oats / 75
	1968 acq Canad. parent / Salada Foods Jam. / 50
	———— / cereals / Caribbean Foods / 75
Mexico	1951 / cereals / Kellogg de Mexico SA / 100
	———— / 1977: sold / snack foods / Kellog de Mexico SA
Venezuela	1961 / cereals / Alimentos Kellogg / 100
	———— / cereals / Alimentos Kellogg SA

King Ranch, Inc.

Argentina	———— / cattle / King Ranch Argentina SA
Brazil	1954 jv / cattle / King Ranch do Brasil SA
Cuba	1952 jv / 1959: nat / cattle ranches / Becerra Cattle

Kraftco, Inc.

Argentina	1937 / dairy products / Alimentos Kraft Argentina / 100
Cuba	1930 acq US parent / dairy products / Kraft-Phenix Cheese / 100
	1957 / 1960: nat / proc cheese / Alimentos Kraft SA / 100
Guatemala	1968 / cheese / Alimentos Kraft / 100
Panama	1962 / dairy products / Kraft Foods SA / 100
	1977 / cheese proc. / Kraft Foods SA / 100
P. Rico	1964 / ice cream

Mexico   1955 / sauces, confections, canned fruits / Kraft Foods SA / 100
　　　　　1965 acq / margarine, cheese / Indust Carrancedo SA / 100
Venezuela 1955 / dairy products / Alimentos Kraft / 100
　　　　　1964 / Inversiones Kraft / 100
　　　　　——— / food prep. / Inversiones Kraft / 100

L.T.V. Corp. (Wilson Meats & Co.)

Argentina 1919 acq / 1962: sold / meatpacking / Frigorifico Argentina / 100
Brazil   1913 / meatpacking / Sultzberger / 23
　　　　　1918 / meatpacking / Frigorifico Wilson SA / 100
　　　　　192– acq / cattle lands / Brazilian Land and Cattle / maj.
Mexico   192– acq / cattle ranch
Uruguay   1918 / holding co. / Cia Wilson International SA / 100

Massey-Ferguson Ltd.

Argentina 1969 acq / tractors / Rheinstahl-Hanomag Cura SA
Brazil   1961 acq / diesel engines / Motores Perkins SA / 100
　　　　　1961 jv / tractors
　　　　　1971 / agri. implements / Massey-Ferguson do Brasil SA / 100
　　　　　1974 / const. machinery / 100
Mexico   1967 / 1979: sold / tractors
　　　　　1969 / 1979: sold / agric. implements / Ransomes de Mexico SA
Peru   1971 jv / tractors / Tractores Andinos SA / 51
　　　　　1976 jv / diesel engines

Nabisco, Inc.

Argentina ——— / toiletries / Farmaceuticos y Cosmeticos SA
　　　　　——— / drugs / JB Williams de Argentina
Brazil   ——— / drugs, toiletries / JB Williams Medicamentose Cosmeticos
Colombia ——— / Landers y Cia / 50.1
Dom. Rep. ——— / cookies, crackers / Tamara / 60
Guatemala ——— / toiletries / JB Williams y Cia / 100
Mexico   1953 acq / bakery prods / Fabricas Modernas SA / 50
　　　　　1970 acq / bakery prods / Prod Alimenticias Aurora SA / 50
　　　　　——— / toiletries / JB Williams SA
　　　　　——— / crackers, bakery prods / Nabisco Famosa SA
Nicaragua 1965 acq / biscuits, crackers / Indust Nabisco Cristal SA / 60
Panama   ——— / bakery, crackers / Nabisco Int'l SA
P. Rico   1961 acq / crackers / Arbona Hermanos 100
Venezuela 1941 / bakery products / 100
　　　　　1950 acq / cookies, crackers / Cia. Nacional de Galletas Nabisco / 60

National Distillers

Argentina	1964 acq / tire valves, motor parts / Bridgeport Argent / 100
	1967 acq / elect & mech auto parts / Indico Argent / 50
Bolivia	1968 acq / polyethylene film / Plastix Boliviana SA / 60
	1968 / alcohol blending / National Distillers SA / 83
Brazil	1969 jv / low density polyethylene / Poliolefinas SA / 28
	1975 acq / wines / Vinhos Danta Rosa SA / 20
	———— / dist liquor, chemicals / National Distillers do Brasil
Chile	———— / plastics, resins / United Polymers / under 50
Cuba	1924 / 1960: nat. / molasses storage & handling / Cuba Distilling / 75
	1951 acq US parent / molasses trans / Cia. Cubana de Transportes de Mieles / 10
Ecuador	1952 / Cia. Ecuatoriana del Piretro SA / 50
Mexico	1966 jv / distillery / Destilby SA
	———— / spec. chems / Quimica Miohoacana SA / 49
Panama	1946 acq / distillery / National Distillers SA / 50
P. Rico	1954 acq / 1959: sold / blending rum / JR Nieves & Co. / 50

Norton Simon

Argentina	1966 / ———: sold / beverage extract / Canada Dry
Bermuda	1964 / beverage extract / 100
Brazil	———— / beverage concentrate / Canada Dry do Brasil
	———— / toiletries / Max Factor do Brasil
Chile	1966 / ———: sold / beverage extract
C. Rica	———— / soft drinks / Canada Dry Bottling
Cuba	1943 / 1960: nat. / soft drinks / Cia de Refrescos Canada Dry de Cuba / 100
Guatemala	1963 acq US parent/ paints / 100
	———— / toiletries / Max Factor de Centro-america SA
Mexico	1963 acq US parent / paints / 100
	1966 / soft drinks, beverage extract
	196– / fruit juices, non-alcoholic bev / Extractos y Derivados SA / 51
	———— / distilled liquor, soft drinks, canned foods / Extractos & Derivado SA / 51
	———— / toiletries / Max Factor Mexicana SA
	———— / distilled liquor / Servicios Indust SA / 100
Nicaragua	———— / concentrate / Canada Dry
Panama	1963 acq US parent / paints / 100
P. Rico	1944 acq / ———: sold / rum distillery / Destileria de los Asociados Borinqen / 58

Pepsi Co

Argentina	1959 / concentrate / Pepsi-Cola Argentina / 100
	1963 / bottling / Embotteladora Pepsi-Cola / 100
	1963 acq / bottling
Bermuda	1957 / 1967 / bottling & concentrate / Pepsi-Cola / 100
Brazil	1951 / bottling / Pepsi-Cola do Brasil SA / 100
	1965 acq / beverages / 77
	1974 acq / fast foods / Chips Productos Alimenticios
	———— / food prep / Holbra-Productos Alimenticios e participacoes / 100
	———— / soft drinks / Pepsi-Cola Refrigerantes
	———— / Refrig Rio de Janiero
	———— / Refrig Sul Riograndenses SA / 86
Colombia	1963 / concentrate / Pepsi-Cola Interamericana SA / 100
C. Rica	———— / soft drinks / Pepsi-Cola
Cuba	1939 / beverage bottling / Cia Pepsi-Cola de Cuba / 100
	1943 acq / 1950: sold / sugar mill, distillery / Ingenios Azucarenos Matanzas / 100
Ecuador	1967 / beverages / Cotopaxi SA / 90
El Salv.	———— / soft drinks / Pepsi-Cola
Haiti	1970 acq US parent / baseballs, softballs / General Sports SA / 100
Mexico	1942 / 1945 / beverage syrup / Mexican-American Flavors SA / 100
	1955 jv / bottling / 51
	1947 / 1957: sold / beverages / Cia. Embotteladora Nacional SA / 51
	1966 / snack foods / 100
	1965 acq / snack foods / Selectos SA / 100
	1968 acq / cookies / Mac'Ma SA / 100
	———— / 1976: sold / vehicle leasing
	———— / soft drinks / Bebidas Purificadas de la Frontera SA / 100
	———— / concentrate / Embotelladora Occidente SA
	———— / concentrate / Embotelladora Bravo SA / 100
	———— / Inversiones Industriales SA / under 50
	———— / Pizza Hut
	———— / Productos Victoria SA / 100
	———— / bottling / 100
Nicaragua	———— / soft drinks / Embotelladora Nacional SA
Peru	———— / chewing gum / MISTI
P. Rico	1964 / concentrate / 100
	1970 acq US parent / sporting goods / Wilrico / 100
	1972 acq US parent / bottling / 100
	———— / can mfg
	———— / 1976: sold / vehicle leasing
Uruguay	1961 acq / bottling / Paso de los Toros SA / 100
	———— / concentrate / Pepsi-Cola Inter-americana

Venezuela 1969 acq / candy, fruit, pasta, ice cream / Pasteleria Viensa / 80
1972 / concentrate / Pepsi-Cola Inter-americana / 100

Pet, Inc.

Bahamas ———— / milk / General Milk / 35
Brazil 1957 / dairy products / Leite Gloria SA / 35
Chile 1966 acq US parent / commercial refrig. / Frio-Lux SA / 20
C. Rica 1967 acq / proc chocolate / Costa Rican Cocoa Products SA / 60
Cuba 1957 / 1960: nat. / metal cans
1937 / 1960: nat. / dairy products / 24
Dom. Rep. ———— / evaporated & condensed milk
Guatemala 1967 acq / commercial refrig. / Cia Americana de Refrigeracion / 30
Jamaica 1931 jv / milk / General Milk / min
Mexico 1946 / dairy products / 35
1964 acq / 1972: sold / frozen strawberries / Congeladora
Empacadora Nac SA / 100
1966 acq / preserves, sauces / Almacenes Refrigerantes SA / 100
1966 acq US parent / sausages, proc fruits, commercial refrig. /
American Refrigeration Products SA / 100
1968 acq / canned meats / Empacadora La India SA / 100
———— / meatpacking / Empacadora La India SA / 100
Panama 1935 / 1966: sold / dairy prods / 10
Peru 1941 / canned milk / Leche Gloria SA / 97
P. Rico 1964 acq / dairy prods / Toddy Venezolana
1964 acq / dairy prods / Milk Products SA / 100
Venezuela 1964 acq / milk, chocolate, bev. powders / Toddy Venezolana / 100

Pillsbury

El Salv. 1960 acq / wheat flour / Molinos de El Sal SA / 9
Guatemala 1966 acq / desserts, baking powder / Prod Alimenticios Imperial SA /
80
1966 acq / flour mill / Molinos Modernas SA / 25
1970 acq / corn chips / Kugarts SA / 100
Jamaica 1966 jv / flour & feed mill, fish proc / Jam Flour Mills / 32
Mexico 1965 / mushroom canning
1966 acq / cookies, crackers, pasta / Galletos 7 Pastas SA / 70
1967 acq / pasta / Alimentos Cora SA / 100
1972 acq / pasta, cookies / Rex Pasta SA / 100
1972 acq / pasta / Pastas Finas Coyocan SA / 100
———— / flour, cookies, crackers / Pillsbury de Mexico
Trinidad 1965 acq / flour mill / 9
Venezuela 1960 acq / flour products / Molinos Caracas Maracaibo / 70

1965 acq / pasta / Milani / 51
196– acq / animal feed / Protinal
1970 acq / leasing firm / Arrendamintas P & P SA / 70

Quaker Oats

Argentina 1954 acq / grain mill prods / Elaboradora Argentina de Cereales SA / 10
Brazil 1954 acq / oats / Productos Alimenticios SA / 100
1973 acq / sardines / Conservas Coquiero SA
Colombia 1954 / corn & oat prods, chocolate, feeds / Productos Alimenticios Quaker SA / 100
Jamaica ———— / Quaker Products Jamaica
Mexico 1935 / breakfast cereals / Productos Quaker de Mexico SA / 100
1959 / breakfast cereals / Productos Alimenticios SA / 100
1959 acq / breakfast cereals / 100
1970 acq / chocolate, biscuits / Fabrica de Chocolates La Azteca / 100
———— / toys, sporting goods / Fisher-Price de Mexico SA
———— / plastic materials / Manufacturas Plasticas SA
———— / plastic materials / Artefactos Plasticos SA
Nicaragua ———— / flour, cereals, wet corn milling / Quaker de Centro-america
Uruguay ———— / Molino Puritas
Venezuela 1960 / flour, malt bev., oats, cereals / Productos Quaker SA / 100
1973 acq / spec. cleaning items / Tempus
———— / pasta prods / Milani / 51
———— / Nevex

Ralston Purina

Argentina 1962 / chow plant / Purina de Argentina / 100
1967 / poultry proc / 100
Brazil 1965 / chow, feed mill / Purina do Brasil Alimentos / 100
1969 / chow
Chile 1966 / 1970: nat. / feed mill, broiler growing / Purina de Chile SA / 80
Colombia 1957 / chow mill / Purina / 75
1961 acq / poultry hatchery / Avicola Colombiana / 33
1962 / chow plant / Purina Colombiana SA / 100
1966 / breeder farm & hatchery
1969 / animal feeds / 100
Cuba 1958 acq / chow plant / 100
Ecuador 1963 acq US parent / fish canning / Industrial Manitobas / 100
Guatemala 1961 acq / poultry broilers / Incubadores Centro-americanos / 55
1961 acq / restaurants / Auto-Cafes Purina / 61
1961 acq / animal & poultry feeds / Purina de Centro-americana / 55

Jamaica 1963 acq / animal feed mill / Jamaica Feeds / 27
Mexico 1956 / chow, oilseed proc / Ralston Purina SA / 49
1961 / poultry farms, hatcheries / Pollitos Unidos de Mexico SA / 75
1964 acq / canned foods / 15
1964 / hatchery, breeder farm / 100
1966 acq / breeder farm, hatchery / 100
1966 jv / chow mill / 50
1966 acq / poultry proc / 100
1967 / chow plant / 100
1967 / poultry proc / 100
───── / 1977 acq US parent / poultry / 80
1978 / holding co. for livestock feed ops. / Industrias Purina SA / 49
───── / 1978 / livestock & poultry feed / 49
1979 acq / wheat- and rice-flour prods / Lance SA / 100
Nicaragua 1966 acq / animal feeds, poultry / Nutrimentos Balanceados SA / 51
1967 acq / grain mill prods / 51
Panama 1974 / shrimp nursery / 100
Peru 1963 acq US parent / 1968: sold / fishmeal / Pesquera Cruz del Sur SA / 100
1963 acq / 1968: sold / fishmeal / 100
1964 / chow plant / Purina Peru / 100
1968 / poultry proc. / Purina Peruana SA / 100
P. Rico 1963 acq US parent / tuna processing / National Packing / 100
───── / 1977 acq US parent / animal feed plant & warehouse
Venezuela 1957 acq / chow, feed mill / Productos & Consumidores Unidos / 100
1962 / poultry proc. / 100
1962 / hatcheries & breeder farm / Cargon de Venezuela / 33

A. E. Staley

Argentina 1969 / corn refining / Staley Argentina / 100
Honduras 1965 jv / 1970: closed / corn refining / Almidones de Centro-america SA / 50
Mexico 1968 acq / corn refining / Almidones Mexicanos SA / 50

Standard Brands, Inc.

Argentina 1934 / yeast / Fleischmann Argentina / 100
Brazil 1931 / yeast, baking powder, desserts / Standard Brands / 100
1957 acq / manioca starch / 100
1957 jv / evap milk, cans, whole milk / Leite Gloria / 100
1958 jv / instant coffee, prepared foods / Brasileira de Cafe Solurel / 40
1975 acq / snack foods / Pommy's / 100
───── / flavorings / Florasynth Industria e Commercio de Aromas

—— / dairy products / Leite Gloria do Nordeste SA / 100
—— / fabricated metal prods / Metalurgica Metacan / 100
—— / flour, tea, shortening / Prods Alimenticos Fleischmann e Royal
—— / tea production / Sociedade Brasileira Beneficiadora de Cha / 60

Colombia 1938 / yeast, tea, sauces / Cia Fleischmann Colombiana / 100
1963 jv / margarine, shortening / Bavaria SA / 51
1966 jv / food colors, flavors / 60
—— / flavors, colors, malt bev / Industria de Colores & Sabores SA / 100

C. Rica 1965 acq / margarine, shortening / Golden SA / 80
1966 acq / margarine, ice cream, veg oil / Aceitera Centro-americana SA / 60
—— / ice cream, desserts / Aceitera Centro-americana SA / 100
—— / fats, cooking oil / Standard Brands

Cuba 1929 acq US parent / 1960: nat. / yeast / Cia. de Levadura Fleischmann SA / 100
1957 / frozen egg packing plant / 100

Ecuador 1945 / yeast / Fleischmann Ecuatoriana SA / 100
El Salv. 1962 / baking powder, desserts / Pan American Standard Brands / 100
Guatemala 1965 acq / margarine, confections / Dely SA / 100
—— / confections, fruits, vegetables / Pan American Standard Brands

Guyana —— / food products / Pan American Standard Brands
Jamaica 1972 jv / yeast / West Indies Yeast / 72
—— / Pan American Standard Brands

Mexico 1966 jv / yeast / Industria Mexicana de Alimentos SA / 49
1967 / meat products / 100
1967 acq / candy / Productos Selmor SA / 51
1967 jv / yeast / 80
1970 jv / flavors, food fragrances
—— / food prep / Marcas Alimenticias Int'les SA / 100
—— / food prep / Pan American Standard Brands
—— / food products, confections / Florasynth SA / 50

Nicaragua —— / shortening, cooking oils / Pan American Standard Brands
Panama 1959 / shortening, desserts, flavorings / Pan American Standard Brands / 100
Paraguay 1959 acq / yeast / Pan American Standard Brands / 100
Peru 1939 / yeast, confections / Fleischmann Peruana / 100
P. Rico 1958 / yeast / Fleischmann Puerto Rico / 100
1970 / yeast
Trinidad 1955 / tea, desserts / 100
Trin. Tob. —— / food prep / Pan American Standard Brands
Uruguay 1945 / yeasts, desserts / Fleischmann Uruguay / 100
—— / ice cream, desserts, confections / Fleischmann Uruguana / 100

Venezuela 1955 / corn prods, yeast, tea, vinegar / Standard Brands Venezolana / 100

Stokeley–Van Camp, Inc.

Dom. Rep. 1968 acq / fruit & veg proc / Industrias Portela
Honduras 1963 jv / pineapple proc
P. Rico 1961 / pineapple proc / Stokeley–Van Camp / 100
Venezuela ———— / Newport de Venezuela / 100

Tenneco (J. I. Case)

Brazil 1971 / tractors, excavators / J. I. Case do Brasil / 100
1978 acq Fr parent / hydr excavators / Podain do Brasil / 100
Mexico 1976 jv / crawler tractors, heavy constr equip. / J. I. Case SA / 40
Nicaragua 1964 jv / mixes, fertilizers / Fertilizantes Superior SA

United Brands Co.

Cayman ———— / plastics, synthetics / Polymer United / 100
———— / shortening, cooking oils / Unimar
Colombia ———— / vegetables / Cia. Frutera de Sevilla SA
C. Rica 1899 / banana lands, railroad / Cia. Bananera de Costa Rica
1902 / railway / Northern Railway
1951 / palm oil proc / 100
1962 / banana boxes / 100
1965 acq / veg oils, margarine / Numar SA / 100
1968 acq / plastic bags & pipes / Polymer SA / 100
1971 jv / thermoformed products / Polipak de Costa Rica SA
Cuba 1901 / 1960: nat. / sugarmills / 100
1907 acq / 1960: nat. / sugarmill / Nipe Bay / 100
1913 acq / sugar lands / Saetia Sugar
1938 acq / dock terminals
Dom. Rep. 1898 acq / banana lands
195– / 196–: sold / mashed banana proc
Ecuador ———— / banana ops.
Guadaloup 1970 / bananas
Guatemala 190– / railways / Int'l Railways of Central America
1924 acq / 1972: sold / banana concession / Cia Agricola de Guatemala
———— / plastics, synthetics / Polymer
———— / Quellenhof Gmbh
Honduras 1913 acq / banana lands, railroad / Tela Railroad / 100

1929 acq US parent / sugarmill / Cuyamel Fruit / 100
1950 / palm oil proc. / Unimar / 100
1963 / banana boxes / 100
1965 / banana puree, babyfoods / Agricola Rio Tinto SA / 100
1968 / edible oils / Cia. Numar de Honduras SA / 100
———— / Empresa Hondurena de Vapores SA / 100
———— / Frig Hondurena SA
———— / crop prep services / Productos Acuaticos y Terrestres SA
———— / rubber, plastics & synthetics / Polymer Industrial SA

Jamaica   1885 / banana land
193– / sugarmill / Bernard Lodge Sugar Co
Mexico   1966 acq / 1977: sold / food proc. & canning / Clemente Jacques y Cia
SA / 100
Nicaragua ———— / 1968 / banana ops., tobacco / Cokra Development Co.
1968 acq / edible oils / Aceitera Corona SA / 77
———— / plastics, synthetics / Polimeros Centro-americanos
———— / fruit & vegetable proc / Aceitera Corona SA / 76
Panama   1899 / bananas / Chiriqui Land Co
1925 / experimental farm, manila fiber / 100
1927 acq / banana concession / Chiriqui Land Co
1962 / banana boxes / 100
1966 acq / polyethylene bags, pipe / Productos Plasticos SA / 100
1966 acq / polyethylene bags, pipe / Polymer Extrusion SA / 100
1969 / banana proc., babyfoods / Cia Processadora de Frutas /
100
Peru   1964 acq US parent / fish meal & oil / 33

Universal Foods Corp.

Brazil   197– / yeast / min
Colombia 197– / yeast / min
197– / yeast / min
C. Rica   197– / yeast / min
Guatemala 197– / yeast / min
Mexico   1962 acq / brewing
———— / Empresa Agricola Industrial SA
Peru   ———— / yeast, baking products
P. Rico   1964 acq
———— / Red Star de Puerto Rico
St. Lucia   197– / yeast / min

Warner-Lambert

Argentina 1938 / drugs / Lambert Pharmacal / 30
1954 acq / drugs / 50

	———— / gum, spec. foods
Brazil	1961 / drugs / Laboratorios Warner / 100
	1962 acq / gum / Chicle Adams / 100
	1966 acq US parent / ophthalmic lenses / American Optical do Brasil SA / 100
Chile	1959 / drugs / 100
	1965 / gum / Chicle Adams / 100
	193– / drugs
Colombia	1962 acq US parent / gum / Chicle Adams / 100
Cuba	193– / 1961: nat. / drugs
Dom. Rep.	———— / gum / Adams Dominicana SA
Ecador	1965
	———— / gum, spec. foods
Guatemala	1962 acq US parent / gum / Chicle Adams
	1961 / drugs / 100
Mexico	1917 / listerine, drugs / Lambert Pharmacal / 100
	1951 acq / ophthalmic goods / 50
	1962 acq US parent / gums / Chicle Adams SA / 100
	1965 acq / confectionery / La Cia Colonel SA / 80
	1966 acq US parent / ophthalmic goods / Cia Aomex SA / 100
	1972 / gum / Chicle Adams SA / 100
	———— / cosmetics / Cia Medicinal La Campana SA
Panama	———— / gum, spec. foods
Peru	1962 acq US parent / gum / Chicle Adam SA
	1964 / drugs
P. Rico	1962 / pharmac. & optical prod.
	1970 / breath mints, drugs / 100
	1971 / drugs / 100
	———— / gum, spec. foods
Uruguay	———— / drugs / Warner Lambert SA
	1962 acq US parent / gum / Chicle Adams SA
Venezuela	1960 / drugs / 80
	1962 acq US parent / gum / Chicle Adams SA / 100
	1970 acq US parent / Eversharp pens / 100
Vir. Is.	1964 acq / men's toiletries / West Indies Bay Co. / 100

Williams Co's

Brazil	1973 jv / phosphatic fertilizers / Uniagro Quimica SA / 40
	1977 / phosphatic rock, concentrate / Fosfago-Fosfatos de Goias SA / 49

Wrigley (Wm.) Jr. Co.

Mexico	1955 acq / confectionery, chewing gum / Productos de Calcio SA / 100
Nicaragua	1973 / gum base / Wrigley Import Co. / 100

Notes

Chapter 1. Crisis and Change in U.S. Agriculture: An Overview

1. *Dollars & Sense,* February 1978.
2. Calculated using figures from *Dollars & Sense,* February 1978 and *The Economist,* February 10, 1979.
3. Harriett Friedmann, "Simple Commodity Production and Wage Labor in the American Plains," *Journal of Peasant Studies* 6, no. 1 (1978): 71–100.
4. Kevin Kelly, "The Independent Mode of Production," *Review of Radical Political Economy* 11, no. 1 (1979): 38–46. Kelly has introduced the concept of the "independent mode of production" as a more general term for a system of independent household producers than Marx's "simple commodity production." In a thoroughly commercialized economy such as the U.S. has been since colonial times, the two terms can be used interchangeably. See also Karl Marx, *Capital* (New York: International Publishers, 1967), Vol. I, Chap. 32, and Friedmann, "Simple Commodity Production," p. 71.
5. From early in U.S. agriculture this has been the case. Contrary to popular myth, few homesteaders were able to start out "from scratch." Land almost always had to be purchased, whether from the federal government, royal grantees, or most important land speculators with roots in the East Coast or Europe. See Roy Robbins, *Our Landed Heritage: The Public Domain, 1776–1970* (Lincoln: University of Nebraska, 1976), and A. M. Sakolski, *The Great American Land Bubble* (New York: Harper & Bros., 1932).
6. Marx, *Capital,* Vol. I, p. 376.
7. *The Economist,* January 5, 1980.
8. Marx, *Capital,* Vol. I, pp. 380–86.
9. Robin Murray, "Value and the Theory of Rent, Part II," *Capital and Class* 4 (Spring 1975): 11–34.
10. Michael Perelman, *Farming for Profit in a Hungry World* (Montclair, N.J.: Allenheld, Osmun, 1977), p. 4.
11. Ibid., p. 75.
12. Ibid., passim. While Perelman is astute in pointing out the importance of the social division of labor for U.S. agriculture, he fails to treat the family farm system as a mode of production embedded in a capitalist system rather than as a branch of capitalist production. He uses terms such as "the new feudalism" to describe the relations between capital and farmers which are quite misleading.
13. Kelly, "The Independent Mode of Production," p. 46, and Richard Walker, "The Transformation of Urban Structure in the Mid-Nineteenth Century

and the Beginnings of Suburbanization," in Kevin Cox, ed., *Urbanization and Conflict in Market Societies* (Chicago: Maaroufa Press, 1978), pp. 165–212. This development has contributed to the confusion about the nature of the U.S. agricultural system and the failure to realize that the family farm system cannot be understood simply as a branch of capitalist production.

14. *The Economist,* January 5, 1978.
15. Roy Barner, "Science and Technology in Western Agriculture," *Agricultural History* 49, no. 1 (January 1975): 56–72. Barner also tries to use climate as an explanation for the advanced state of California's mechanization. The question as to why large holdings have prevailed in California more than elsewhere is one that has never been satisfactorily answered. The usual explanations, cheap labor and reliance on specialty crops in a mild climate, do not work, since big growers never relied extensively on either. (This has been pointed out to us by Ellen Liebman, Department of Geography, University of California, Berkeley, and is based on her doctoral research.)
16. Tenneco Corporation, *Agricultural Report* (Houston), November 1975. The growth of contract farming in recent years has been substantial and has fueled critics of monopoly power who hold that the plight of small farmers can be traced to this source alone.
17. Murray, "Value and the Theory of Rent."
18. *Time,* November 6, 1978.
19. Luther Tweeten and W. Huffman, "Structural Change: an Overview," paper presented at the National Rural Center Conference on Small Farms, Lincoln, Nebraska, February 1–3, 1979, p. 26.
20. *Miami Herald,* October 10, 1976.
21. Tweeten and Huffman, "Structural Change," p. 5. This level of concentration still puts agriculture well below any other industry in degree of concentration—which serves as another reminder of the lack of transformation to fully capitalist and corporate production relations.
22. *The Nation,* June 2, 1979.
23. As a result, the smallest farms have less debt and fewer bankruptcies than their larger brethren. Perelman, *Farming for Profit,* pp. 85, 88.
24. George Sternlieb and James Hughes, *Post-Industrial America: Metropolitan Decline and Interregional Job Shifts* (New Brunswick: Rutgers University Center for Urban Policy Research, 1976).
25. *The Progressive,* June 28, 1978, p. 23.
26. R. Rodefeld, "Farm Structure and Structural Type Characteristics: Recent Trends, Causes, Implication and Research Needs," revision of paper presented at National Rural Center, Small Farms Workshop (Phase II), Lincoln, Nebraska, February 1, 1979, p. 43.
27. *Forbes,* March 5, 1979.
28. Rodefeld, "Farm Structure," p. 63.
29. *The Economist,* January 5, 1980.
30. *The Nation,* June 2, 1979.
31. *The Economist,* January 5, 1980.

32. For a fuller analysis of labor and the family farm see Friedmann, "Simple Commodity Production."
33. Rodefeld, "Farm Structure," p. 64.
34. L. P. Schertz, et al., *Another Revolution in U.S. Farming* (Washington, D.C.: U.S. Department of Agriculture, 1979), pp. 303–34.
35. Ibid.
36. *The Economist*, February 10, 1979.
37. *Dollars & Sense*, February 1978.

Chapter 2. Exports for Empire: U.S. Agricultural Policies in the 1970s

1. Speech by Vice-President Walter Mondale in U.S. Department of Agriculture, *Foreign Agriculture*, August 1979.
2. For more on the monetary crisis see Harry Magdoff and Paul M. Sweezy, *The End of Prosperity: The American Economy in the 1970s* (New York: Monthly Review Press, 1977).
3. Duane Kujawa, ed., *American Labor and the Multinational Corporation* (New York: Praeger, 1973), p. 185, quoted in Steve Volk, "U.S. Workers in the International Economy: Trade and Production in Steel and Electronics," paper presented at a conference on the United States, U.S. Foreign Policy, and Latin American and Caribbean Regimes, Washington, D.C., March 1978.
4. For in-depth studies on the international restructing of industry see "Steelyard Blues: New Structures in Steel," *NACLA Report on the Americas* 13, no. 1 (January–February 1979), and "Car Wars," *NACLA Report on the Americas* 13, no. 4 (July–August 1979).
5. U.S. Department of Commerce, Bureau of Economic Analysis, *Survey of Current Business*, February and July 1977.
6. Hugh Mosley, "Is There a Fiscal Crisis of the State?" *Monthly Review* 30, no. 1 (May 1978): 34–45.
7. José de la Torre, "Latin American Exports of Manufactures to the United States: The Outlook for the Future," in Robert B. Williamson, William P. Glade, Jr., and Karl M. Schmitt, eds., *Latin American–U.S. Economic Interactions* (Washington, D.C.: American Enterprise Institute for Public Policy Research, 1974), p. 51, quoted in Volk, "U.S. Workers in the International Economy."
8. *United States International Economic Policy in an Interdependent World*, Report to the President submitted by the Commission on International Trade and Investment Policy (Washington, D.C., July 1971). Cited hereafter as the Williams Report.
9. Another influential report produced by a presidential task force in 1971 was "The United States in a Changing World Economy" (the Peterson Report). See NACLA, "Facing the Blockade," *NACLA's Latin America and Empire Report* 7, no. 1 (January 1973).
10. For discussion of agriculture's central role in U.S. international economic policy in the early 1970s see Raford Boddy and James Crotty, "Food Prices:

Planned Crisis in Defense of the Empire," *Socialist Revolution* 5, no. 1 (April 1975): 111–15, and "Can Agriculture Save the Dollar?" *Forbes*, March 15, 1973.

11. *Foreign Agriculture*, March 5, 1973.
12. See numerous issues of *Foreign Agriculture* for data and U.S. official views on overseas markets for U.S. farm exports.
13. *Foreign Agriculture*, December 5, 1977.
14. *Foreign Agriculture*, October 24, 1977.
15. For an account of the history of U.S. agricultural policy see Henry John Frundt, "American Agribusiness and U.S. Foreign Agricultural Policy," Ph.D. Dissertation, Rutgers University, New Brunswick, New Jersey, May 1975.
16. For a discussion of changes in the U.S. farm program during the Nixon administration see Jim Hightower, "Food, Farmers, Corporations, Earl Butz . . . And You" (Washington, D.C.: Agribusiness Accountability Project, 1973), mimeo; Daniel Balz, "Economic Report: Exports, High Food Prices Boost Administration Efforts to Reverse Farm Policy," *National Journal*, February 24, 1973; and Susan Sechler and Susan DeMarco, "The Fields Have Turned Brown" (Washington, D.C.: Agribusiness Accountability Project, 1975), mimeo.
17. Frundt, *American Agribusiness*.
18. "The New Economic Policy and Agricultural Trade," *Foreign Agriculture*, September 27, 1971.
19. Interview with the president of the National Grain and Feed Association, July 1975.
20. Frundt, *American Agribusiness*, p. 275; and William Robbins, *The American Food Scandal* (New York: William Morrow, 1974), p. 180.
21. Interview with Richard Bell, the assistant secretary of agriculture for international affairs and commodity programs, July 1975.
22. This account of U.S. government involvement in the Soviet grain sales is based primarily on information revealed in the hearings held by the Permanent Subcommittee on Investigations of the Senate Committee on Government Operations, *Russian Grain Transactions*, July 1973 (Washington, D.C.: Government Printing Office, 1973).
23. Ibid., p. 15.
24. *Foreign Agriculture*, August 1979.
25. *Christian Science Monitor*, October 23, 1978.
26. Williams Report.
27. Department of Agriculture data cited in Frundt, *American Agribusiness*, p. 272.
28. *National Journal*, February 19, 1977.
29. *Foreign Agriculture*, December 4, 1978.
30. *New York Times*, April 13, 1979.
31. *National Journal*, March 17, 1979 and June 17, 1979.
32. *Foreign Agriculture*, January 16, 1978.
33. *Wall Street Journal*, February 23, 1979.
34. *Business Week*, March 14, 1977.

35. Ibid., April 30, 1979.
36. *National Journal,* July 16, 1977.
37. *Business Week,* September 12, 1977.
38. See *New York Times,* various issues in January and February 1980, especially January 14, 1980.
39. *Business Week,* September 12, 1977.
40. Ibid.
41. See James Grant, "The Trilateral Stake: More Food in the Developing Countries or More Inflation in the Industrial Democracies," *Trialogue* 17 (Spring 1978).

Chapter 3. The U.S. Grain Arsenal: Food as a Weapon

1. Quoted in *Time,* November 11, 1974.
2. Harry Cleaver, "Will the Green Revolution Turn Red?" in Steve Weissman, ed., *The Trojan Horse* (San Francisco: Ramparts Press, 1974). See also Walter Cohen, "Herbert Hoover Feeds the World," in Weissman, ed., *The Trojan Horse.*
3. For more background on PL 480 see Israel Yost, "The Food for Peace Arsenal," *NACLA Newsletter* 5, no. 3 (May–June 1971).
4. Betsy Hartmann and James Boyce, *Bangladesh: Aid to the Needy* (Washington, D.C.: Center for International Policy, 1978) and Donald McHenry and Kai Bird, "Food Bungle in Bangladesh," *Foreign Policy* 27 (Summer 1977), quoted in Frances Moore Lappé and Joseph Collins, *Food First* (New York: Houghton Mifflin, 1977; Ballantine Books, 1979).
5. Institute for Food and Development Policy, *The Aid Debate* (San Francisco: Institute for Food and Development Policy, 1979), p. 13.
6. Judy Carnoy and Louise Levison, "The Humanitarians," in Weissman, ed., *The Trojan Horse.* See also "Christian Missions for the Empire," NACLA's *Latin America and Empire Report,* December 1973.
7. Israel Yost, "The Food for Peace Arsenal."
8. U.S. Agency for International Development, Office of Financial Management, *Status of Loan Agreements as of December 31, 1974* (W-22) (Washington, D.C.: AID, 1975).
9. U.S. General Accounting Office, *Use of Food Aid for Diplomatic Purposes,* January 1977 (Washington, D.C.: Government Printing Office, 1977), p. 26.
10. See Roger Burbach and Patricia Flynn, "U.S. Grain Arsenal," *NACLA's Latin America and Empire Report* 9, no. 7 (October 1975), p. 9.
11. See series of articles by Dan Morgan in the *Washington Post,* March 10, March 12, and July 5, 1975.
12. See for example, Melvin Burke, "Does 'Food for Peace' Assistance Damage the Bolivian Economy?" *Inter-American Economic Affairs* 25 (1971); and Leonard Dudley and Roger Sandilands, "The Side Effects of Foreign Aid: The Case of PL 480 Wheat in Colombia," *Economic Development and Cultural Change,* January 1975.

13. U.S. Congress, Senate Committee on Agriculture and Forestry, Hearings, *Policies and Operations of PL 480,* 84th Cong., 1st Sess. (1957), p. 129.

14. See Leslie Gelb and Anthony Lake, "Less Food, More Politics," *Foreign Policy* (Winter 1974–75); and Emma Rothschild, "The Politics of Food," *New York Review of Books,* May 16, 1974.

15. Central Intelligence Agency, Directorate of Intelligence, Office of Political Research, *Potential Implications of Trends in World Population, Food Production, and Climate,* August 1974.

16. For more on congressional control over foreign aid channels see "Foreign Aid: Evading the Control of Congress," *International Policy Reports,* January 1977 (Washington, D.C.).

17. For more on the operation of the Commodity Credit Corporation see U.S. Congress, Senate Committee on Appropriations, Hearings, *Agriculture and Related Agencies Appropriations for Fiscal Year 1978, Part 2,* 95th Congress, lst Session (1977), pp. 309–15.

18. *Washington Post,* March 14, 1975; *Des Moines Register,* February 19, 1975; NACLA interview with Department of Agriculture official, July 1975.

19. For background on U.S. policy and events in Chile during this period, see Elizabeth Farnsworth et al., "Facing the Blockade," in *New Chile,* (New York: NACLA, 1973).

20. Stephen Rosenfeld, "The Politics of Food," *Foreign Policy,* Spring 1974, p. 22.

21. Based on State Department figures.

22. For more on U.S. efforts to prop up the junta with aid, see "The United States: Propping Up the Junta," NACLA's *Latin America and Empire Report 8,* no. 8 (October 1974).

23. Interview with former official with the Commodity Credit Corporation, July 1975.

24. *Miami Herald,* November 26, 1973.

25. Center for International Policy, *Human Rights and the U.S. Foreign Assistance Program, Fiscal Year 1978, Part 1: Latin America* (Washington, D.C.: Center for International Policy, 1979), p. 45.

26. *Los Angeles Times,* September 22, 1974.

27. ECLA data quoted by Orlando Letelier "Economic Freedom's Awful Toll: The Chicago Boys in Chile," *The Nation,* August 28, 1976.

28. Data from a study by the vicariate of Chile quoted in "Chile's Politics of Hunger," *Pacific News Service,* July 22, 1976.

29. Unpublished study by William Goodfellow.

30. Testimony of William Goodfellow before the House Appropriations Committee on Agriculture, *Congressional Record,* May 9, 1974.

31. Interview with officials at the Department of Agriculture, including a former administrator of the Barter Program, July 1975.

32. Figures on the Barter Program were made available at the Department of Agriculture. The figures listed in the PL 480 Annual Reports under Title III do not accurately reflect the actual spending level, since the Barter Program had spending authority under the Commodity Credit Corporation Charter in addition to Title III.

33. *New York Times,* January 21 and February 19, 1975.
34. For more on the Carter administration human rights policy see "Carter and the Generals," *NACLA Report on the Americas* 8, no. 2 (March–April 1979).
35. See James Morrell, "The Big Stick: The Use and Abuse of Food Aid," *Food Monitor,* December 1977.
36. U.S. Congress, Senate Committee on Appropriations, Hearings, p. 314.
37. Ibid., p. 324.
38. U.S. Congress, Senate Committee on Agriculture, Nutrition and Forestry, *Future of Food Aid,* 95th Congress, 1st Session, 1977, p. 131.
39. Ibid.
40. *Washington Post,* November 22, 1977.
41. *Seven Days,* March 24, 1978.
42. *New Directions for U.S. Food Assistance: A Report of the Special Task Force on the Operation of Public Law 480* (Washington, D.C., May 1978).
43. U.S. Congress, House of Representatives, Report of a Staff Study Mission to the Committee on Foreign Affairs, *Economic Support Fund Programs in the Middle East,* 96th Congress, 1st Session, April 1979, p. 1.
44. *New York Times,* May 9, 1975.
45. U.S. House of Representatives, *Economic Support Fund Programs,* p. 7.
46. Morrell, "The Big Stick."

Chapter 4: Modernization Capitalist Style: An Introduction

1. Inter-American Development Bank figure quoted in *Miami Herald,* April 6, 1977. See also William C. Thiesenhausen, *Current Development Patterns in Latin America with Special Reference to Agricultural Policy* (Madison: Land Tenure Center, University of Wisconsin, January 1977).
2. For a critique of this modernization approach during the 1960s see James Petras and Robert LaPorte, "U.S. Policy Towards Agrarian Reform," in *Politics and Social Structure in Latin America* (New York: Monthly Review Press, 1970).
3. U.N. Food and Agriculture Organization, *Monthly Bulletin of Agricultural Economics and Statistics,* March 1976, pp. 5, 9.
4. Inter-American Development Bank, *IDB News,* (Washington, D.C.), October 1974.
5. A comprehensive compilation of agricultural production and trade statistics for Latin America is contained in U.S. Department of Agriculture, *Agriculture in the Americas. Statistical Tables* (Washington, D.C.: U.S. Department of Agriculture, 1977).
6. G. Mueller, *Les Oléagineux et la récente expansion du Soja au Brésil* (Paris: Centre de Recherche sur L'Amérique Latine et le Tiers Monde, 1979). Regular coverage of the soybean industry in Brazil also appears in U.S. Department of Agriculture, *Foreign Agriculture.*
7. The importance of focusing on *internal* social forces and contradictions (rather than *external* determinants) to explain the nature of social and economic

development in the third world has been convincingly argued by numerous Marxist scholars in recent years. See the important article by Robert Brenner, "The Origins of Capitalist Development. A Critique of Neo-Smithian Marxism," *New Left Review* 104 (May–June 1977): 25–92. This framework has been used to analyze contemporary Latin American reality and to critique the "dependency" theory originally formulated by A. G. Frank, in *Capitalism and Underdevelopment in Latin America* (New York: Monthly Review Press, 1969). See, for example, the articles in "Peasants, Capitalism and the Class Struggle in Rural Latin America," *Latin American Perspectives* 5, no. 4 (Fall 1978). For a skillful and well-researched application of this approach to analyzing agricultural development in Latin America see Salamón Kalmonovitz, *Desarrollo de la Agricultura en Colombia* (Bogota: Editorial la Carreta, 1978).

8. This treatment of agrarian social structures in Latin America is, for reasons of space, an oversimplification of a complex historical reality. Among the many works that discuss the evolution of Latin American agrarian structures in some depth are Solon Barraclough, *Agrarian Structures in Latin America* (Lexington, Mass.: D.C. Heath, 1973); Rodolfo Stavenhagen, *Agrarian Problems and Peasant Movements in Latin America* (New York: Doubleday, 1970); Andrew Pearse, *The Latin American Peasant* (London: Frank Cass, 1975) and "Agrarian Change Trends in Latin America," *Latin American Research Review*, Summer 1966; Ernest Feder, *The Rape of the Peasantry* (Garden City, N.Y.: Doubleday–Anchor, 1971); Frank, *Capitalism and Underdevelopment.*

9. See Pearse, *The Latin American Peasant,* for a discussion of the hacienda system throughout Latin America. A classic work on the hacienda system as it developed in Mexico is François Chevalier, *Land and Society in Colonial Mexico: The Great Hacienda* (Berkeley: University of California Press, 1963); see also William Taylor, *Landlord and Peasant in Colonial Oaxaca* (Stanford, Cal.: Stanford University Press, 1972). For a discussion of Peru see James Lockhardt, *Spanish Peru Fifteen Thirty to Fifteen Sixty: A Colonial Study* (Madison: University of Wisconsin Press, 1968).

10. See Taylor, *Landlord and Peasant.*

11. This argument is made in Ernesto Laclau, "Feudalism and Capitalism in Latin America," *New Left Review* 67 (May–June 1971). For another view see Frank, *Capitalism and Underdevelopment.*

12. The development of plantation agriculture in the Caribbean is discussed in John P. Augelli and Robert C. West, *Middle America: Its Land and Peoples* (Englewood Cliffs, N.J.: Prentice-Hall, 1976) and Pearse, "Agrarian Change," and various articles in *Plantation Systems of the New World* (Washington, D.C.: Pan American Union, 1959). On Brazil see Kit S. Taylor, *Sugar and the Underdevelopment of Northeastern Brazil 1500–1970* (Gainesville: University Presses of Florida, 1978); and "Brazil's Northeast: Sugar and Surplus Value," *Monthly Review* 20, no. 10 (March 1969): 20–29.

13. See Augelli and West, *Middle America,* and George Beckford, *Persistent Poverty: Underdevelopment and Plantation Economies of the Third World* (New York: Oxford University Press, 1972).

14. See Eric Williams, *Capitalism and Slavery* (New York: Capricorn Books, 1966);

and Richard Graham, *Britain and the Onset of Modernisation in Brazil 1850–1914* (Cambridge and New York: Cambridge University Press, 1968).

15. See K. S. Taylor, *Sugar;* Gervasio Castro de Rezende, "Plantation Systems, Land Tenure and Labor Supply" (Ph.D. dissertation, University of Wisconsin, Madison, 1976); Teresa Meade, "Transition to Capitalism in Brazil: Notes on a Third Road," *Latin American Perspectives* 5, no. 3 (Summer 1978): 7–26.

16. See Manuel Moreno Fraginals, *The Sugarmill* (New York: Monthly Review Press, 1976); and Fernando Ortiz, *Cuban Counterpoint: Tobacco and Sugar* (New York: Alfred A. Knopf, 1940).

17. The modernizing impact of the coffee planters in Central America is discussed by Anthony Winson, "Class Structure and Agrarian Transition in Central America," *Latin American Perspectives* 5, no. 4 (Fall 1978). On Brazil see Warren Dean, "The Planter as Entrepreneur: The Case of São Paulo," *Hispanic American National Review* 46, no. 2 (May 1966): 144–45.

18. The early development of capitalist agriculture in Mexico is discussed in Peter Baird and Ed McCaughan, *Beyond the Border: Mexico and the U.S. Today* (New York: North American Congress on Latin America, 1979), ch. 2.

19. Anthony Winson, "Class Structure and Agrarian Transition in Central America," *Latin American Perspectives* 5, no. 4 (Fall 1978): 32.

20. Juarez Rubens Brandão Lopez, "Capitalist Development and Agrarian Structure in Brazil," São Paulo: CEBRAP, n.d., mimeo.

21. See James Scobie, *Revolution in the Pampas: A Social History of Argentine Wheat* (Austin, University of Texas Press, 1964).

22. Oscar Pino-Santos, *El Asalto a Cuba Por La Oligarquía Financiera Yanqui* (Havana: Casa de las Américas, 1972), pp. 99–120. On W. R. Grace's investments in Latin America see NACLA, "Amazing Grace—The W. R. Grace Corporation," *NACLA Latin America and Empire Report* 10, no. 3 (March 1976). The United Fruit Company's operations in Latin America are discussed in David Tobis, "United Fruit Is Not Chiquita," in NACLA, *Guatemala* (New York: North American Congress on Latin America, 1974).

23. On Cuba see Fraginals, *Sugarmill.* On Puerto Rico see Angel G. Quintero Rivera, "Background to the Emergence of Imperialist Capitalism in Puerto Rico"; and Diane Christopulos, "Puerto Rico in the Twentieth Century: A Historical Survey," in Adalberto Lopez and James Petras, eds., *Puerto Rico and Puerto Ricans: Studies in History and Society* (New York: John Wiley and Sons, 1974).

24. See NACLA, *Guatemala;* and Suzanne Jonas, "Guatemala: Land of Eternal Struggle," in Ronald Chilcote and Joel Edelstein, eds., *Latin America: The Struggle with Dependency* (Cambridge, Mass.: Schenkman, 1974).

25. For a discussion of import substitution industrialization in Latin America see Frank, *Capitalism and Underdevelopment;* James Cockroft, A. G. Frank, and Dale Johnson, *Dependency and Underdevelopment: Latin America's Political Economy* (Garden City, N.Y.: Doubleday-Anchor, 1972); and Celso Furtado, *The Economic Growth of Brazil* (Berkeley: University of California Press, 1968). For a good synthetic overview of the post-World War II development of

Latin American agriculture see Gonzalo Arroyo, "Modelos de Acumulación, Clases Sociales y Agricultura" (Quito: Centro de Planificación y Estudios Sociales, 1977) reprinted in Arroyo, *Bases Theoriques et Méthodologiques d'un Projet* (Paris: Centre de Recherche Sur L'Amérique Latine et le Tiers Monde, 1979); and Alain de Janvry, "The Political Economy of Rural Development in Latin America: An Interpretation," *Journal of Agricultural Economics,* August 1975.

26. Baird and McCaughan, *Beyond the Border;* and Cheryl Payer, "The World Bank and Agribusiness," unpublished manuscript, 1977.

27. Orlando Núñez Soto, "El Somocismo: Desarrollo y Contradicciones del Modelo Capitalista Agro Exportadora En Nicaragua 1950–1975," Nicaragua, n.d., mimeo.

28. Kalmonovitz, *Desarrollo de la Agricultura,* p. 261. These figures are not corrected for inflation.

29. Mueller, *Les Oléagineux,* p. 73.

30. *Latin American Economic Report,* July 15, 1977; *San Francisco Chronicle,* June 23, 1978; and *Wall Street Journal,* September 15, 1977.

31. Edmond Missiaen and Samuel Ruff, *Agricultural Development in Brazil: A Case Study of São Paulo* (Washington, D.C.: U.S. Department of Agriculture, 1975); and Mueller, *Les Oléagineux.*

32. Payer, "The World Bank." For more on the World Bank's role in agriculture see Susan George, *How the Other Half Dies* (Montclair, N.J.: Allanheld, Osmun, 1976); and Frances Moore Lappé and Joseph Collins, *Food First* (New York: Ballantine, 1979), pp. 388–412.

33. Baird and McCaughan, *Beyond the Border.*

34. Brandão Lopez, "Capitalist Development"; and Missiaen and Ruff, *Agricultural Development in Brazil.*

35. Winson, "Class Structure and Agrarian Transition."

36. D. E. Goodman, "Rural Structure, Surplus Mobilization and Modes of Production in a Peripheral Region: The Brazilian Northeast," *Journal of Peasant Studies* 5, no. 5 (October 1977).

37. Alain de Janvry, Carlos Benito, and Efrain Franco, "The Political Economy of Accumulation and Poverty in Latin America," unpublished paper, n.d.

38. *Statistical Abstract on Latin America,* Latin American Center, University of California, Los Angeles.

39. Carlos Samaniego, "Movimiento Campesino o Lucha del Proletariado Rural en El Salvador," San Salvador, 1978, mimeo.

40. For a critique of the failure of Latin American agrarian reform programs in the 1960s to achieve substantive results see Feder, *Rape of the Peasantry.*

41. See Baird and McCaughan, *Beyond the Border;* Rodrigo Montoya, "Changes in Rural Class Structure under the Peruvian Agrarian Reform," and Alain de Janvry and Lynn Ground, "Types and Consequences of Agrarian Reform in Latin America," both in *Latin American Perspectives* 5, no. 4 (Fall 1978), and Alain de Janvry, "Political Economy of Reformism: Land Reform and Rural Development Projects," unpublished paper.

42. Carmen Diana Deere, "Changing Social Relations of Production and Peru-

vian Peasant Women's Work," *Latin American Perspectives* 4, nos. 1 and 2 (Winter and Spring 1977).

43. Winson, "Class Structure and Agrarian Transition," p. 40. Orlando Núñez Soto, "El Somocismo," p. 32; and Howard Blustein, et al., *Area Handbook for El Salvador* (Washington, D.C.: American University, 1971).

44. Kalmonovitz, *Desarrollo de la Agricultura*, p. 59.

45. Baird and McCaughan, *Beyond the Border*.

46. For a discussion of different sectors of the agrarian bourgeoisie see James Petras, "The Latin American Agro Transformation from Above and Outside," in *Critical Perspectives on Imperialism and Social Classes in the Third World* (New York: Monthly Review Press, 1978).

47. "Brazil's Coffee (with Sugar) Billionaire," *Fortune* 96, no. 1 (July 1977).

48. Baird and McCaughan, *Beyond the Border*.

49. See Tobis, "United Fruit."

50. This beef packing and export company, GISA, was formed in 1971 and is currently owned by Agrodynámica Holding Co., which in turn is one-third owned by ADELA (the multinational investment consortium). Agrodynámica, based in Panama, is an integrated agribusiness enterprise with operations in several countries. In Costa Rica it supplies agricultural machinery, owns a tannery and a chain of butcher shops; it owns a beef import company in Miami, United Beef Packer; and its subsidiary Haciendas Ganaderas owns 30,000 acres of cattle land in Costa Rica and Nicaragua. See Beverly Keene, "La Agro-Industria de la Carne en Costa Rica," CSUCA/ Programa Centroamericano de Ciencias Sociales, Costa Rica, 1978.

51. Carlos Figueroa Ibarra, *El Proletariado Rural en el Agro Guatemalteco* (Guatemala: Instituto de Investigaciones Económicas y Sociales, 1976).

52. "Brazil's Agricultural Policy: Fine Tuning under Delfim Neto," Report from the U.S. agricultural attaché, Brasilia, April 26, 1979 (U.S. Department of Agriculture files).

53. *Latin America Economic Report,* July 15, 1977.

54. Ibid., March 9, 1979.

55. Missiaen and Ruff, *Agricultural Development in Brazil*.

56. *Latin America Economic Report,* May 25, 1979.

57. *Latin America Economic Report,* March 9, 1979.

58. Baird and McCaughan, *Beyond the Border*.

59. Latin America Economic Report, quoted in NACLA, "Brazil: Controlled Decompression," *NACLA Report on the Americas* 12, no. 3 (May–June 1979).

60. *Inforpress,* May 26, 1977.

61. Baird and McCaughan, *Beyond the Border*.

Chapter 5. *The Grim Reapers: Transnationals and Their Impact*

1. This information was provided by M. Herold, "Multinational Enterprise Data Base," University of New Hampshire, Dover.

2. See for example some of the very important studies done by Gonzalo Arroyo

and the Transnational Agribusiness Project at the Université de Paris X, Nanterre, Paris, France. One such study is *Firmas Transnacionales Agroindustriales, reforma agraria y desarrollo rural.*

3. The growth of the Latin American economies is discussed by C. Fred Bergsten, Asst. Secretary of the Treasury for International Affairs, Statement Before the Western Hemisphere Subcommittee Senate Foreign Relations Committee, October 3, 1979. See also Inter-American Development Bank, *Annual Report 1980* (Washington, D.C., 1980).

4. Some banana companies are also diversifying their plantation production. Castle & Cooke in Honduras, for example, grows coconuts, grapefruits, and pineapples, and is experimenting with cucumbers and tomatoes for the U.S. market. Interview with Castle & Cooke executive, Honduras, November 1977.

5. W. G. Phillips, *The Agricultural Implement Industry in Canada* (Toronto: University of Toronto Press, 1956), p. 12–15.

6. U.N. Food and Agriculture Organization, *Monthly Bulletin of Agricultural Economics and Statistics* (Geneva: FAO, 1976), pp. 5, 9.

7. Michael Perelman, "The Green Revolution: American Agriculture in the Third World," in *Radical Agriculture,* ed. Richard Merrill (New York: New York University Press, 1976), p. 120.

8. NACLA interview, December 1977.

9. *NACLA Report on the Americas,* March 1976, p. 20.

10. *New York Times,* October 20, 1975.

11. *Business Week,* December 5, 1977, p. 76.

12. Ibid.

13. Williams Companies, *Annual Report, 1977* (New York, 1978).

14. For a thorough study of the Green Revolution in Mexico see Cynthia Hewitt de Alcántara, *The Social and Economic Implications of Large-Scale Introduction of New Varieties of Food Grains, Country Report: Mexico* (Geneva: U.N. Research Institute for Social Development, 1974).

15. "Brazil's Agricultural Situation, 1978." Report from U.S. Embassy in Brazil to the U.S. Department of Agriculture, January 26, 1979 (available in Department of Agriculture files).

16. *Washington Post,* December 26, 1976.

17. *Farm Chemicals,* September 1976, pp. 28–30.

18. *Business Week,* May 23, 1977, p. 69.

19. Herold, "Multinational Enterprise Data Base."

20. Based on an analysis of various annual reports by U.S. food processors.

21. Herold, "Multinational Enterprise Data Base."

22. Anderson Clayton, *Annual Reports* (Houston).

23. Frances Moore Lappé and Joseph Collins, *Food First: Beyond the Myth of Scarcity* (Boston: Houghton Mifflin, 1977), p. 304. See also Robert J. Ledogar, *Hungry for Profits* (New York: IDOC/North America, 1975), p. 113.

24. NACLA, *Guatemala, 1974,* pp. 96–98.

25. *Business Week,* December 5, 1977, p. 81.

26. See hearings of U.S. Senate Select Committee on Nutrition and Human

Needs, *Diet Related to Killer Diseases*. Studies on the nutritional impact of U.S. food processors are also being done by: Center for Science in the Public Interest, 1757 F St., N.W., Washington, D.C. 20009.

27. Ledogar, *Hungry for Profits*, p. 96.
28. NACLA interview, November 1977.
29. The authors wish to thank Manuel Lajo for making available an unpublished study: "Empresa transnacional y desarrollo capitalista de la agricultura, La Carnation—Leche Gloria en el Sur del Peru," Pontífica Universidad Católica del Peru, Departamento de Economía, Lima, Peru, 1977.
30. Manuel Lajo and Mariluz Morgan, "Económica campesina y desarrollo capitalista agroindustrial," Departamento de Economía, Pontífica Universidad Católica del Peru, Lima Peru, 1977, p. 11.
31. U.S. Department of Agriculture, *Foreign Agriculture*, April 10, 1978.
32. Tabulation of statistical material available in government statistical office, Cali, Colombia.
33. NACLA interview, October 1977.

Chapter 6. Latin America in the World Market: The Ties that Bind

1. U.N. Food and Agriculture Organization, *Trade Yearbook, 1976* (New York, 1977), pp. 35, 41.
2. U.S. Department of Agriculture, *Foreign Agriculture*, August 21, 1978, pp. 7–9, 15.
3. U.S. Department of Agriculture, "Agriculture in the Americas," unpublished statistical data on the Americas, Washington, D.C., 1975.
4. James P. Grant, "The Trilateral Stake: More Food in the Developing Countries or More Inflation in the Industrial Democracies," *Trialogue* 17 (Spring 1978): 4.
5. See *NACLA Report on the Americas*, "Carter and the Generals: Human Rights in the Southern Cone," March–April 1979.
6. *Business Week*, October 4, 1976.
7. Unpublished paper from GATT-Fly, Toronto, and "Coffee: The Corporate Roast," in *NACLA Report on the Americas*, April 1977. For more on the world sugar market see GATT-Fly pamphlet, *Sugar: Who Pays the Price?* (Toronto: GATT-Fly, 1975).
8. *Fortune*, July 1977.
9. See Frances Moore Lappé and Joseph Collins, *Food First: Beyond the Myth of Scarcity* (Boston: Houghton, Mifflin, 1977), p. 228. Also based on interview with Joseph Collins.
10. See *NACLA Report on the Americas*, July–August 1976.
11. *Latin America Commodities Report* (London), September 1, 1978.
12. "Terms of Trade Squeeze Third World Nations," *Dollars & Sense*, May–June 1978.
13. "Seeking a New Accommodation in World Commodity Markets," *Trilateral Commission Task Force Report No. 9* (New York: New York University Press, 1978), p. 64.

14. GATT-Fly, *Coffee—A GATT-Fly Commodity Profile* (Toronto: GATT-Fly, 1976).
15. *Latin America Commodities Report,* March 3, 1978.
16. Ibid., February 9, 1978.
17. Ibid., April 21, 1978 and May 26, 1978.
18. Ibid., May 12, 1978.

Chapter 7. The Agricultural Workforce: From Peasant to Proletarian

1. *Miami Herald,* May 6, 1977.
2. Edmond Missiaen and Samuel Ruff, *Agricultural Development in Brazil: A Case Study of São Paulo* (Washington, D.C.: U.S. Department of Agriculture, 1975).
3. Peter Baird and Ed McCaughan, *Beyond the Border* (New York: North American Congress on Latin America, 1979).
4. A general description of different types of "peasants" in Latin America is given in Ernest Feder, *The Rape of the Peasantry* (New York: Doubleday-Anchor, 1971). For a general discussion of the category of "peasant" in Marxist economic theory see Judith Enner et al., " 'Peasantry' as an Economic Category," *Journal of Peasant Studies* 5, no. 4 (July 1977).
5. The development of cotton production in El Salvador is described by Rafael Manhivar, *Crisis del Desarrollismo* (Costa Rica: Educa, 1977).
6. Carlos Samaniego, "Movimiento Campesino o Lucha del Proletariado Rural en El Salvador," San Salvador, 1978, mimeo.
7. See Carlos Figueroa Ibarra, *El Proletariado Rural en el Agro Guatemalteco* (Guatemala: Instituto de Investigaciones Económicas y Sociales, Universidad de San Carlos, 1976), pp. 170–72, 213.
8. *Washington Post,* June 13, 1977.
9. Penny Lernoux, "The Somozas of Nicaragua," *The Nation,* July 23, 1977.
10. Mateo Mina, *Esclavitud y Libertad en el valle del río Cauca* (Bogota: Publicaciones de la Rosca, 1975), pp. 83–127.
11. NACLA interviews in the Cauca Valley, November 1977.
12. M. Taussig, "Peasant Economics and the Development of Capitalist Agriculture in the Cauca Valley, Colombia," unpublished study, Department of Anthropology, University of Michigan, 1976, pp. 16–25.
13. NACLA interview, November 1977.
14. Baird and McCaughan, *Beyond the Border.*
15. Samaniego, "Movimiento."
16. *New York Times,* September 16, 1976 and November 6, 1976.
17. There is a good deal of controversy among Marxists in Latin America over how to characterize the persistence of small peasant production. Some writers such as Roger Bartra characterize this sector as constituting a "simple mercantile mode of production" which coexists with and is integrated into the dominant capitalist mode. See Roger Bartra, "Peasants and Political Power in Mexico: A Theoretical Model," *Latin American Perspectives* 2, no. 3 (Summer 1975): 125–45. See also Richard Harris, "Marxism and the Agrarian Question in Latin America," *Latin American Perspectives* 5, no. 4 (Fall 1978): 2–27.

18. Samaniego, "Movimiento."
19. In the principal coffee producing regions of Colombia, the number of mini-fundia coffee farms of less than one hectare decreased from 42 to 13 percent between 1960 and 1970. See Asociación Nacional de Usuarios Campesinos, "El Café y El Movimiento Campesino," *Latin American Perspectives* 2, no. 3 (Fall 1975).
20. Figueroa Ibarra, *El Proletariado Rural.*
21. Baird and McCaughan, *Beyond the Border,* p. 48.
22. Ibid., p. 50.
23. Orlando Núñez Soto, "El Somocismo: Desarrollo y Contradicciones del Modelo Capitalista Agro-Exportadora en Nicaragua 1950–1975," n.d., mimeo.
24. Figure from *Revista Brasileira de Geographía* (April–June 1973) quoted in E. Gonzales and M. Bastos, "O Trabalho Volante Na Agricultura Brasileira," 1975, mimeo.
25. Baird and McCaughan, *Beyond the Border.*
26. *Inforpress* 269, November 24, 1977.
27. For a discussion of general working conditions of rural workers in Latin America see Feder, *Rape of the Peasantry.* Figueroa Ibarra, *El Proletariado Rural,* is rich with information on the situation of and working conditions of agricultural workers in Guatemala. On Colombia see Salamón Kalmonovitz, *Desarrollo de la Agricultura en Colombia* (Bogotá: Editorial la Carreta, 1978), chapter 5. On Mexico see Baird and McCaughan, *Beyond the Border.*
28. *Inforpress* 269, November 24, 1977.
29. See NACLA, *Guatemala* (Berkeley: North American Congress on Latin America, 1974); Suzanne Jonas, "Guatemala: Land of Eternal Struggle" in Ronald Chilcote and Joel Edelstein, eds., *Latin America: The Struggle with Dependency* (Cambridge: Schenkman, 1974); and "El Proceso Historico-Estructural de la Producción Bananera en Centroamérica y Panama," Costa Rica, CSUCA, 1977. See also various issues of the *Guatemala & Central America Report* (Berkeley; no longer published).
30. For more on the peasant leagues of Brazil see Gerrit Huizer, *The Revolutionary Potential of Peasants in Latin America* (Lexington & Toronto: D.C. Heath, 1972); H. A. Landsberger, *Latin American Peasant Movements* (Ithaca: Cornell University Press, 1969); and Joseph Page, *The Revolution that Never Was* (New York: Grossman Publishers, 1972).
31. Recent repression of union leaders is discussed in Henry J. Frundt, "Gulf and Western in the Dominican Republic: An Evaluation," New York, Interfaith Center on Corporate Responsibilities, 1979.
32. This account of the situation of agricultural workers in Guatemala is based on Figueroa Ibarra, *El Proletariado Rural.*
33. This profile of the boias-frias is compiled from several sources: Maria Conceicão D'Incão e Mello, *O Boia Fria: Accumulacão e Miseria* (Petropolis, Brazil: Editoria Voxes Ltda, 1975); David Goodman and Michael Redclift, "The Boias-Frias: Rural Proletarianization and Urban Marginality in Brazil," *International Journal of Urban and Regional Research* 1, no. 2 (1977); *Movimiento* (São Paulo), January 10, 1977; and *Opinião* (São Paulo), June 11, 1973.

34. Figueroa Ibarra, *El Proletariado Rural.*
35. *Salud Ocupacional en el Sector Bananero Centroamericano: Trabajadores Del Valle de la Estrella* (San José, Costa Rica, Confederación Superior Universitaria de Centroamérica, 1977).
36. Data provided by Frank Ellis, who has since published "Commodity Exports and Employment in Developing Countries: A Study of Employment in the Banana Export Industry of Panama and Central America," University of Sussex, 1977.
37. U.N. Environment Program and Central American Research Institute for Industry, *An Environmental and Economic Study of the Consequences of Pesticide Use in Central American Cotton Production* (Guatemala: ICAITI Project No. 1412, 1977), pp. 2, 3.
38. *New York Times,* November 9, 1977.
39. K. C. Abercrombie, "Agricultural Mechanisation and Employment in Latin America," in *Mechanization and Employment in Agriculture* (Geneva: International Labor Office, 1973), p. 63.
40. Missiaen and Ruff, *Agricultural Development in Brazil.*
41. Baird and McCaughan, *Beyond the Border.*
42. Abercrombie, "Agricultural Mechanisation," p. 68.
43. For a fuller analysis of the development of rural unions and peasant organizations in Mexico see "Harvest of Anger," in Baird and McCoughan, *Beyond the Border.*

Chapter 8. The Del Monte Corporation: Planting the Seeds of Empire

1. Carey McWilliams, *Factories in the Field* (Layton, Utah: Peregrine Smith, 1971), pp. 101–32.
2. Quoted in ibid., p. 56.
3. Ibid., pp. 66–80.
4. *Del Monte Shield,* October 1959, p. 4.
5. *Fortune,* November 1938, pp. 80–81.
6. Thomas Horst, *At Home Abroad: A Study of the Domestic and Foreign Operations of the American Food-Processing Industry* (Cambridge, Mass.: Ballinger, 1974), pp. 1–5, 30, 55.
7. *Fortune,* November 1938, p. 81.
8. Ibid., p. 102.
9. Horst, *At Home Abroad,* pp. 2–4. See also National Commission on Food Marketing, *The Structure of Food Manufacturing,* Technical Study No. 8, June 1966, pp. 103–04.
10. *Fortune,* November 1938, p. 79.
11. U.S. Department of Labor, *Labor Unionism in American Agriculture,* Bulletin No. 836 (Washington, D.C.: Government Printing Office, 1945), pp. 19–21.
12. Quoted in McWilliams, *Factories in the Field,* p. 215.
13. U.S. Department of Labor, *Labor Unionism,* p. 94.
14. *Fortune,* November 1938, p. 109.

15. McWilliams, *Factories in the Field*, pp. 233–34.
16. U.S. Department of Labor, *Labor Unionism*, p. 113.
17. McWilliams, *Factories in the Field*, p. 228.
18. U.S. Department of Labor, *Labor Unionism*, pp. 149–66.
19. McWilliams, *Factories in the Field*, pp. 259–60.
20. Don Watson, "Teamsters-Canneries Connivance Destroys Rank and File Movement," *El Macriado, Voice of the Farm Worker*, July 31, 1974, p. 18.
21. J. Paul St. Sure, "Some Comments on Employer Organizations and Collective Bargaining in Northern California Since 1934." Interview conducted by Corinne Gilb, Institute of Industrial Relations, Berkeley, 1957.
22. Don Watson, "Illegal Canner-IBT Pact Defies 1945 Vote," *El Macriado*, September 4, 1974, p. 20.
23. California Packing Corporation, *Annual Report, 1945*.
24. Report on Meeting with Del Monte vice-president, *Public Affairs*, April 20, 1976.
25. *Del Monte Shield*, Winter 1973, p. 20.
26. Al Krebs, *Del Monte Corporation, A Report of the Agribusiness Accountability Project*, December 1973, p. 7.
27. Standard & Poore's Corporation, "Standard N.Y.S.E. Stock Reports, Del Monte," March 20, 1975. See also Davis, Skaggs & Co., Inc., *Basic Report: Del Monte Corporation*, April 27, 1976.
28. Interviews with UFW organizers and farmworkers.
29. *San Francisco Chronicle*, March 2, 1978.
30. "Why Food Firms Have Become Appetizing Takeover Targets," *San Francisco Examiner*, May 27, 1979.
31. *Business Week*, November 13, 1978, pp. 83–84.
32. Ibid., p. 93.

Chapter 9. Canned Imperialism: Del Monte in Mexico

1. Interview with Del Monte group vice-president, International Division, July 1976. For an in-depth study of U.S. agribusiness in Mexico, see NACLA's recent *Report on the Americas*, "Harvest of Anger, Agro-Imperialism in Mexico's Northwest," 10, no. 6, July–August 1976.
2. *Del Monte Shield*, October 1974, p. 17.
3. Ibid., p. 18.
4. Simon Williams, *Agricultural Credit for Small Farmers—Case Histories from Mexico* (Mexico City: Coordinacion Rural A.C.), p. 224.
5. *Del Monte Shield*, October 1974, pp. 18–19.
6. Ibid.
7. Interview with Del Monte's head agricultural supervisor in the Bajio Valley, June 1976.
8. Interview with Oskar Kuellar, agricultural technician in the Association of Small Strawberry Producers, June 1976.
9. Williams, *Agricultural Credit*, p. 222.

10. Vivian St. Clair, "Foreign Agribusiness—An Area of Sensitivity," *Mexican-American Chamber of Commerce Review*, March 1975, p. 47.
11. Interview with grower in Bajío Valley, June 1976.
12. Interview with Del Monte's head agricultural supervisor in the Bajío. See also *Del Monte Shield*, April 1968, p. 4.
13. *Del Monte Shield*, October 1974, p. 19.
14. Interview with Del Monte plant workers, June 1976.
15. Ibid.
16. Ibid.
17. Ibid.
18. Interview with Del Monte group vice-president, International Division, July 1976.
19. Interview in Bajío Valley, June 1976.
20. Ibid.
21. *Del Monte Shield*, October 1968, p. 13.
22. Ibid., p. 16.
23. Ibid., January 1968, p. 20.
24. Manuel Mejido, "Interview with Fernando Carmona," *Excelsior*, November 17, 1972.

Chapter 10. Modern Plantation Systems: Del Monte in the Pacific

1. "Pineapples in Paradise," *Fortune*, November 1930, and "Hawaii Faces the Pacific," *Pacific Research and World Empire Telegram*, January–February 1975.
2. *Fortune*, November 1930.
3. Ibid.
4. Frederick Simpich, Jr., *Dynasty in the Pacific* (New York: McGraw Hill, 1974), and *Pacific Research and World Empire Telegraph*, January–February 1975.
5. International Longshoremen's and Warehousemen's Union, "ILWU and the Pineapple Worker"; and interview with ILWU officials in Honolulu.
6. *Wall Street Journal*, April 11, 1974.
7. *Honolulu Advertiser*, June 17, 1976.
8. *Honolulu Star Bulletin*, June 16, 1976.
9. *Del Monte Shield*, Special Issue on Del Monte in the Philippines, Winter 1975.
10. "The Philippines: American Corporations, Martial Law and Underdevelopment" (New York: IDOC, 1973).
11. California Packing Corporation, *Annual Report, 1946*.
12. Ibid.
13. IDOC, "The Philippines."
14. California Packing Corporation, *Annual Report, 1947*.
15. IDOC, "The Phillipines," p. 37.
16. *Del Monte Shield*, May 1965.
17. *Far Eastern Economic Review*, July 8, 1974.
18. *Pacific Basin Reports*, October 1972 and September 1973.

19. *New Yorker,* May 3, 1976; and *Asia Yearbook, 1976* (Hong Kong: Far Eastern Economic Review, 1977).
20. Eleanor McCallie and Frances Moore Lappé, "An Informal On-Site Report on the Banana Industry in the Philippines" (unpublished ms., 1979).
21. *Far Eastern Economic Review,* May 8, 1974.
22. Wage figures from National Economic Development Authority; and McCallie and Lappé, "On-Site Report," p. 3.
23. McCallie and Lappé, "On-Site Report."
24. *Sign of the Times,* Manila, June 12, 1976, and *Pahayag,* Honolulu, July 1976.
25. Liberation News Service, June 22, 1974.
26. See Ernst Utrecht, "The Separationist Movement in the Southern Philippines," *Race and Class,* April 1975; and Ligaya del Mundo, "Mindanao: Strife in the Land of Promise," *Bahayag,* April 1973.
27. *Far Eastern Economic Review,* October 10, 1975.
28. IDOC, "The Philippines."
29. *Manila Journal,* July 13, 1975.
30. IDOC, "The Philippines," p. 43.
31. *Far Eastern Economic Review,* May 8, 1974. This estimate was made by a Dole official.

Chapter 11. A New "Banana Republic": Del Monte in Guatemala

1. *Forbes,* December 15, 1970.
2. UNCTAD, *The Marketing and Distribution System for Bananas* (Geneva: UNCTAD, 1974).
3. For a comprehensive history of Guatemala, including U.S. political and corporate involvement, see *Guatemala* (Berkeley: NACLA, 1974).
4. *El Gráfico,* July 14, 1975; and *Diario de la Tarde,* July 16, 1975.
5. *Wall Street Journal,* July 14, 1975.
6. See *Wall Street Journal,* July 14, 1975; and *Guatemala and Central America Report,* October 1972 and July 1975.
7. Interview in Guatemala, 1976.
8. *Inforpress,* nos. 60, 64, and 151, *El Gráfico,* February 10, 1972, "Nicaragua," NACLA *Report on the Americas,* February 1976, p. 16, and interviews in Guatemala.
9. Interview with Del Monte official in Guatemala, 1976.
10. *El Gráfico,* July 25, 1975.
11. Carlos Figueroa Ibarra, *El Proletariado Rural en el Agro Guatemalteco* (Guatemala: Instituto de Investigaciones Económicas y Sociales de la Universidad de San Carlos, 1976), p. 187.
12. Ibid.
13. *Guatemala,* p. 75.
14. *Inforpress,* no. 191, and *Guatemala and Central America Report* (Berkeley), February 1976.

15. When NACLA researchers visited BANDEGUA, the union office was being used for a three-month course sponsored by the International Federation of Plantation, Agricultural and Allied Workers, an international secretariat that has worked in the past with the CIA, according to Philip Agee. As one of the instructors, a Colombian, explained, the purpose of the course was to train potential leaders in "social problem solving." The other course instructor was a BANDEGUA office employee, a graduate of AIFLD courses with extensive travel experience in Central America and the U.S. Besides workers from the plantation, there were five Salvadoreans and twenty local peasant farmers recruited for the course.

16. UNCTAD, *The Marketing and Distribution System,* p. 11.

17. Frederick F. Clairmonte, "Bananas: A Commodity Case History," in Cheryl Payer, ed., *Commodity Trade of the Third World* (New York: McGraw Hill, 1975).

18. *La Nación,* April 18, 1974.

19. *New York Times,* May 21, 1975.

20. *San Francisco Examiner,* May 21, 1975.

21. *Inforpress,* no. 114.

22. *Diario La Hora,* September 10, 1975.

23. *Central America Report* (Guatemala); November 24, 1975.

24. Information from Frank Ellis.

25. *Inforpress,* no. 165.

26. *La Nación,* May 23, 1974; *Inforpress,* nos. 93, 101.

27. See *Guatemala,* pp. 122–31 for an article on the United Fruit Company's changing strategy.

28. Information from Frank Ellis.

29. Estimated acreage in UNCTAD, *The Marketing and Distribution System,* p. 24.

Chapter 12. The Grain Trade: A Seedy Business

Unless otherwise noted, interviews cited were conducted by the authors during July–August 1975.

1. Dan Morgan, *Merchants of Grain* (New York: Viking, 1979), pp. 199–200, 337–39.

2. Interview with official at the U.S. General Accounting Office.

3. Ibid. See also *Business Week,* March 11, 1972, p. 85.

4. Interview with Washington, D.C. representative of the Bunge Corporation.

5. Interview with an aide to a senator on Committee on Agriculture and Forestry, Washington, D.C.

6. Interview with official at the U.S. General Accounting Office.

7. *Business Week,* April 16, 1979.

8. Interview with John Schnittker, who has written on the grain trade and worked in the Department of Agriculture.

9. *Business Week,* April 16, 1979.

10. Interview with Clarence Palmby, vice-president of Continental Grain.

11. *Business Week,* March 11, 1972.
12. Morgan, *Merchants of Grain,* p. 39.
13. *New York Times,* June 12, 1975.
14. Martha M. Hamilton, *The Great American Grain Robbery & Other Stories* (Washington, D.C.: Agribusiness Accountability Project, 1972).
15. Morgan, *Merchants of Grain,* p. 175.
16. Ibid., p. 178.
17. *Southwestern Miller* (Kansas City), April 11, 1967.

Chapter 13. Harvest of Profits: World Empire of Cargill, Inc.

Unless otherwise noted, interviews cited were conducted by the authors during July–August 1975.

1. *Cargill Today,* no publication date, issued by Cargill between 1965 and 1968.
2. *Business Week,* April 16, 1979.
3. John L. Work, *Cargill Beginnings—An Account of Early Years* (Minneapolis, Cargill Incorporated, 1965), pp. 53–56, 48–49.
4. *The History of Cargill, Incorporated, 1865–1945* (Minneapolis, Minn., 1945), p. 14.
5. Work, *Cargill Beginnings,* p. 76.
6. *History of Cargill,* pp. 85–87. See also Federal Trade Commission, *Agricultural Income Inquiry,* submitted to Congress March 2, 1937, Part I, pp. 349–51.
7. "Cargill Reaps New Harvest," *Business Week,* April 16, 1949.
8. *The History of Cargill,* p. 95.
9. Harry Fornari, *Bread Upon the Waters* (Nashville, Tenn.: Aurora Publishers, 1973), pp. 93, 112–13.
10. "The Two-Billion-Dollar Company That Lives by the Cent," *Fortune,* December 1965, p. 168.
11. Interview with Washington, D.C. representative of the Bunge Corporation.
12. Interview with George Shanklin, Assistant Administrator, Commercial Export Programs.
13. Interview with Washington, D.C. representative of the Bunge Corporation.
14. United States Department of Agriculture, Commodity Credit Corporation, *Storage and Handling Payments, 1965–1968* (Washington, D.C.: Government Printing Office, 1969).
15. Interview with Neal Smith, House of Representatives. See also "The Effect of Corn Marketing by the Commodity Credit Corporation upon Small Business," Hearings before the Subcommittee on Special Investigations of Small Business Problems, June 14, 15, 22, 23, and 29, 1966.
16. Interview with an aide to a Senate Subcommittee investigating the grain trade.
17. General Accounting Office, *Alleged Discriminations and Concessions in the Allocation of Railcars to Grain Shippers* (Washington, D.C.: Government Printing Office, 1974), pp. 1–8.

18. *Business Week*, April 16, 1979.
19. Interviews with a Cargill official and a vice-president of Continental Bank of Illinois. See also "Sales Soar, Nearly Triple Cargill Profits," *Minneapolis Tribune*, December 2, 1973.
20. Interview with a Cargill official.
21. *The History of Cargill*, p. 99.
22. Interview with a vice-president of Continental Bank of Illinois.
23. *New York Times*, January 2, 1974.
24. Interview with a Cargill official.
25. Agency for International Development, *The War on Hunger: A Challenge to Business* (Washington, D.C.: AID, 1967), p. 5.
26. Interview with an aide to a Senate Subcommittee investigating the grain trade. See also Don Mitchell, *The Politics of Food* (Toronto: James Lorimer, 1975), pp. 68–72.
27. Interviews with farmers in Saskatchewan province, Canada.
28. Dan Morgan, *Merchants of Grain* (New York: Viking Press, 1979).
29. Interview with a retired Cargill official.
30. Interview with an aide to a senator on Committee on Agriculture and Forestry.
31. "Payoffs: Common in Foreign Grain Sales," *Des Moines Register*, July 13, 1975.
32. *Cargill Today*. See also *Minneapolis Tribune*, February 10, 1970.
33. United States Department of Agriculture files on Private Trade Entity loans. These files include private correspondence and data submitted by companies such as Cargill.
34. Ibid.
35. Ibid.
36. Ibid.
37. Interview with a retired Cargill official. See also Overseas Private Investment Corporations (OPIC), Direct Loan Investment Guaranty, Brazil: Cargill Agricola, S.A. The OPIC papers were obtained through a Freedom of Information Act request, and although extensively edited by OPIC officials, the papers contain information on Cargill's Brazilian operations.
38. OPIC papers. See also a September 5, 1975 letter from the Eximbank.
39. Interview with Minnesota Democratic Party official who is close to Cargill executives.
40. Quote attributed to ex-president of General Mills by retired official of Minnesota Democratic Party.
41. Interview with John Schnittker, who has written on the grain trade and worked in the Department of Agriculture.
42. Interview with official at General Accounting Office.
43. Interview with vice-president of Continental Grain.
44. Financial Report submitted in December 1973 to Securities and Exchange Commission. Cargill was required to submit the report when it tried to purchase the Missouri Portland Cement Company, a public corporation.
45. *Business Week*, April 16, 1979.

Index